STRONGHOLD™

VOLUME

1

THE PRIMACY

PHIL HESTER

RYAN KELLY

DEE CUNNIFFE

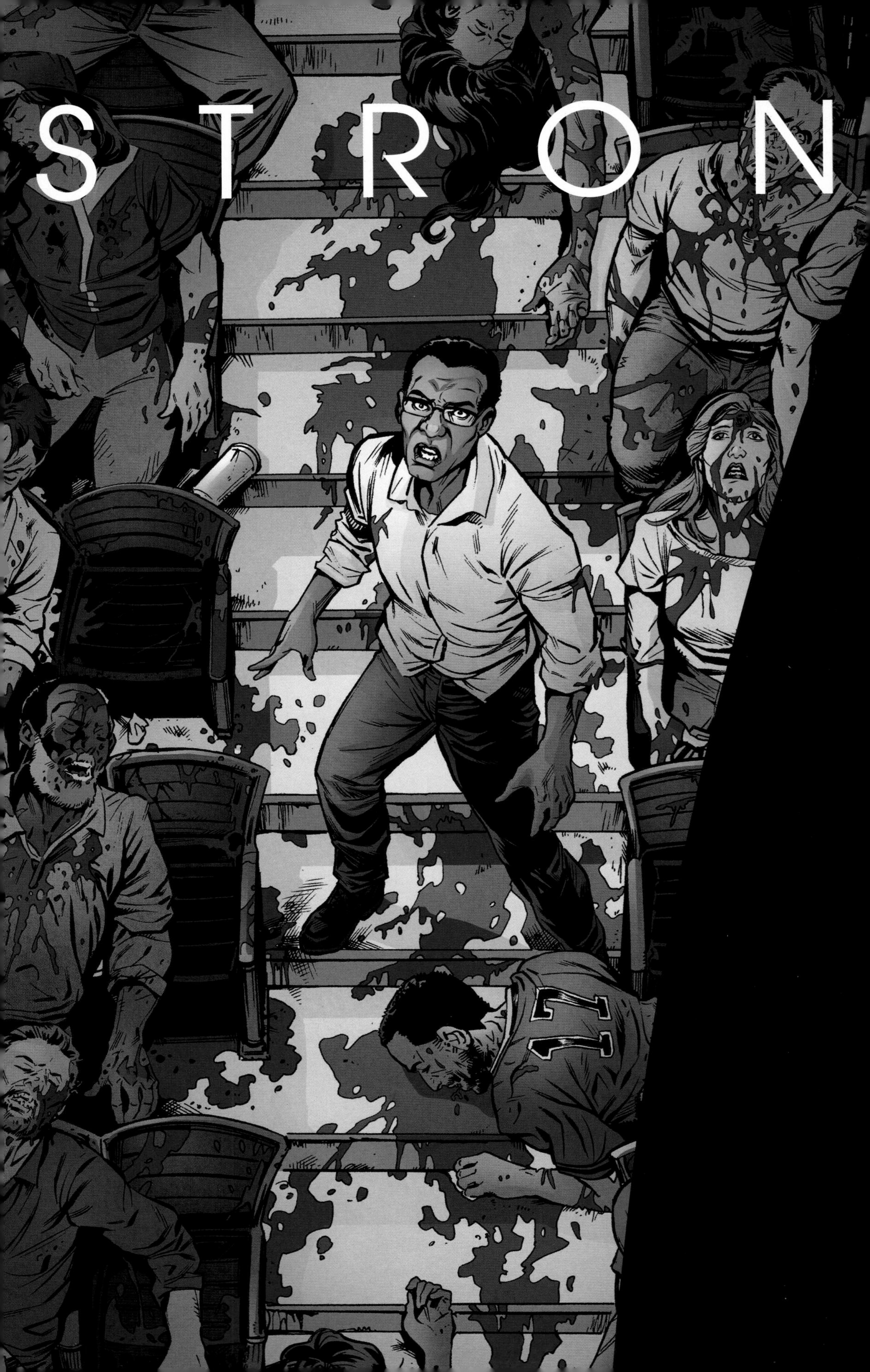
S T R O N

GHOLD™

VOLUME 1

THE PRIMACY

PHIL HESTER co-creator & writer

RYAN KELLY co-creator & artist

TYLER WALPOLE co-creator

DEE CUNNIFFE colorist

SIMON BOWLAND letterer

RYAN KELLY w/ **DEE CUNNIFFE** front & original covers

PHIL HESTER w/ **DEE CUNNIFFE** & **TYLER WALPOLE** variant covers

EMMA PRICE logo designer

COREY BREEN book designer

MIKE MARTS editor

AFTERSHOCK™

MIKE MARTS - Editor-in-Chief • **JOE PRUETT** - Publisher/CCO • **LEE KRAMER** - President • **JON KRAMER** - Chief Executive Officer
STEVE ROTTERDAM - SVP, Sales & Marketing • **DAN SHIRES** - VP, Film & Television UK • **CHRISTINA HARRINGTON** - Managing Editor
MARC HAMMOND - Sr. Retail Sales Development Manager • **RUTHANN THOMPSON** - Sr. Retailer Relations Manager • **BLAKE STOCKER** - Chief Financial Officer
AARON MARION - Publicist • **LISA MOODY** - Finance • **RYAN CARROLL** - Development Coordinator • **STEPHAN NILSON** - Publishing Operations
CHARLES PRITCHETT - Comics Production • **COREY BREEN** - Collections Production • **TEDDY LEO** - Editorial Assistant
STEPHANIE CASEBIER & **SARAH PRUETT** - Publishing Assistants

AfterShock Logo Design by **COMICRAFT**
Publicity: contact **AARON MARION** (aaron@publichausagency.com) & **RYAN CROY** (ryan@publichausagency.com) at **PUBLICHAUS**
Special thanks to: **IRA KURGAN**, **MARINE KSADZHIKYAN**, **ANTONIA LIANOS** & **JULIE PIFHER**

AFTERSHOCKCOMICS.COM Follow us on social media 🐦 📷 f

I N T R O D U C T I O N

How long does it take to make a comic book?

That's a question I get asked a lot, especially by people who aren't dyed-in-the-wool comic book fans. It's nearly as popular as "Don't they do all that on computers now?" or "Have you met Stan Lee?" But you, dear reader, know better than to ask. You're an informed consumer. You've been told countless times that it takes anywhere from a week to a month to write a monthly comic book, then at least another month to pencil it, maybe a bit less to ink it, a few weeks to color, with whatever's left before press time allotted to the beleaguered letterer, sometimes lucky to get more than a day to turn a book around.

All in all, you need a good three months to make that flimsy pamphlet you're going to tear through in just a few minutes. Ideally, all the talented folks employed in this process are working assembly-line style, all advancing their share of each new issue every day so that your favorite comic hits the stands once a month.

But that's not the truth.

A comic book's lifecycle really begins the day its creator wakes up from a dead sleep to jot down a note of inspiration, or doodles a character in the margin of a biology notebook, or stares at a blank parking garage wall long enough to watch an otherwise unseen epic unfold before their eyes. Technically, Frank Miller created SIN CITY in his mid-thirties, but he started working on it when he was a teenager, before he knew exactly what form it would take. It may have taken him only a few weeks to draw the first Violent Marv tale, but that baby had actually been gestating for twenty years. It had been a comic for decades before it saw print, only in Frank's head...where you couldn't read it yet.

There are occasional bolts from the blue that go from inspiration to bookshelves in just a few months, but I think you'll find most creators carry around their stories for years before they get to properly tell them. I know that's certainly true for STRONGHOLD. But unlike most comics projects, our long gestation took place in public.

Some of you may recall that a first issue much like the first chapter of this book came out in the mid-2000s. Yes, we tried STRONGHOLD once before. Fresh off the critical success of THE COFFIN and DEEP SLEEPER (both with Mike Huddleston), I was eager to get my next "big idea" out into the world. I was lucky to know the talented Tyler Walpole, and convinced him to join me in the project. Eager to make a splash, we unleashed a giant, forty-eight page first issue on the world in 2005. Then...nothing. There was no second issue. We were cancelled right out of the gate. It happens. To paraphrase the aforementioned Mr. Miller, "This. Is. COMICS!"

But I couldn't let STRONGHOLD go. Over the next decade and a half I tweaked the plot, rethought the themes, changed characters' genders and races, and—most importantly—became a better writer. I never gave up on this comic. Hell, I've never given up on any comic. Reality does that for me.

But this time reality took some favorable turns and let me bring STRONGHOLD back to the surface. I was lucky enough to have great relationships with Joe Pruett and Mike Marts, the creative forces behind AfterShock. When I told them STRONGHOLD wouldn't leave me alone, they decided if an idea bugged me that much, it must have some merit.

Tyler, the book's original co-creator (and masterful fantasy illustrator—see his BLOOD OF DRAGONS project for proof) agreed to allow another artist to take the reins, and we were lucky enough to catch all-star artist Ryan Kelly in a moment of rare availability. Our luck clearly heightened when we recruited the great Dee Cunniffe on colors, and master letterer Simon Bowland. Or maybe it wasn't luck as much as the guiding hands of editors Christina Harrington and Mike Marts, who brought this team together. The work which follows is, regardless of my efforts as a writer, an indisputable testament to their talents.

In about a year, our team took STRONGHOLD from pitch to the collected volume you now hold. So did it take a year to make STRONGHOLD? Or did it take the dozen or so years between today and our original first issue? Or did it take the thirty years between today and the day I daydreamed a man who didn't know who he was and the woman who did, but was forbidden to tell him?

Maybe it's none of the above. You could say this comic doesn't really exist until it's shared between us. Until you read it, this story may as well still be in my head, my tattered notebooks, my retired computers. Until you see them, Ryan's drawings may as well still be in his sketchbook, Dee's colors on a hard drive somewhere, Simon's letters confined to a journal. STRONGHOLD won't exist for you the way it does for us until you reach the last page of this book you now hold.

So how long does it really take to make a comic book? As long as it takes you to read it.

Turn the page and let's get to work.

PHIL HESTER
Iowa, July 2019

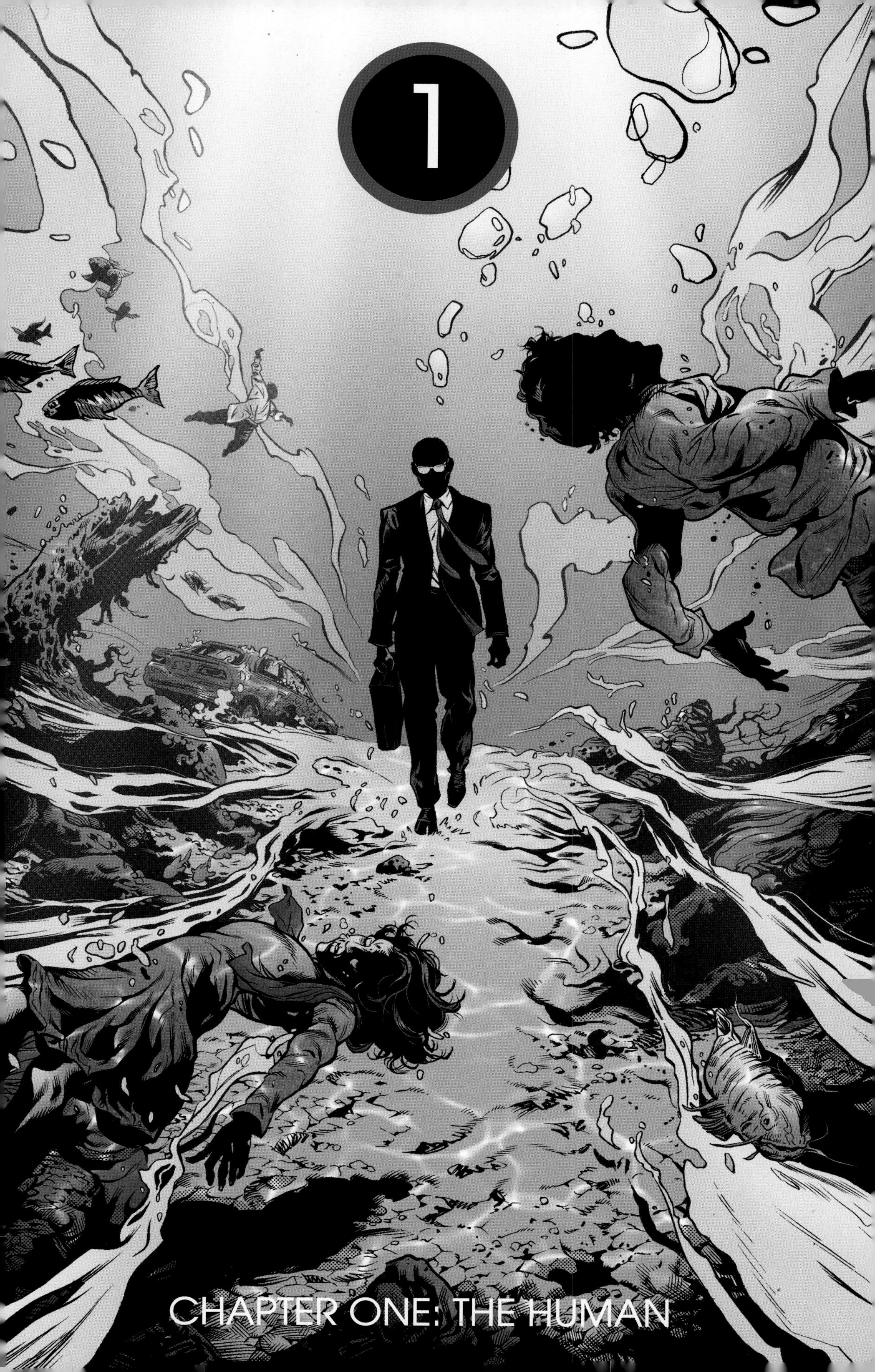
1

CHAPTER ONE: THE HUMAN

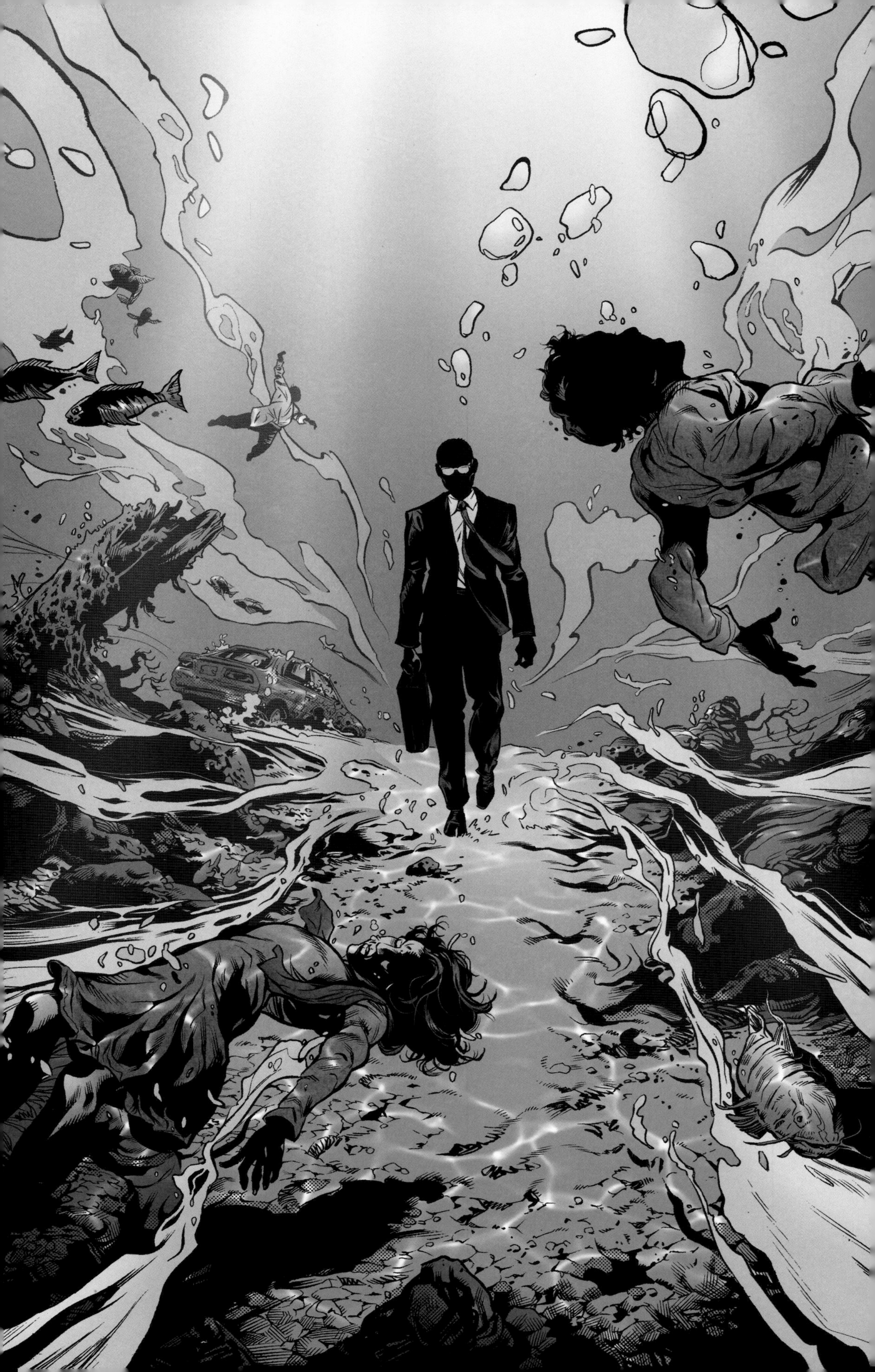

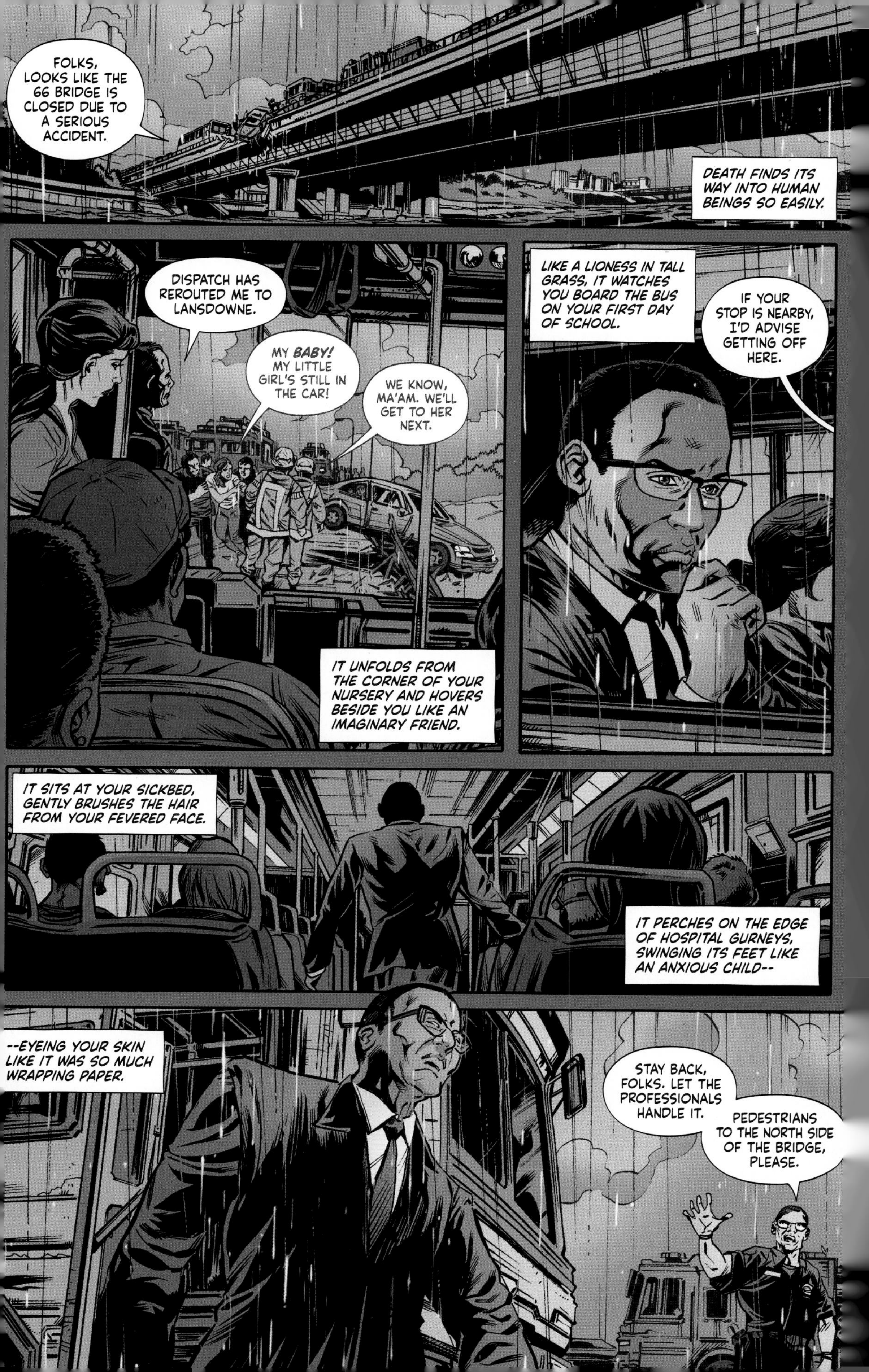
FOLKS, LOOKS LIKE THE 66 BRIDGE IS CLOSED DUE TO A SERIOUS ACCIDENT.
DEATH FINDS ITS WAY INTO HUMAN BEINGS SO EASILY.
DISPATCH HAS REROUTED ME TO LANSDOWNE.
MY BABY! MY LITTLE GIRL'S STILL IN THE CAR!
WE KNOW, MA'AM. WE'LL GET TO HER NEXT.
IT UNFOLDS FROM THE CORNER OF YOUR NURSERY AND HOVERS BESIDE YOU LIKE AN IMAGINARY FRIEND.
LIKE A LIONESS IN TALL GRASS, IT WATCHES YOU BOARD THE BUS ON YOUR FIRST DAY OF SCHOOL.
IF YOUR STOP IS NEARBY, I'D ADVISE GETTING OFF HERE.
IT SITS AT YOUR SICKBED, GENTLY BRUSHES THE HAIR FROM YOUR FEVERED FACE.
IT PERCHES ON THE EDGE OF HOSPITAL GURNEYS, SWINGING ITS FEET LIKE AN ANXIOUS CHILD--
--EYEING YOUR SKIN LIKE IT WAS SO MUCH WRAPPING PAPER.
STAY BACK, FOLKS. LET THE PROFESSIONALS HANDLE IT.
PEDESTRIANS TO THE NORTH SIDE OF THE BRIDGE, PLEASE.

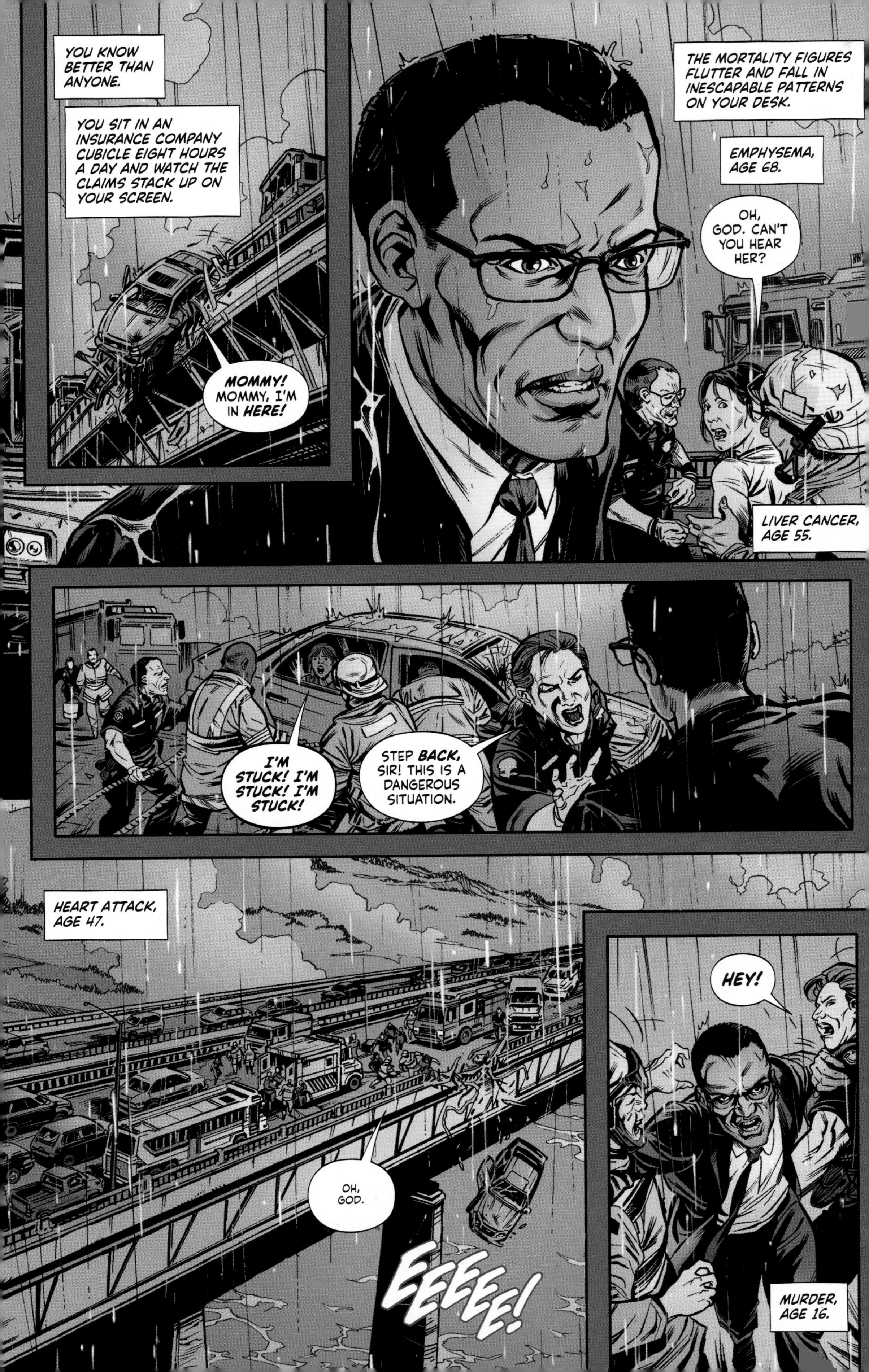

YOU KNOW BETTER THAN ANYONE.
YOU SIT IN AN INSURANCE COMPANY CUBICLE EIGHT HOURS A DAY AND WATCH THE CLAIMS STACK UP ON YOUR SCREEN.
MOMMY! MOMMY, I'M IN HERE!
THE MORTALITY FIGURES FLUTTER AND FALL IN INESCAPABLE PATTERNS ON YOUR DESK.
EMPHYSEMA, AGE 68.
OH, GOD. CAN'T YOU HEAR HER?
LIVER CANCER, AGE 55.
I'M STUCK! I'M STUCK! I'M STUCK!
STEP BACK, SIR! THIS IS A DANGEROUS SITUATION.
HEART ATTACK, AGE 47.
OH, GOD.
EEEEEE!
HEY!
MURDER, AGE 16.

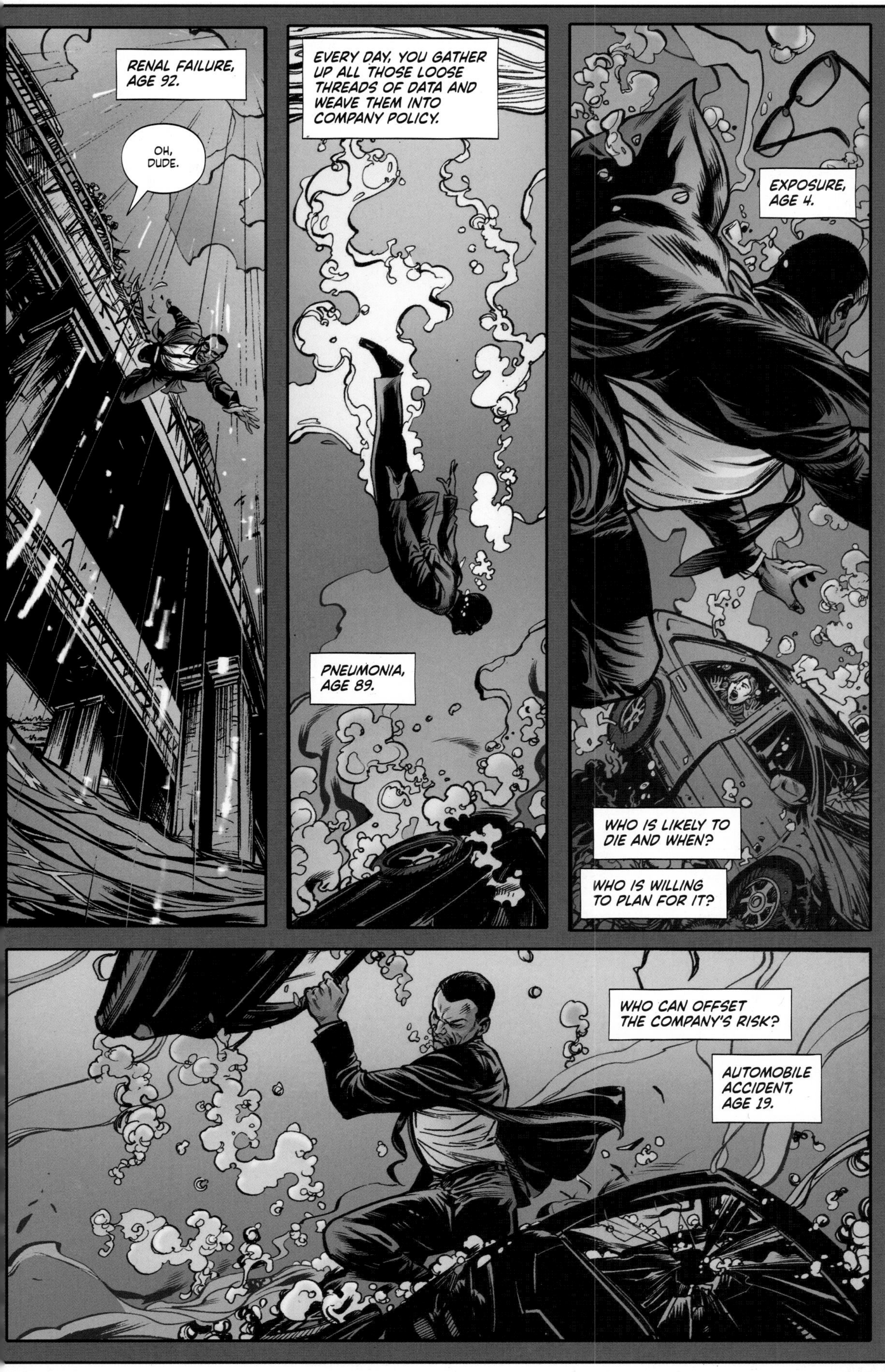
RENAL FAILURE, AGE 92.
OH, DUDE.
EVERY DAY, YOU GATHER UP ALL THOSE LOOSE THREADS OF DATA AND WEAVE THEM INTO COMPANY POLICY.
PNEUMONIA, AGE 89.
EXPOSURE, AGE 4.
WHO IS LIKELY TO DIE AND WHEN?
WHO IS WILLING TO PLAN FOR IT?
WHO CAN OFFSET THE COMPANY'S RISK?
AUTOMOBILE ACCIDENT, AGE 19.

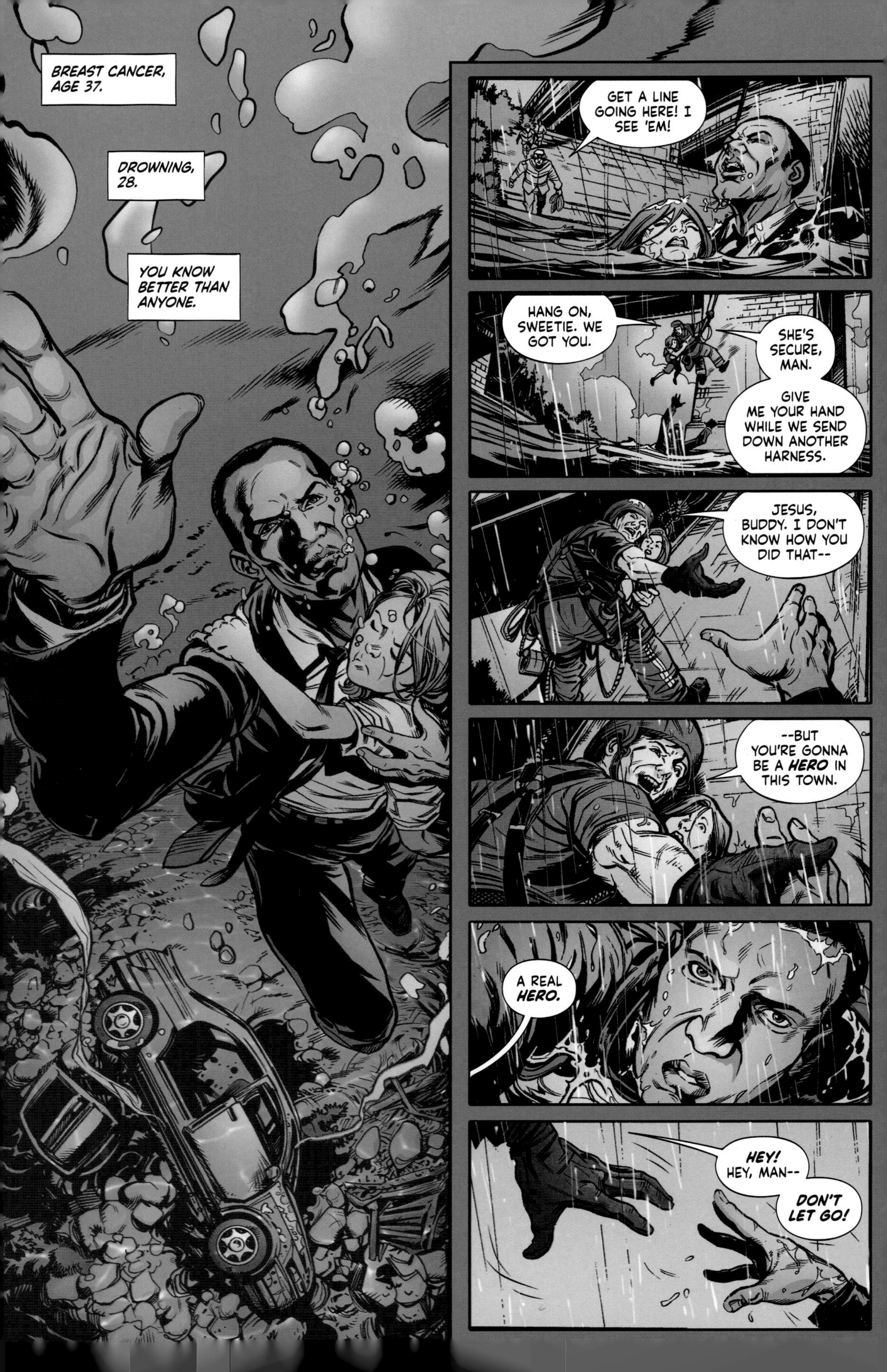

BREAST CANCER, AGE 37.
DROWNING, 28.
YOU KNOW BETTER THAN ANYONE.
GET A LINE GOING HERE! I SEE 'EM!
HANG ON, SWEETIE. WE GOT YOU.
SHE'S SECURE, MAN.
GIVE ME YOUR HAND WHILE WE SEND DOWN ANOTHER HARNESS.
JESUS, BUDDY. I DON'T KNOW HOW YOU DID THAT--
--BUT YOU'RE GONNA BE A HERO IN THIS TOWN.
A REAL HERO.
HEY! HEY, MAN--
DON'T LET GO!

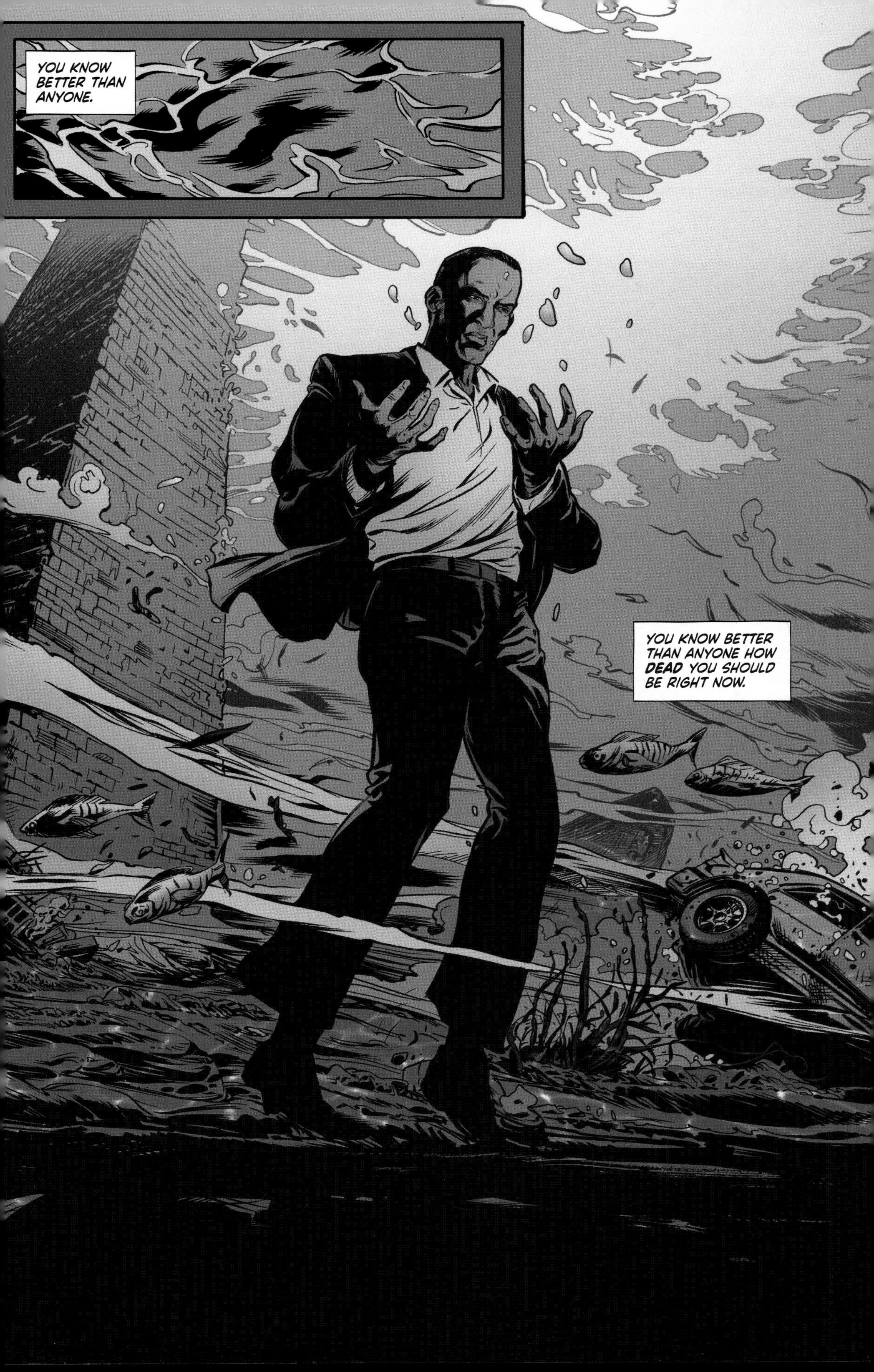
YOU KNOW BETTER THAN ANYONE.
YOU KNOW BETTER THAN ANYONE HOW DEAD YOU SHOULD BE RIGHT NOW.

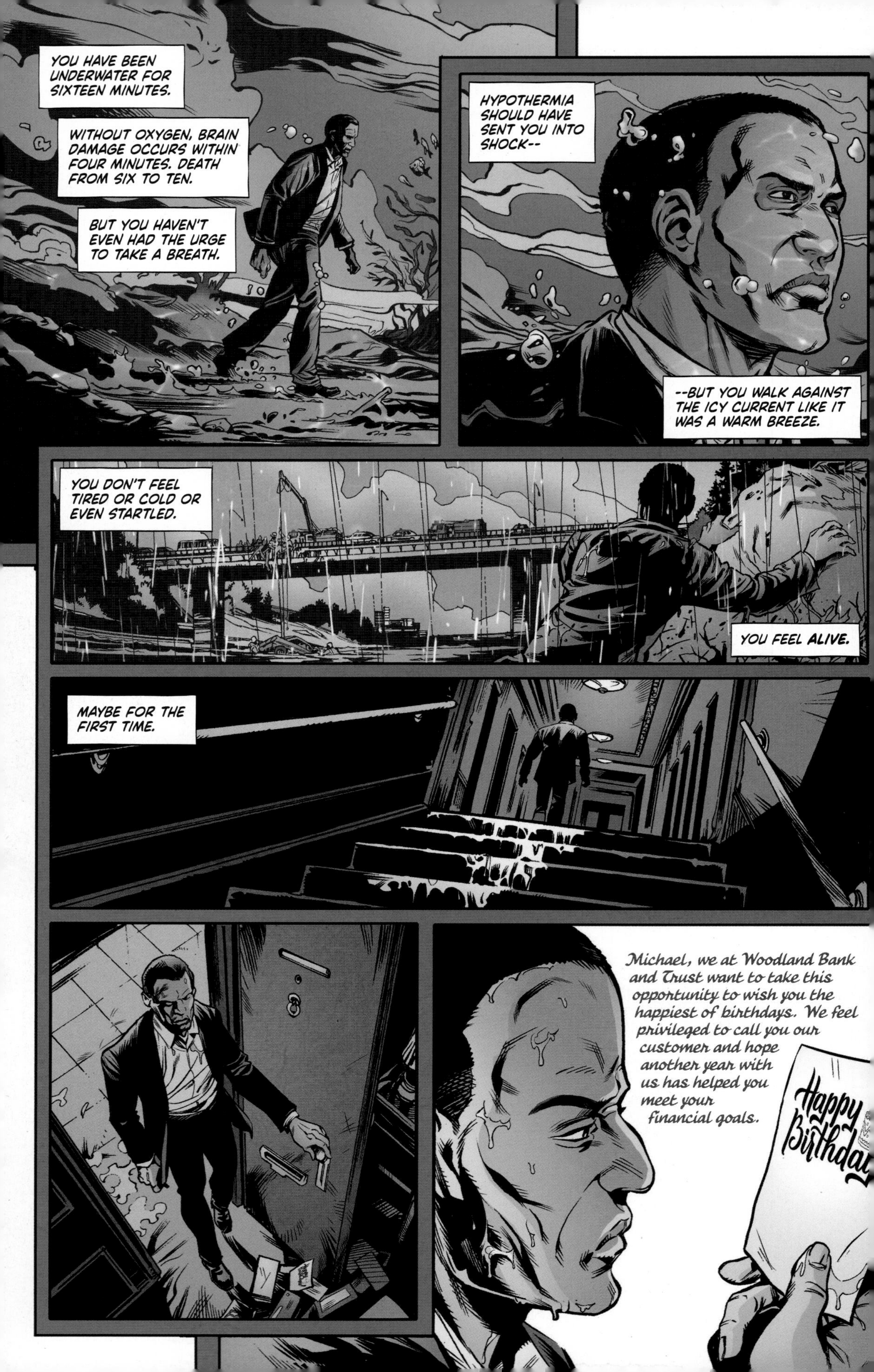
YOU HAVE BEEN UNDERWATER FOR SIXTEEN MINUTES.
WITHOUT OXYGEN, BRAIN DAMAGE OCCURS WITHIN FOUR MINUTES. DEATH FROM SIX TO TEN.
BUT YOU HAVEN'T EVEN HAD THE URGE TO TAKE A BREATH.
HYPOTHERMIA SHOULD HAVE SENT YOU INTO SHOCK--
--BUT YOU WALK AGAINST THE ICY CURRENT LIKE IT WAS A WARM BREEZE.
YOU DON'T FEEL TIRED OR COLD OR EVEN STARTLED.
YOU FEEL ALIVE.
MAYBE FOR THE FIRST TIME.
Michael, we at Woodland Bank and Trust want to take this opportunity to wish you the happiest of birthdays. We feel privileged to call you our customer and hope another year with us has helped you meet your financial goals.
Happy Birthday

YOU TURN ON THE TELEVISION, ACHING FOR PROOF THAT IT WAS MORE THAN JUST A DREAM.

THE NEWS DETAILS THE SEARCH FOR THE GIRL'S UNKNOWN RESCUER, PRESUMED DEAD.

THERE ARE THANKFULLY FEW IMAGES OF YOU, JUST A FEW GRAINY CELL PHONE CLIPS.

THE CHANNELS TUMBLE BY, BLURTING AND FLASHING BEFORE BEING SWALLOWED UP BY THE NEXT.

NOTHING STAYS ON SCREEN LONG ENOUGH TO BE DEFINED.

THE SHUFFLING INCOHERENCE IS COMFORTING.

IT'S HOW YOU WATCH TELEVISION EVERY NIGHT.

THE LAPPING WAVES LULLING YOU TO SLEEP.

PATTERNS OF INFORMATION RISE FROM THE FLICKERING LIGHT.

UNCANNY REPETITIONS. INEXPLICABLE RECURRENCES.

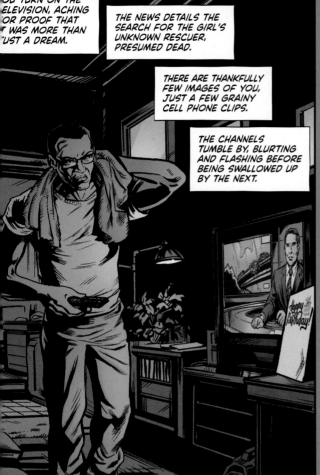

A CODE UNCONSCIOUSLY WRITTEN, NEVER MEANT TO BE READ.

A WEB UNKNOWINGLY STRUNG.

IF YOU CLIMB ONTO THAT WEB, SOMETHING FROM ITS CENTER WILL SCUTTLE OUT TO MEET YOU.

BUT IF YOU REST, IT WILL SPREAD ACROSS YOU LIKE A NET.

AND HOLD YOU STILL FOR THE NIGHT.

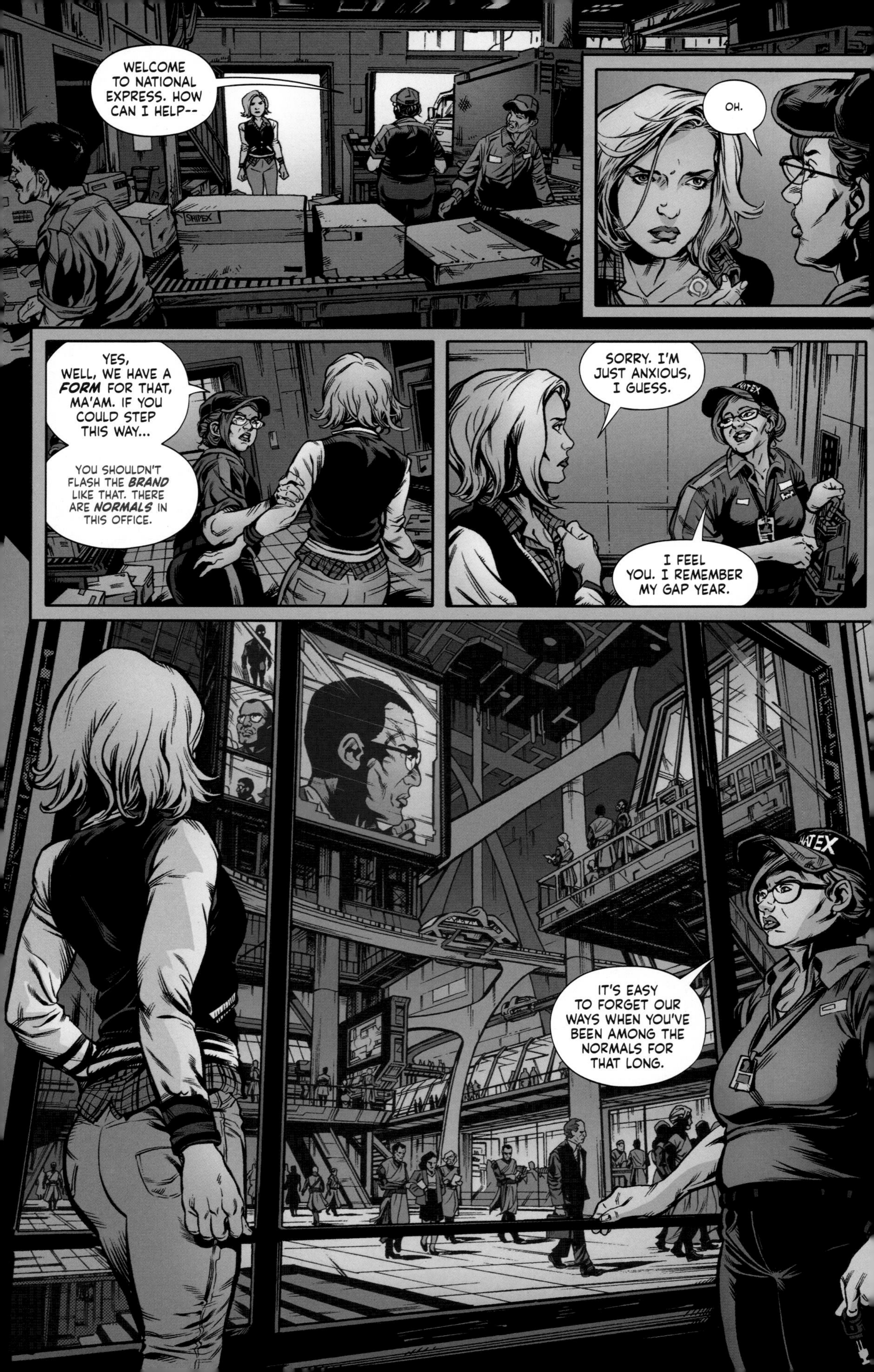
WELCOME TO NATIONAL EXPRESS. HOW CAN I HELP--
OH.
YES, WELL, WE HAVE A FORM FOR THAT, MA'AM. IF YOU COULD STEP THIS WAY...
YOU SHOULDN'T FLASH THE BRAND LIKE THAT. THERE ARE NORMALS IN THIS OFFICE.
SORRY. I'M JUST ANXIOUS, I GUESS.
I FEEL YOU. I REMEMBER MY GAP YEAR.
IT'S EASY TO FORGET OUR WAYS WHEN YOU'VE BEEN AMONG THE NORMALS FOR THAT LONG.

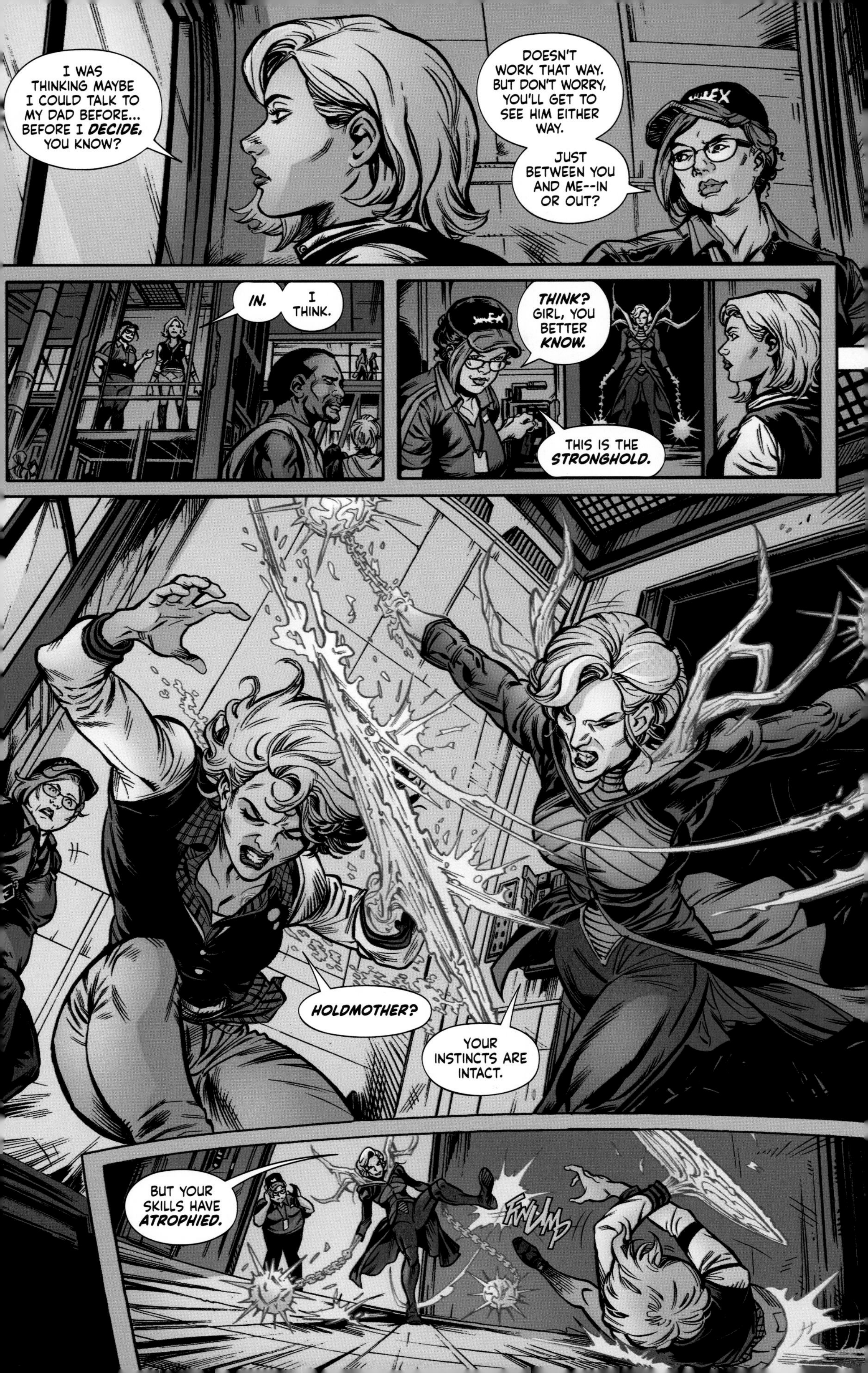
I WAS THINKING MAYBE I COULD TALK TO MY DAD BEFORE... BEFORE I DECIDE, YOU KNOW?
DOESN'T WORK THAT WAY. BUT DON'T WORRY, YOU'LL GET TO SEE HIM EITHER WAY.
JUST BETWEEN YOU AND ME--IN OR OUT?
IN.
I THINK.
THINK? GIRL, YOU BETTER KNOW.
THIS IS THE STRONGHOLD.
HOLDMOTHER?
YOUR INSTINCTS ARE INTACT.
BUT YOUR SKILLS HAVE ATROPHIED.
FWUMP

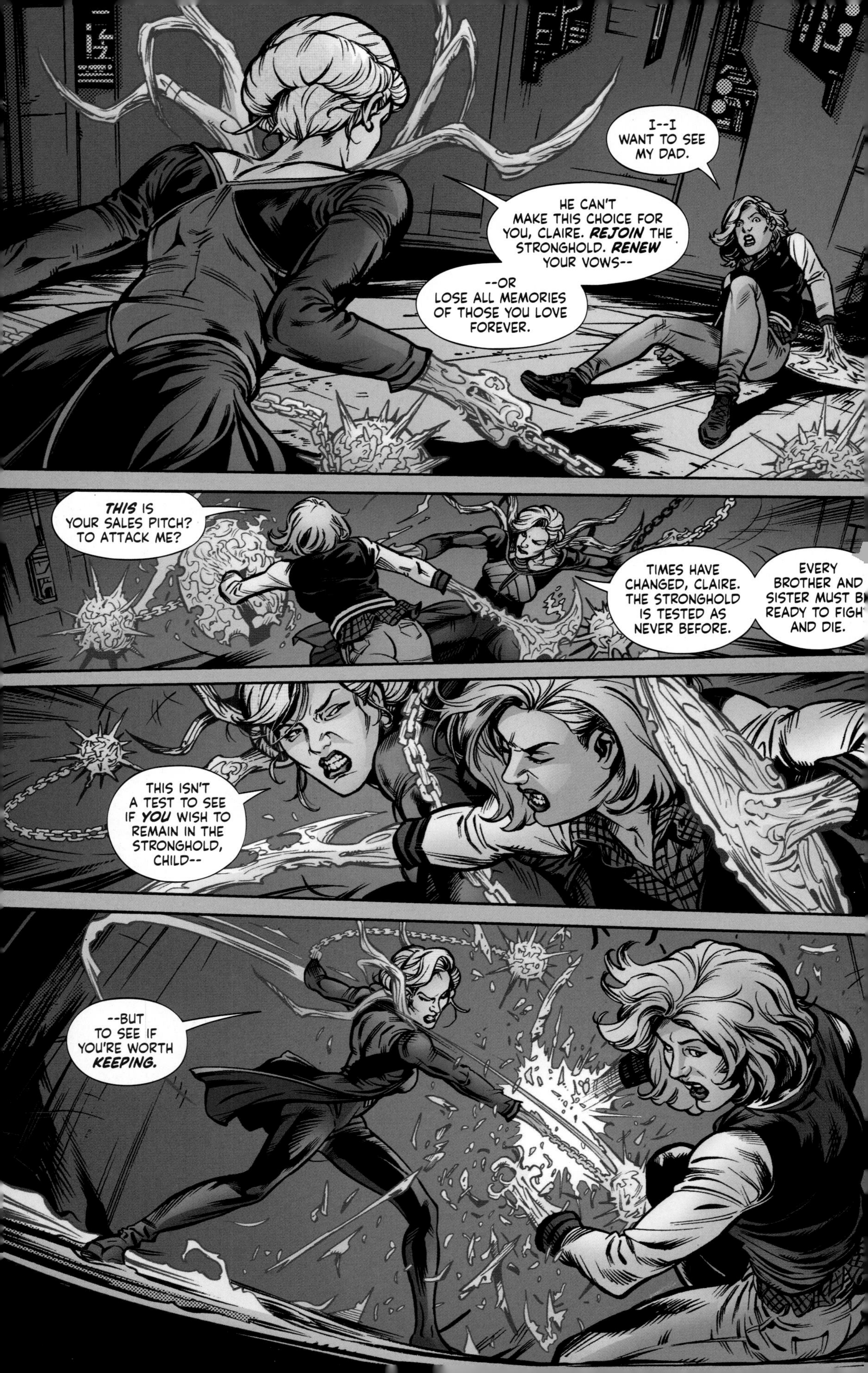
I--I WANT TO SEE MY DAD.
HE CAN'T MAKE THIS CHOICE FOR YOU, CLAIRE. ***REJOIN*** THE STRONGHOLD. ***RENEW*** YOUR VOWS--
--OR LOSE ALL MEMORIES OF THOSE YOU LOVE FOREVER.
THIS IS YOUR SALES PITCH? TO ATTACK ME?
TIMES HAVE CHANGED, CLAIRE. THE STRONGHOLD IS TESTED AS NEVER BEFORE.
EVERY BROTHER AND SISTER MUST B READY TO FIGH AND DIE.
THIS ISN'T A TEST TO SEE IF ***YOU*** WISH TO REMAIN IN THE STRONGHOLD, CHILD--
--BUT TO SEE IF YOU'RE WORTH ***KEEPING.***

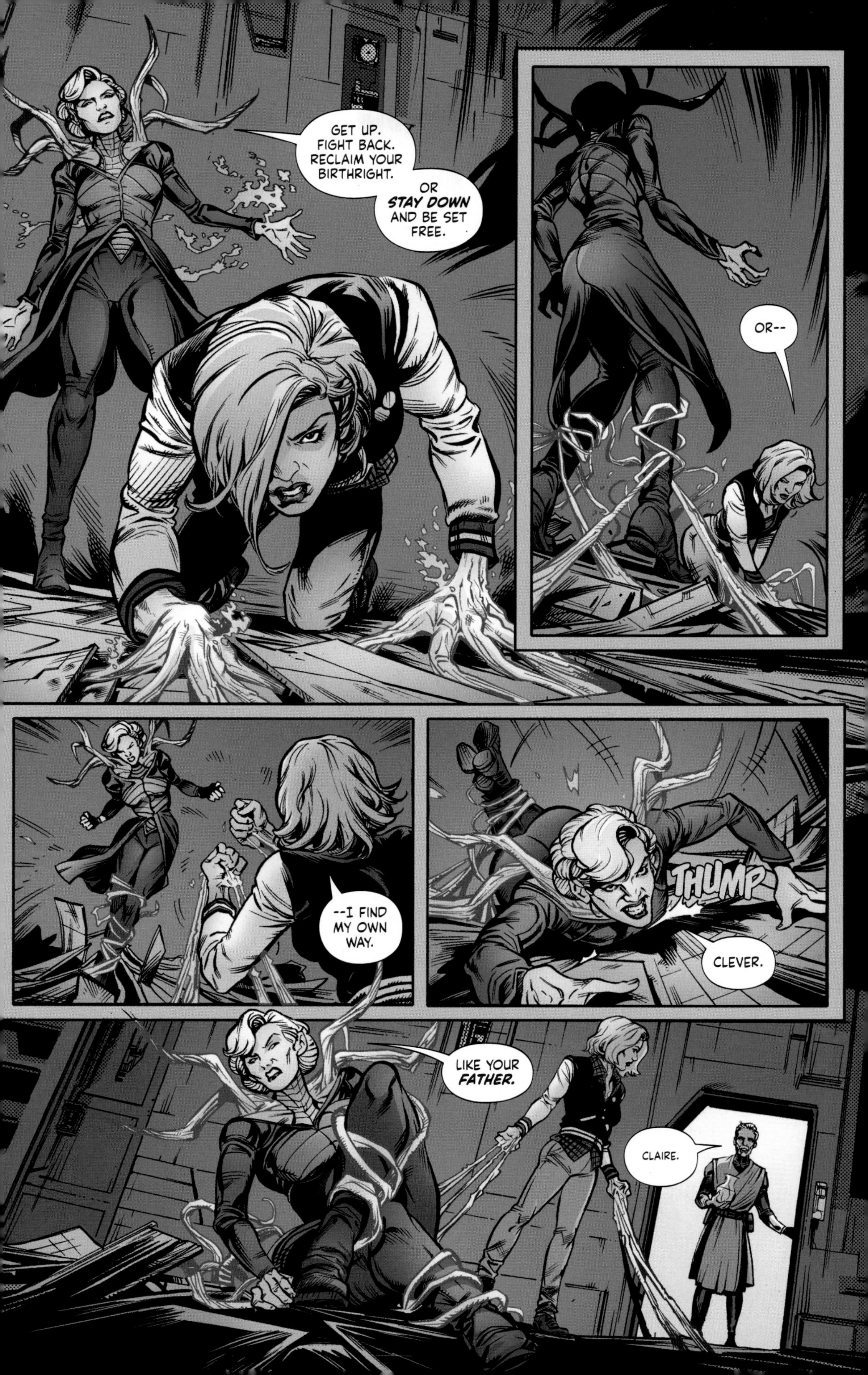
GET UP. FIGHT BACK. RECLAIM YOUR BIRTHRIGHT.
OR *STAY DOWN* AND BE SET FREE.
OR--
--I FIND MY OWN WAY.
THUMP
CLEVER.
LIKE YOUR *FATHER.*
CLAIRE.

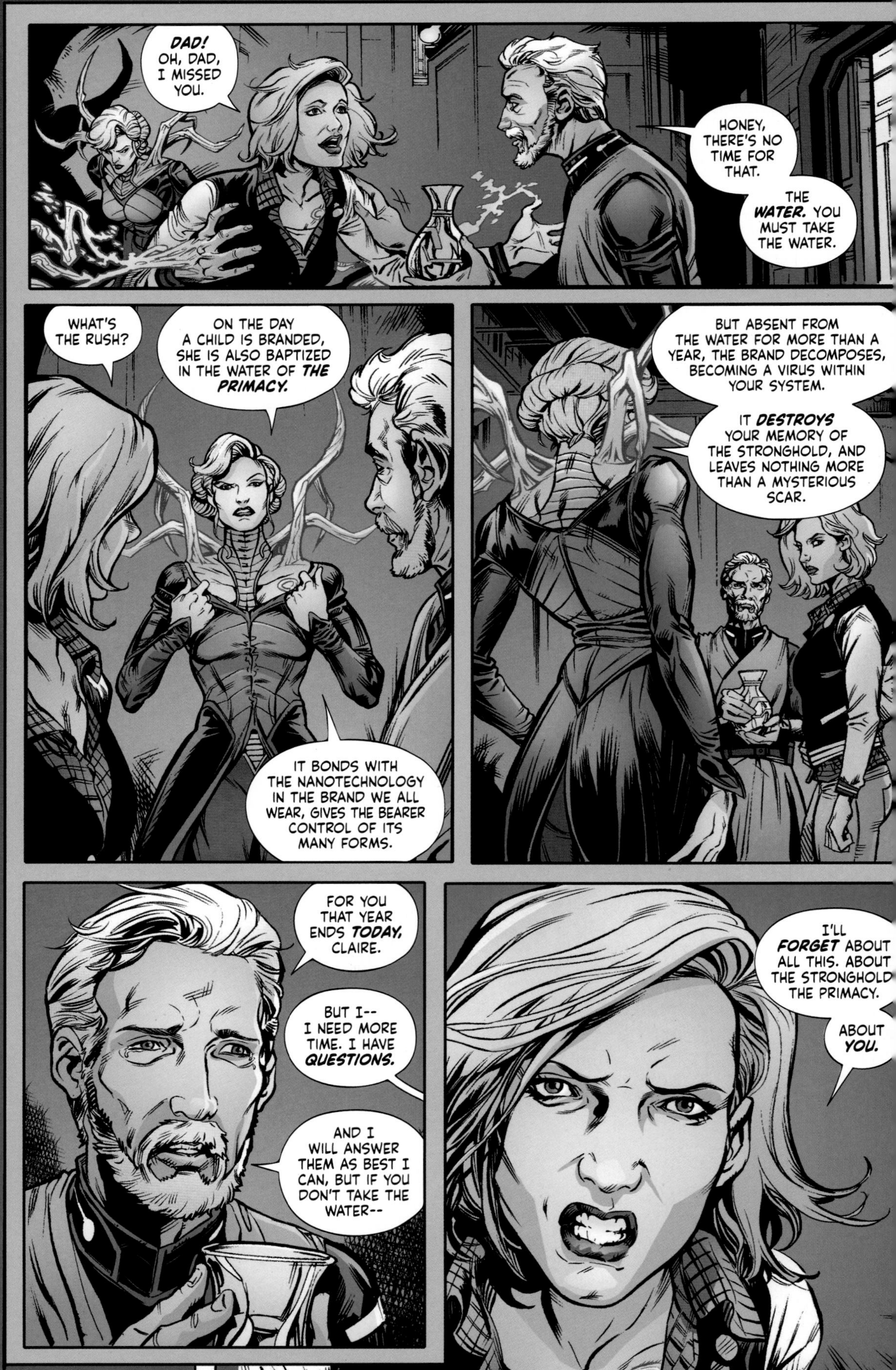

DAD! OH, DAD, I MISSED YOU.
HONEY, THERE'S NO TIME FOR THAT.
THE WATER. YOU MUST TAKE THE WATER.
WHAT'S THE RUSH?
ON THE DAY A CHILD IS BRANDED, SHE IS ALSO BAPTIZED IN THE WATER OF THE PRIMACY.
IT BONDS WITH THE NANOTECHNOLOGY IN THE BRAND WE ALL WEAR, GIVES THE BEARER CONTROL OF ITS MANY FORMS.
BUT ABSENT FROM THE WATER FOR MORE THAN A YEAR, THE BRAND DECOMPOSES, BECOMING A VIRUS WITHIN YOUR SYSTEM.
IT DESTROYS YOUR MEMORY OF THE STRONGHOLD, AND LEAVES NOTHING MORE THAN A MYSTERIOUS SCAR.
FOR YOU THAT YEAR ENDS TODAY, CLAIRE.
BUT I-- I NEED MORE TIME. I HAVE QUESTIONS.
AND I WILL ANSWER THEM AS BEST I CAN, BUT IF YOU DON'T TAKE THE WATER--
I'LL FORGET ABOUT ALL THIS. ABOUT THE STRONGHOLD THE PRIMACY.
ABOUT YOU.

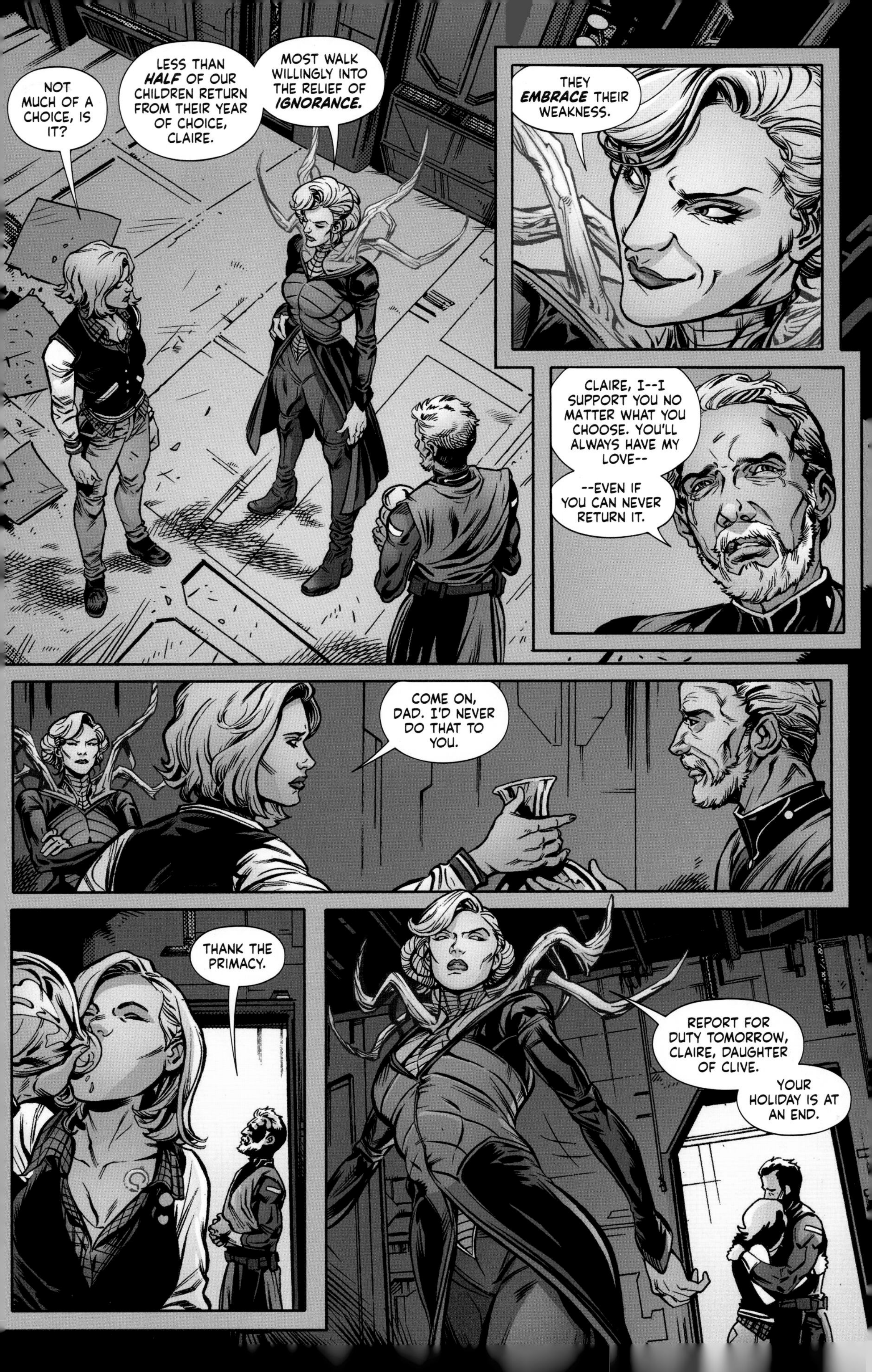
NOT MUCH OF A CHOICE, IS IT?
LESS THAN HALF OF OUR CHILDREN RETURN FROM THEIR YEAR OF CHOICE, CLAIRE.
MOST WALK WILLINGLY INTO THE RELIEF OF IGNORANCE.
THEY EMBRACE THEIR WEAKNESS.
CLAIRE, I--I SUPPORT YOU NO MATTER WHAT YOU CHOOSE. YOU'LL ALWAYS HAVE MY LOVE--
--EVEN IF YOU CAN NEVER RETURN IT.
COME ON, DAD. I'D NEVER DO THAT TO YOU.
THANK THE PRIMACY.
REPORT FOR DUTY TOMORROW, CLAIRE, DAUGHTER OF CLIVE.
YOUR HOLIDAY IS AT AN END.

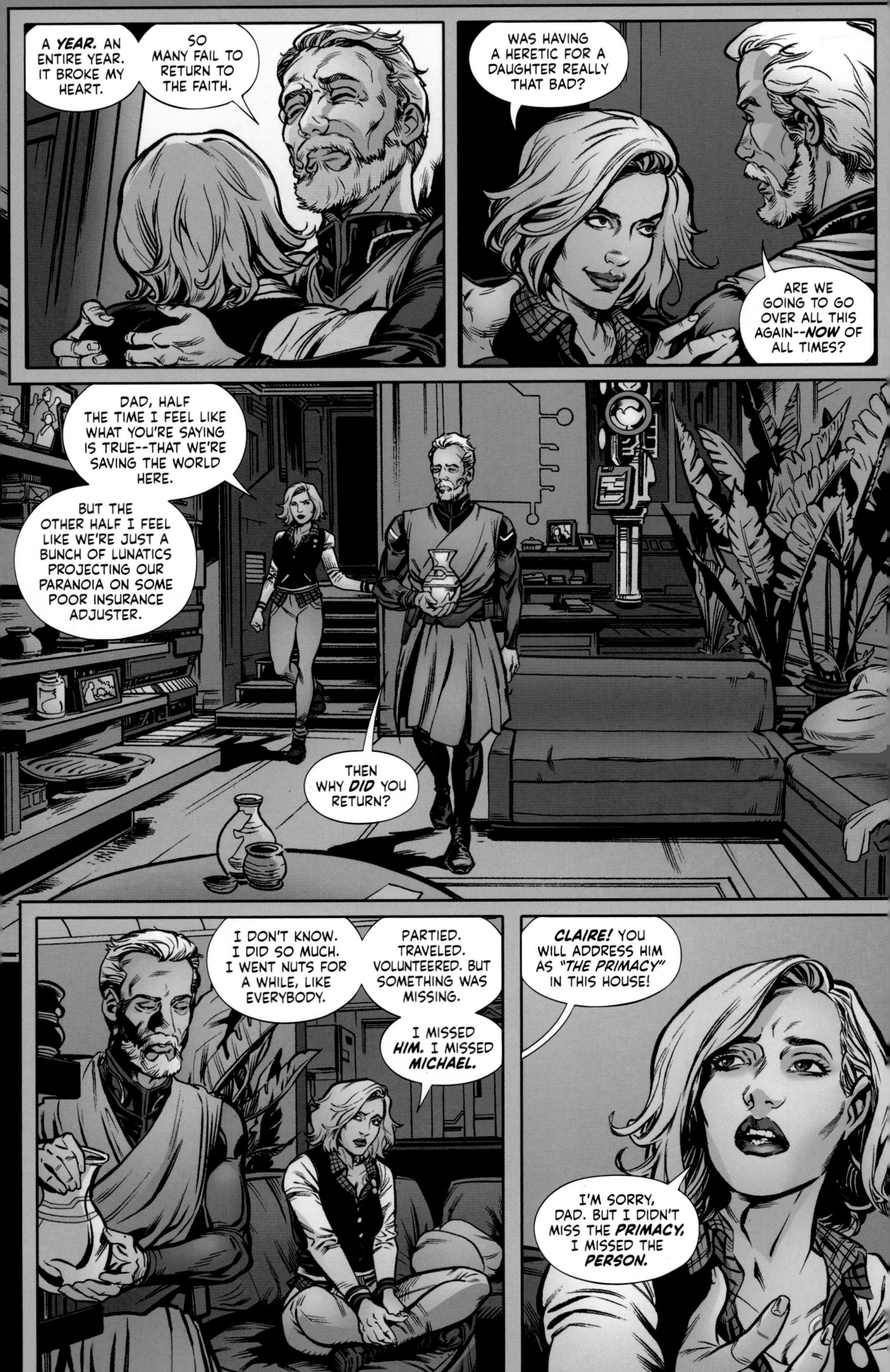
A **YEAR.** AN ENTIRE YEAR. IT BROKE MY HEART.
SO MANY FAIL TO RETURN TO THE FAITH.
WAS HAVING A HERETIC FOR A DAUGHTER REALLY THAT BAD?
ARE WE GOING TO GO OVER ALL THIS AGAIN--**NOW** OF ALL TIMES?
DAD, HALF THE TIME I FEEL LIKE WHAT YOU'RE SAYING IS TRUE--THAT WE'RE SAVING THE WORLD HERE.
BUT THE OTHER HALF I FEEL LIKE WE'RE JUST A BUNCH OF LUNATICS PROJECTING OUR PARANOIA ON SOME POOR INSURANCE ADJUSTER.
THEN WHY ***DID*** YOU RETURN?
I DON'T KNOW. I DID SO MUCH. I WENT NUTS FOR A WHILE, LIKE EVERYBODY.
PARTIED. TRAVELED. VOLUNTEERED. BUT SOMETHING WAS MISSING.
I MISSED ***HIM.*** I MISSED ***MICHAEL.***
CLAIRE! YOU WILL ADDRESS HIM AS *"THE PRIMACY"* IN THIS HOUSE!
I'M SORRY, DAD. BUT I DIDN'T MISS THE ***PRIMACY,*** I MISSED THE ***PERSON.***

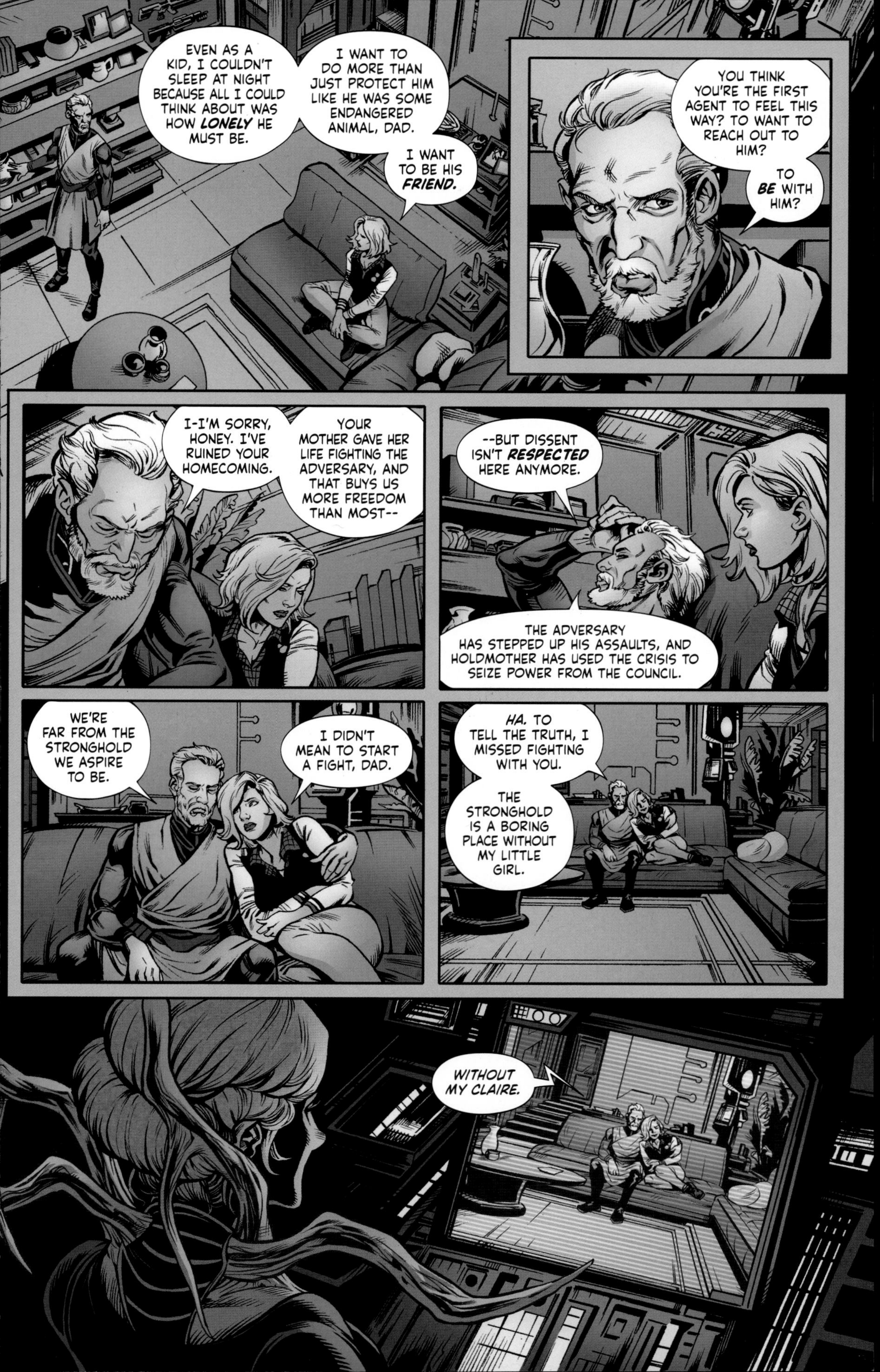
EVEN AS A KID, I COULDN'T SLEEP AT NIGHT BECAUSE ALL I COULD THINK ABOUT WAS HOW *LONELY* HE MUST BE.
I WANT TO DO MORE THAN JUST PROTECT HIM LIKE HE WAS SOME ENDANGERED ANIMAL, DAD.
I WANT TO BE HIS *FRIEND.*
YOU THINK YOU'RE THE FIRST AGENT TO FEEL THIS WAY? TO WANT TO REACH OUT TO HIM?
TO *BE* WITH HIM?
I-I'M SORRY, HONEY. I'VE RUINED YOUR HOMECOMING.
YOUR MOTHER GAVE HER LIFE FIGHTING THE ADVERSARY, AND THAT BUYS US MORE FREEDOM THAN MOST--
--BUT DISSENT ISN'T *RESPECTED* HERE ANYMORE.
THE ADVERSARY HAS STEPPED UP HIS ASSAULTS, AND HOLDMOTHER HAS USED THE CRISIS TO SEIZE POWER FROM THE COUNCIL.
WE'RE FAR FROM THE STRONGHOLD WE ASPIRE TO BE.
I DIDN'T MEAN TO START A FIGHT, DAD.
HA. TO TELL THE TRUTH, I MISSED FIGHTING WITH YOU.
THE STRONGHOLD IS A BORING PLACE WITHOUT MY LITTLE GIRL.
WITHOUT MY CLAIRE.

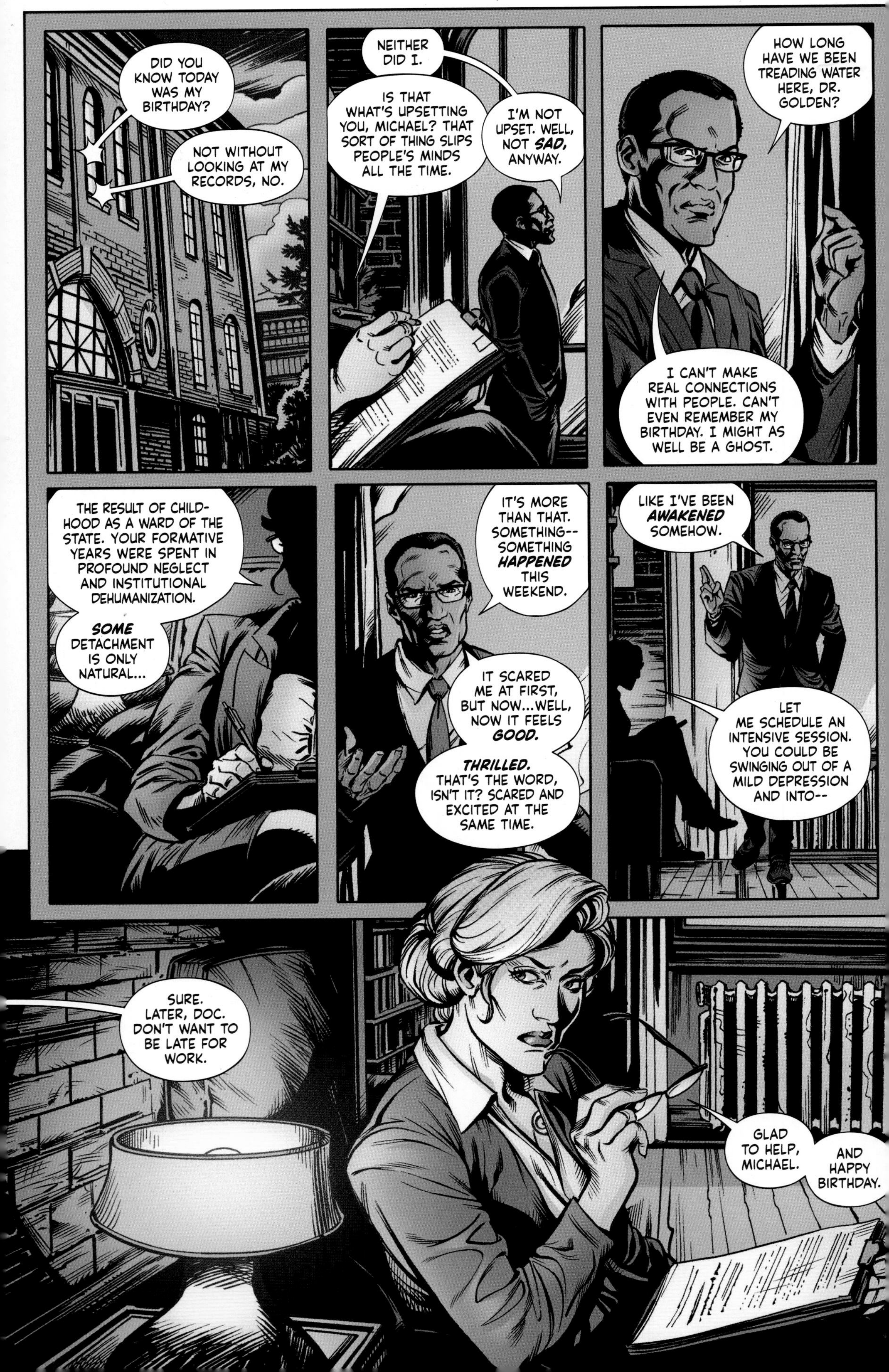
DID YOU KNOW TODAY WAS MY BIRTHDAY?
NOT WITHOUT LOOKING AT MY RECORDS, NO.
NEITHER DID I.
IS THAT WHAT'S UPSETTING YOU, MICHAEL? THAT SORT OF THING SLIPS PEOPLE'S MINDS ALL THE TIME.
I'M NOT UPSET. WELL, NOT SAD, ANYWAY.
HOW LONG HAVE WE BEEN TREADING WATER HERE, DR. GOLDEN?
I CAN'T MAKE REAL CONNECTIONS WITH PEOPLE. CAN'T EVEN REMEMBER MY BIRTHDAY. I MIGHT AS WELL BE A GHOST.
THE RESULT OF CHILDHOOD AS A WARD OF THE STATE. YOUR FORMATIVE YEARS WERE SPENT IN PROFOUND NEGLECT AND INSTITUTIONAL DEHUMANIZATION.
SOME DETACHMENT IS ONLY NATURAL...
IT'S MORE THAN THAT. SOMETHING--SOMETHING HAPPENED THIS WEEKEND.
IT SCARED ME AT FIRST, BUT NOW...WELL, NOW IT FEELS GOOD.
THRILLED. THAT'S THE WORD, ISN'T IT? SCARED AND EXCITED AT THE SAME TIME.
LIKE I'VE BEEN AWAKENED SOMEHOW.
LET ME SCHEDULE AN INTENSIVE SESSION. YOU COULD BE SWINGING OUT OF A MILD DEPRESSION AND INTO--
SURE. LATER, DOC. DON'T WANT TO BE LATE FOR WORK.
GLAD TO HELP, MICHAEL.
AND HAPPY BIRTHDAY.

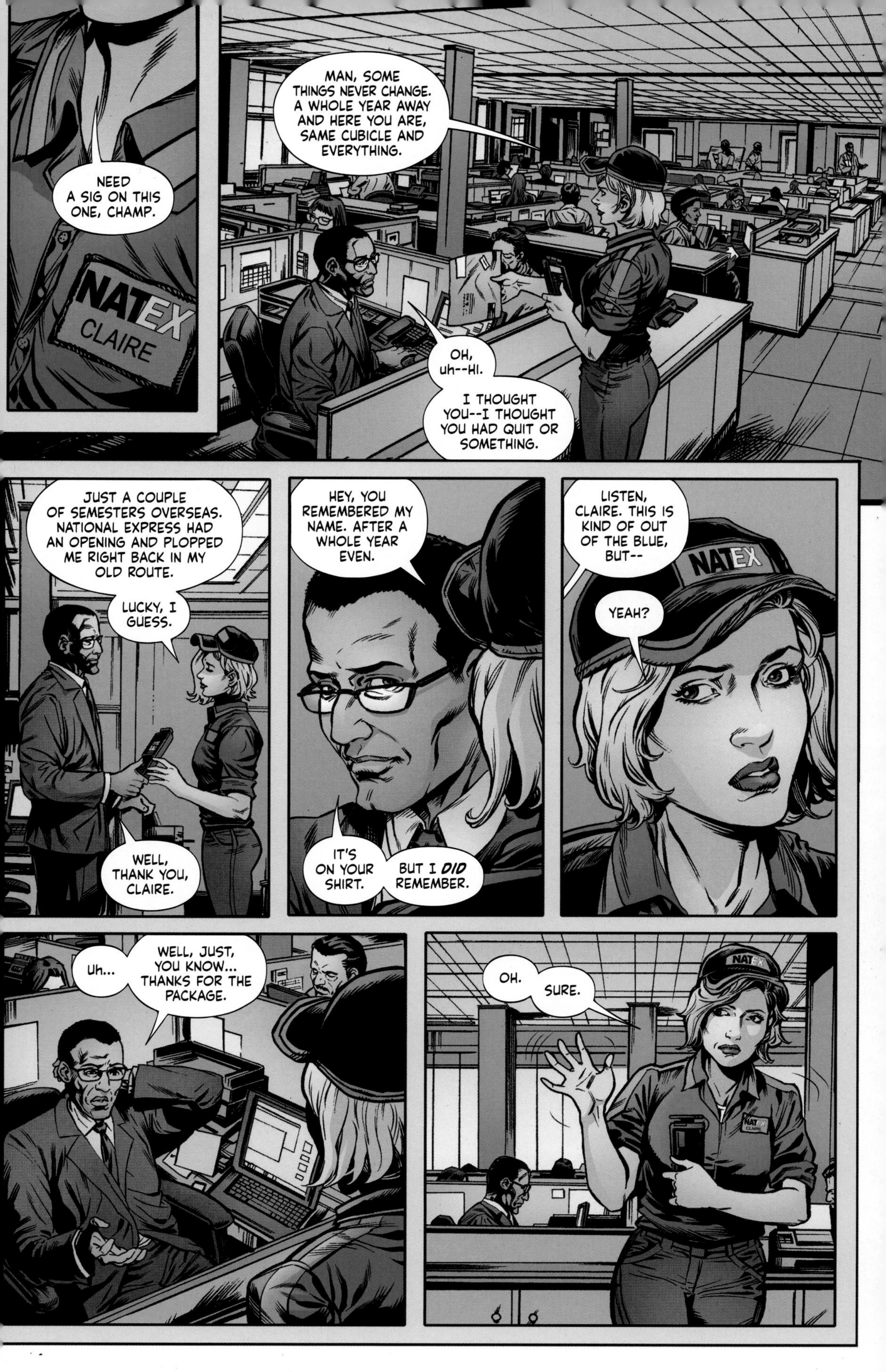
NATEX
CLAIRE
NEED A SIG ON THIS ONE, CHAMP.
MAN, SOME THINGS NEVER CHANGE. A WHOLE YEAR AWAY AND HERE YOU ARE, SAME CUBICLE AND EVERYTHING.
OH, uh--HI.
I THOUGHT YOU--I THOUGHT YOU HAD QUIT OR SOMETHING.
JUST A COUPLE OF SEMESTERS OVERSEAS. NATIONAL EXPRESS HAD AN OPENING AND PLOPPED ME RIGHT BACK IN MY OLD ROUTE.
LUCKY, I GUESS.
WELL, THANK YOU, CLAIRE.
HEY, YOU REMEMBERED MY NAME. AFTER A WHOLE YEAR EVEN.
IT'S ON YOUR SHIRT.
BUT I *DID* REMEMBER.
LISTEN, CLAIRE. THIS IS KIND OF OUT OF THE BLUE, BUT--
NATEX
YEAH?
Uh...
WELL, JUST, YOU KNOW... THANKS FOR THE PACKAGE.
OH.
SURE.
NATEX

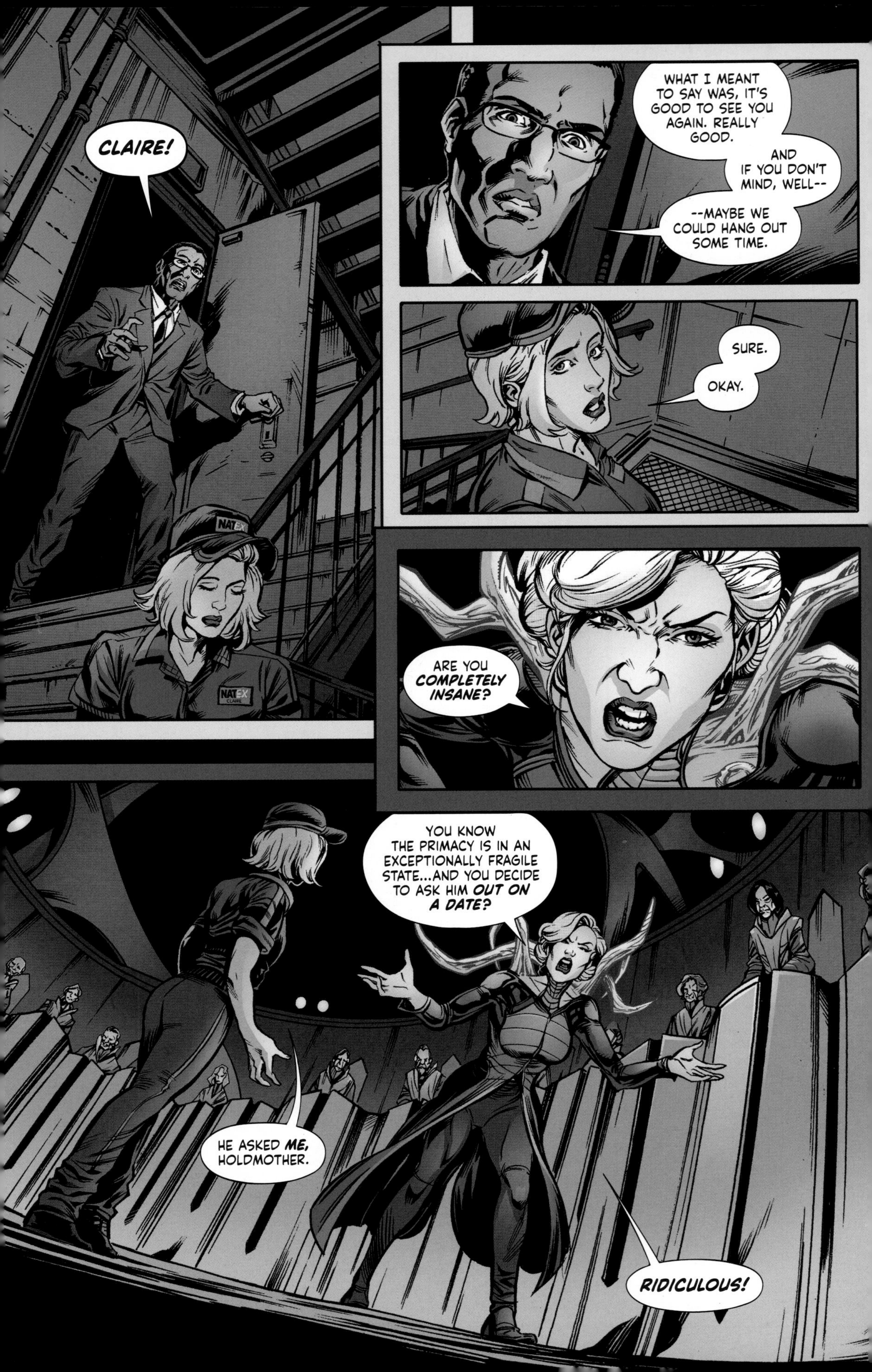
CLAIRE!
WHAT I MEANT TO SAY WAS, IT'S GOOD TO SEE YOU AGAIN. REALLY GOOD.
AND IF YOU DON'T MIND, WELL--
--MAYBE WE COULD HANG OUT SOME TIME.
SURE.
OKAY.
NATEX
NATEX CLAIRE
ARE YOU COMPLETELY INSANE?
YOU KNOW THE PRIMACY IS IN AN EXCEPTIONALLY FRAGILE STATE...AND YOU DECIDE TO ASK HIM OUT ON A DATE?
HE ASKED ME, HOLDMOTHER.
RIDICULOUS!

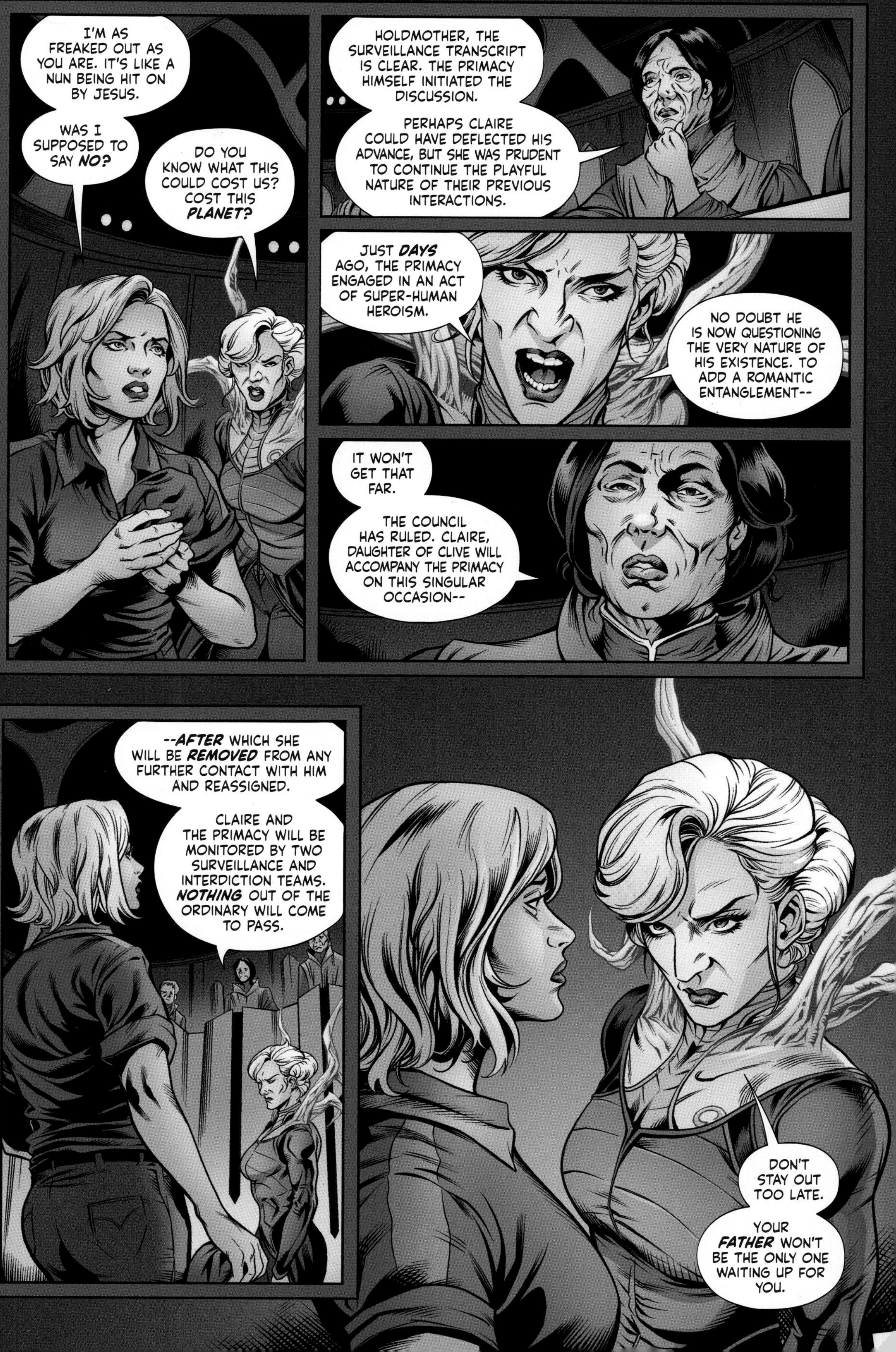

I'M AS FREAKED OUT AS YOU ARE. IT'S LIKE A NUN BEING HIT ON BY JESUS.
WAS I SUPPOSED TO SAY *NO?*
DO YOU KNOW WHAT THIS COULD COST US? COST THIS *PLANET?*
HOLDMOTHER, THE SURVEILLANCE TRANSCRIPT IS CLEAR. THE PRIMACY HIMSELF INITIATED THE DISCUSSION.
PERHAPS CLAIRE COULD HAVE DEFLECTED HIS ADVANCE, BUT SHE WAS PRUDENT TO CONTINUE THE PLAYFUL NATURE OF THEIR PREVIOUS INTERACTIONS.
JUST *DAYS* AGO, THE PRIMACY ENGAGED IN AN ACT OF SUPER-HUMAN HEROISM.
NO DOUBT HE IS NOW QUESTIONING THE VERY NATURE OF HIS EXISTENCE. TO ADD A ROMANTIC ENTANGLEMENT--
IT WON'T GET THAT FAR.
THE COUNCIL HAS RULED. CLAIRE, DAUGHTER OF CLIVE WILL ACCOMPANY THE PRIMACY ON THIS SINGULAR OCCASION--
--*AFTER* WHICH SHE WILL BE *REMOVED* FROM ANY FURTHER CONTACT WITH HIM AND REASSIGNED.
CLAIRE AND THE PRIMACY WILL BE MONITORED BY TWO SURVEILLANCE AND INTERDICTION TEAMS. *NOTHING* OUT OF THE ORDINARY WILL COME TO PASS.
DON'T STAY OUT TOO LATE.
YOUR *FATHER* WON'T BE THE ONLY ONE WAITING UP FOR YOU.

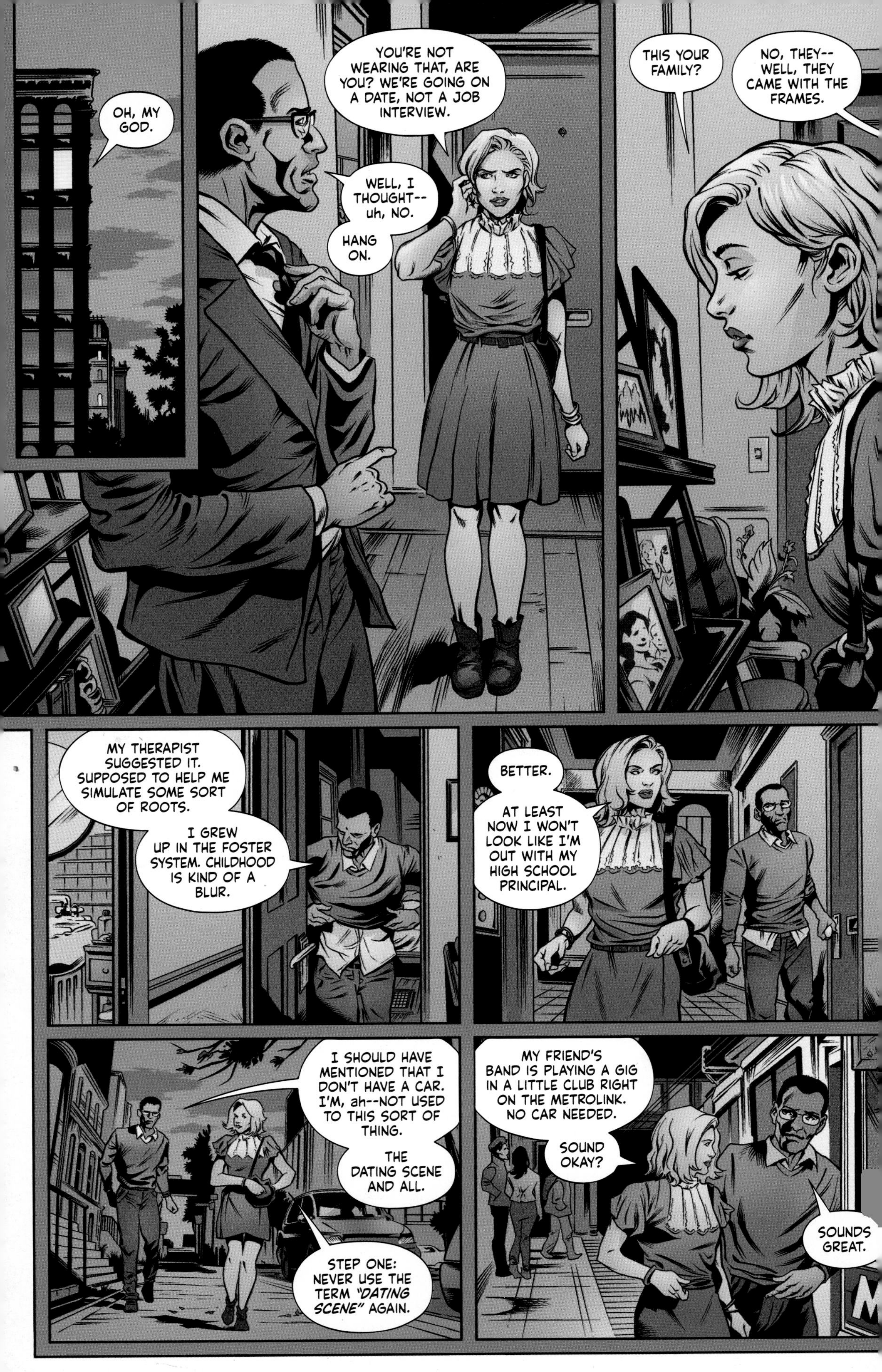
OH, MY GOD.
YOU'RE NOT WEARING THAT, ARE YOU? WE'RE GOING ON A DATE, NOT A JOB INTERVIEW.
WELL, I THOUGHT-- uh, NO.
HANG ON.
THIS YOUR FAMILY?
NO, THEY-- WELL, THEY CAME WITH THE FRAMES.
MY THERAPIST SUGGESTED IT. SUPPOSED TO HELP ME SIMULATE SOME SORT OF ROOTS.
I GREW UP IN THE FOSTER SYSTEM. CHILDHOOD IS KIND OF A BLUR.
BETTER.
AT LEAST NOW I WON'T LOOK LIKE I'M OUT WITH MY HIGH SCHOOL PRINCIPAL.
I SHOULD HAVE MENTIONED THAT I DON'T HAVE A CAR. I'M, ah--NOT USED TO THIS SORT OF THING.
THE DATING SCENE AND ALL.
STEP ONE: NEVER USE THE TERM *"DATING SCENE"* AGAIN.
MY FRIEND'S BAND IS PLAYING A GIG IN A LITTLE CLUB RIGHT ON THE METROLINK. NO CAR NEEDED.
SOUND OKAY?
SOUNDS GREAT.

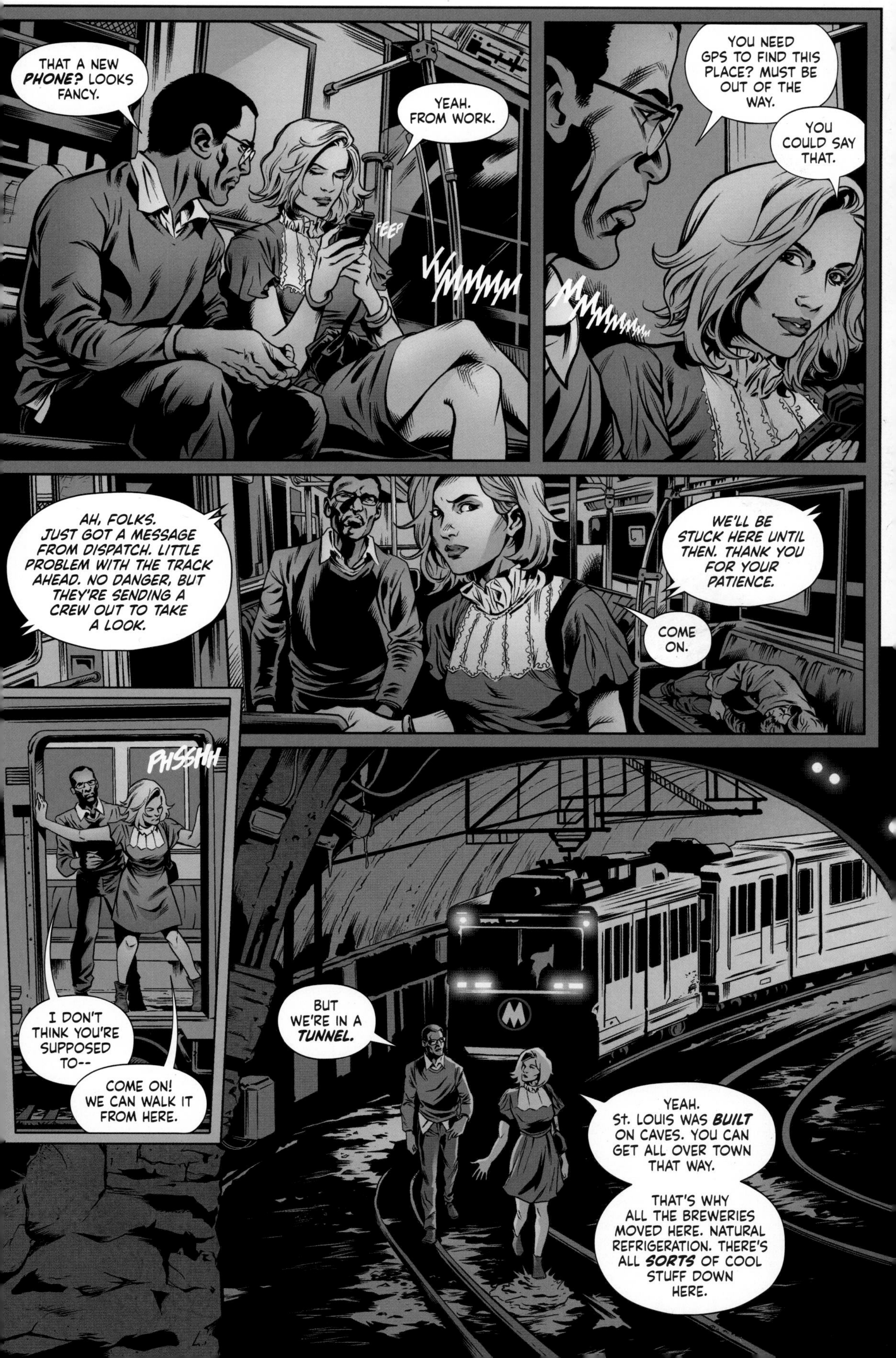
THAT A NEW PHONE? LOOKS FANCY.
YEAH. FROM WORK.
FEEP
VVMMMMM
YOU NEED GPS TO FIND THIS PLACE? MUST BE OUT OF THE WAY.
YOU COULD SAY THAT.
MMMMMMM
AH, FOLKS. JUST GOT A MESSAGE FROM DISPATCH. LITTLE PROBLEM WITH THE TRACK AHEAD. NO DANGER, BUT THEY'RE SENDING A CREW OUT TO TAKE A LOOK.
WE'LL BE STUCK HERE UNTIL THEN. THANK YOU FOR YOUR PATIENCE.
COME ON.
PHSSHH
I DON'T THINK YOU'RE SUPPOSED TO--
COME ON! WE CAN WALK IT FROM HERE.
BUT WE'RE IN A TUNNEL.
YEAH. St. LOUIS WAS BUILT ON CAVES. YOU CAN GET ALL OVER TOWN THAT WAY.
THAT'S WHY ALL THE BREWERIES MOVED HERE. NATURAL REFRIGERATION. THERE'S ALL SORTS OF COOL STUFF DOWN HERE.

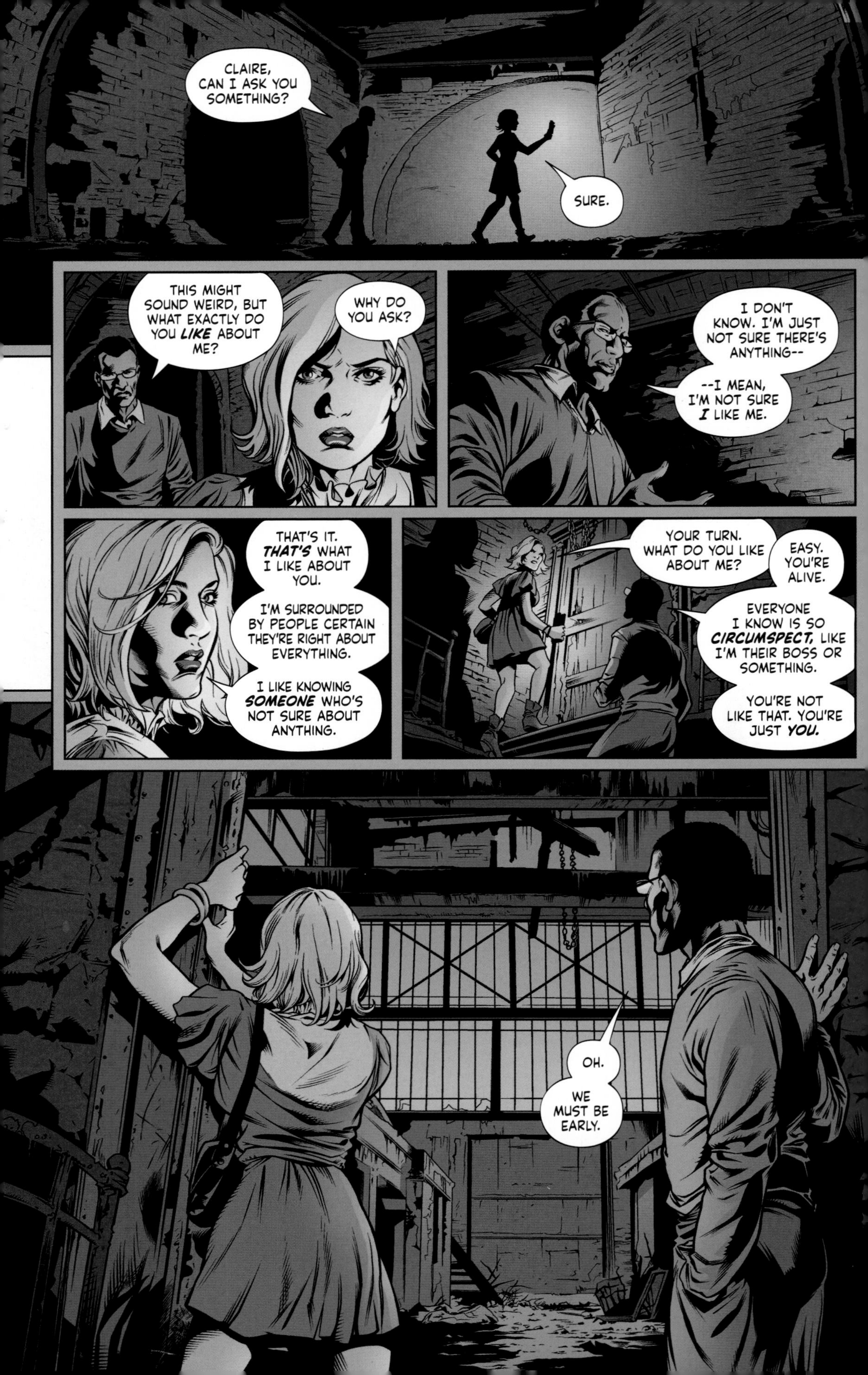
CLAIRE, CAN I ASK YOU SOMETHING?
SURE.
THIS MIGHT SOUND WEIRD, BUT WHAT EXACTLY DO YOU *LIKE* ABOUT ME?
WHY DO YOU ASK?
I DON'T KNOW. I'M JUST NOT SURE THERE'S ANYTHING--
--I MEAN, I'M NOT SURE *I* LIKE ME.
THAT'S IT. *THAT'S* WHAT I LIKE ABOUT YOU.
I'M SURROUNDED BY PEOPLE CERTAIN THEY'RE RIGHT ABOUT EVERYTHING.
I LIKE KNOWING *SOMEONE* WHO'S NOT SURE ABOUT ANYTHING.
YOUR TURN. WHAT DO YOU LIKE ABOUT ME?
EASY. YOU'RE ALIVE.
EVERYONE I KNOW IS SO *CIRCUMSPECT,* LIKE I'M THEIR BOSS OR SOMETHING.
YOU'RE NOT LIKE THAT. YOU'RE JUST *YOU.*
OH.
WE MUST BE EARLY.

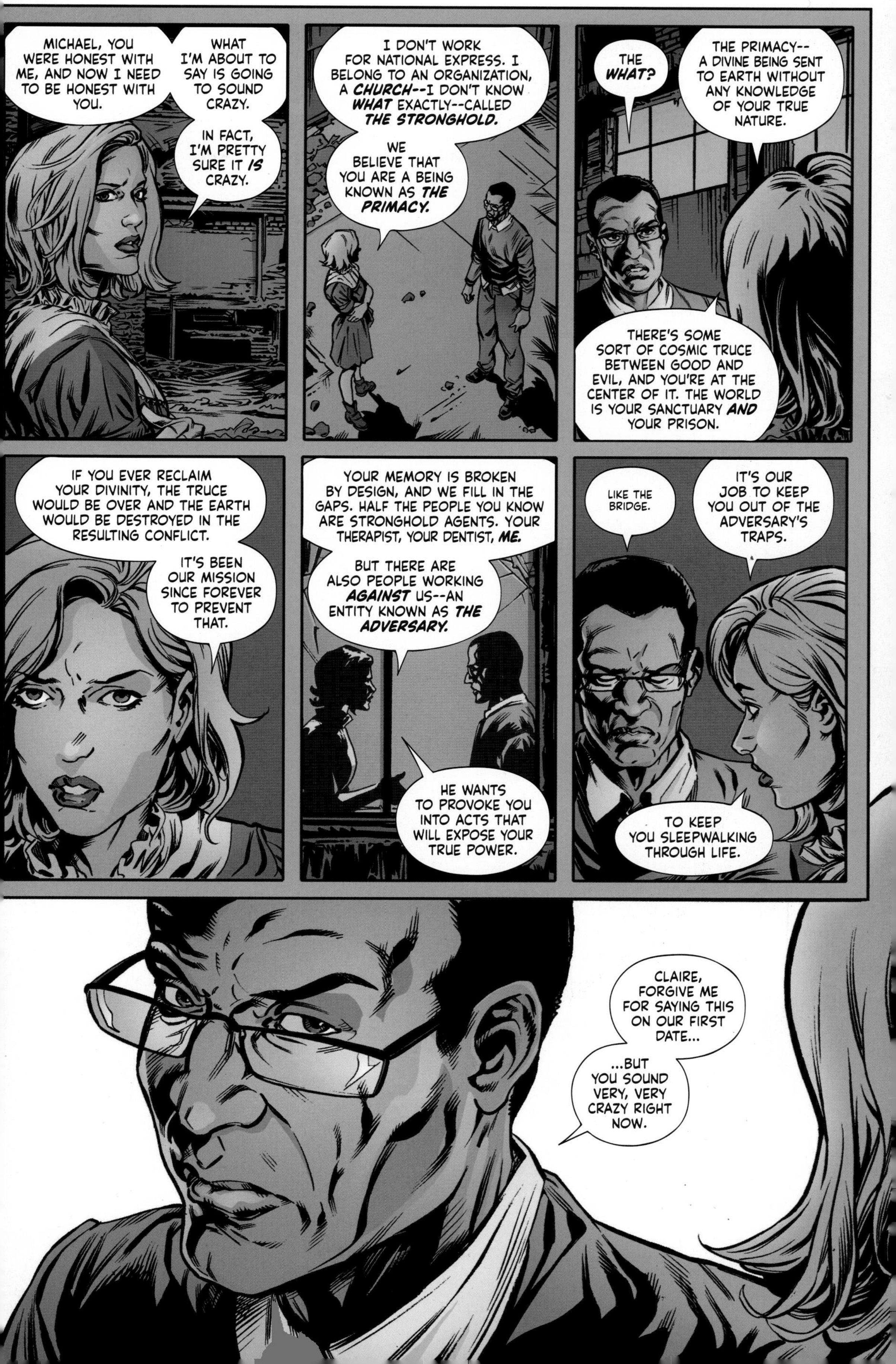
MICHAEL, YOU WERE HONEST WITH ME, AND NOW I NEED TO BE HONEST WITH YOU.
WHAT I'M ABOUT TO SAY IS GOING TO SOUND CRAZY.
IN FACT, I'M PRETTY SURE IT *IS* CRAZY.
I DON'T WORK FOR NATIONAL EXPRESS. I BELONG TO AN ORGANIZATION, A *CHURCH*--I DON'T KNOW *WHAT* EXACTLY--CALLED *THE STRONGHOLD.*
WE BELIEVE THAT YOU ARE A BEING KNOWN AS *THE PRIMACY.*
THE *WHAT?*
THE PRIMACY-- A DIVINE BEING SENT TO EARTH WITHOUT ANY KNOWLEDGE OF YOUR TRUE NATURE.
THERE'S SOME SORT OF COSMIC TRUCE BETWEEN GOOD AND EVIL, AND YOU'RE AT THE CENTER OF IT. THE WORLD IS YOUR SANCTUARY *AND* YOUR PRISON.
IF YOU EVER RECLAIM YOUR DIVINITY, THE TRUCE WOULD BE OVER AND THE EARTH WOULD BE DESTROYED IN THE RESULTING CONFLICT.
IT'S BEEN OUR MISSION SINCE FOREVER TO PREVENT THAT.
YOUR MEMORY IS BROKEN BY DESIGN, AND WE FILL IN THE GAPS. HALF THE PEOPLE YOU KNOW ARE STRONGHOLD AGENTS. YOUR THERAPIST, YOUR DENTIST, *ME.*
BUT THERE ARE ALSO PEOPLE WORKING *AGAINST* US--AN ENTITY KNOWN AS *THE ADVERSARY.*
HE WANTS TO PROVOKE YOU INTO ACTS THAT WILL EXPOSE YOUR TRUE POWER.
LIKE THE BRIDGE.
IT'S OUR JOB TO KEEP YOU OUT OF THE ADVERSARY'S TRAPS.
TO KEEP YOU SLEEPWALKING THROUGH LIFE.
CLAIRE, FORGIVE ME FOR SAYING THIS ON OUR FIRST DATE...
...BUT YOU SOUND VERY, VERY CRAZY RIGHT NOW.

TELL ME ABOUT IT. BUT YOU CAN PROVE IT ONE WAY OR ANOTHER.

THAT'S WHY I BROUGHT YOU HERE THROUGH THE CAVES. DEAD SPOTS IN OUR SURVEILLANCE NET. THEY WON'T FIND US FOR HOURS.

NOT *BEFORE.*

BEFORE *WHAT,* CLAIRE?

BEFORE THE KNIGHTS COME.

OKAY. THESE *KNIGHTS,* THEY BELONG TO YOUR GROUP?

NO. *WHITE KNIGHTS.* A BIKER GANG. THEY CONTROL THE FLOW OF METH-AMPHETAMINES INTO ST. LOUIS.

OUR CRIME INTEL PREDICTS THEY'LL BE HERE SOON, AND IF THEY FIND US IN THEIR SECRET DROP LOCATION, WELL--IT WON'T BE GOOD.

BUT IF I'M THIS *PRIMACY* THING, I'LL BE ABLE TO HANDLE IT.

AND IF I'M *NOT?*

I GUESS I'LL FINALLY HAVE MY ANSWERS.

VRRRMM

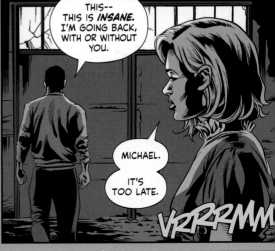
THIS-- THIS IS *INSANE.* I'M GOING BACK, WITH OR WITHOUT YOU.

MICHAEL.

IT'S TOO LATE.

VRRRMM

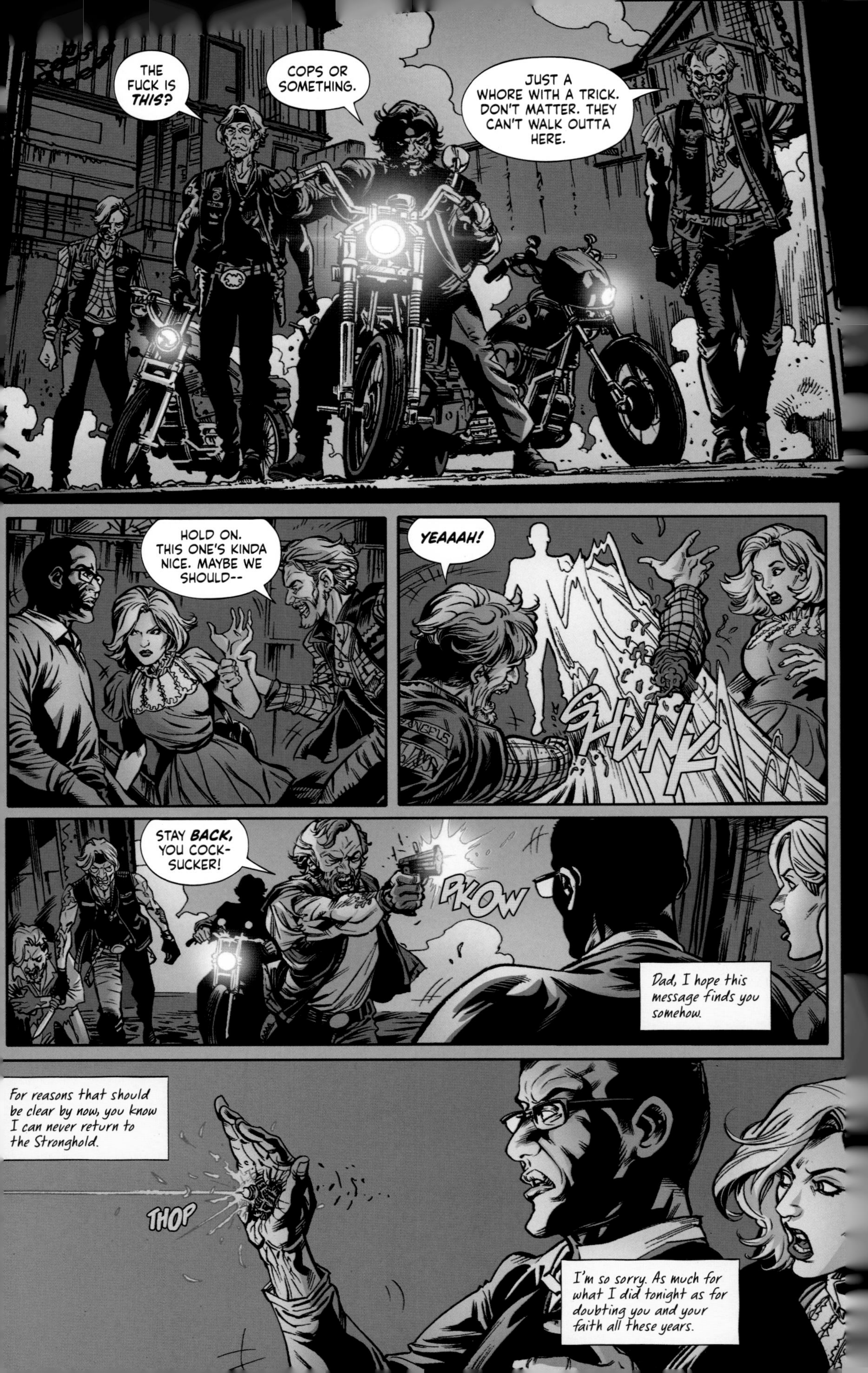

THE FUCK IS THIS?
COPS OR SOMETHING.
JUST A WHORE WITH A TRICK. DON'T MATTER. THEY CAN'T WALK OUTTA HERE.
HOLD ON. THIS ONE'S KINDA NICE. MAYBE WE SHOULD--
YEAAAH!
SHUNK
STAY BACK, YOU COCK-SUCKER!
PKOW
Dad, I hope this message finds you somehow.
For reasons that should be clear by now, you know I can never return to the Stronghold.
THOP
I'm so sorry. As much for what I did tonight as for doubting you and your faith all these years.

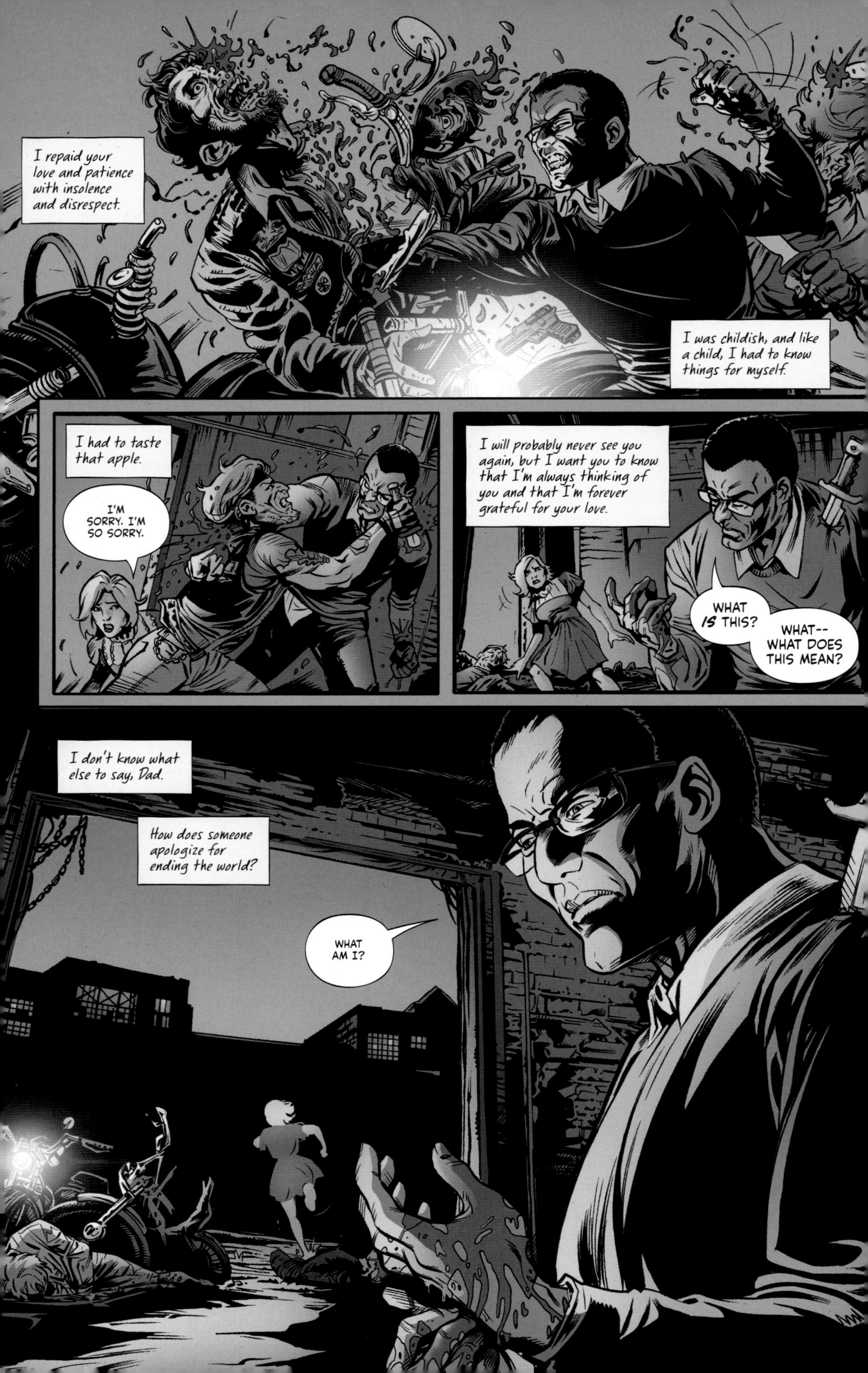

I repaid your love and patience with insolence and disrespect.
I was childish, and like a child, I had to know things for myself.
I had to taste that apple.
I'M SORRY. I'M SO SORRY.
I will probably never see you again, but I want you to know that I'm always thinking of you and that I'm forever grateful for your love.
WHAT *IS* THIS?
WHAT-- WHAT DOES THIS MEAN?
I don't know what else to say, Dad.
How does someone apologize for ending the world?
WHAT AM I?

2

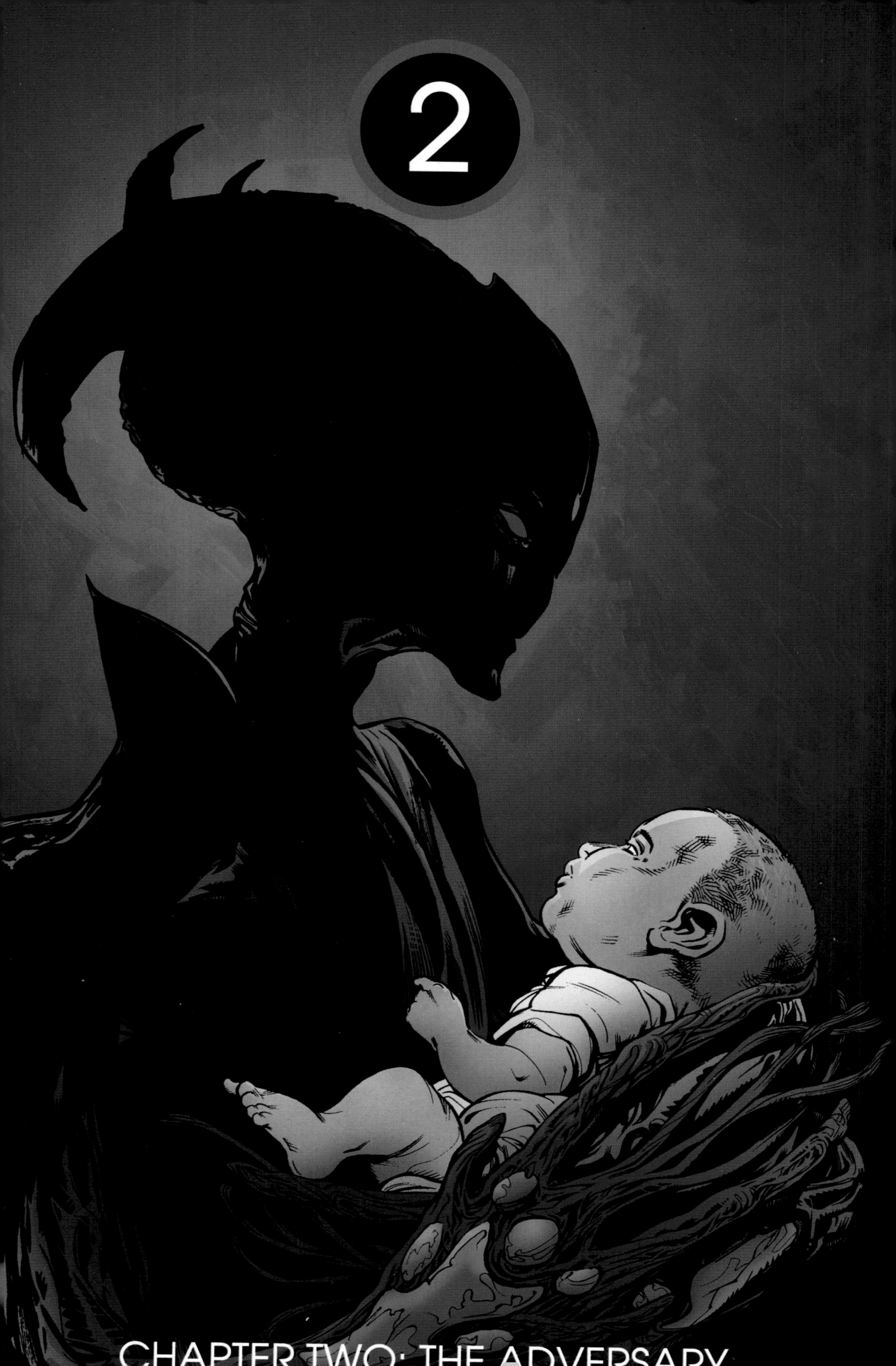

CHAPTER TWO: THE ADVERSARY

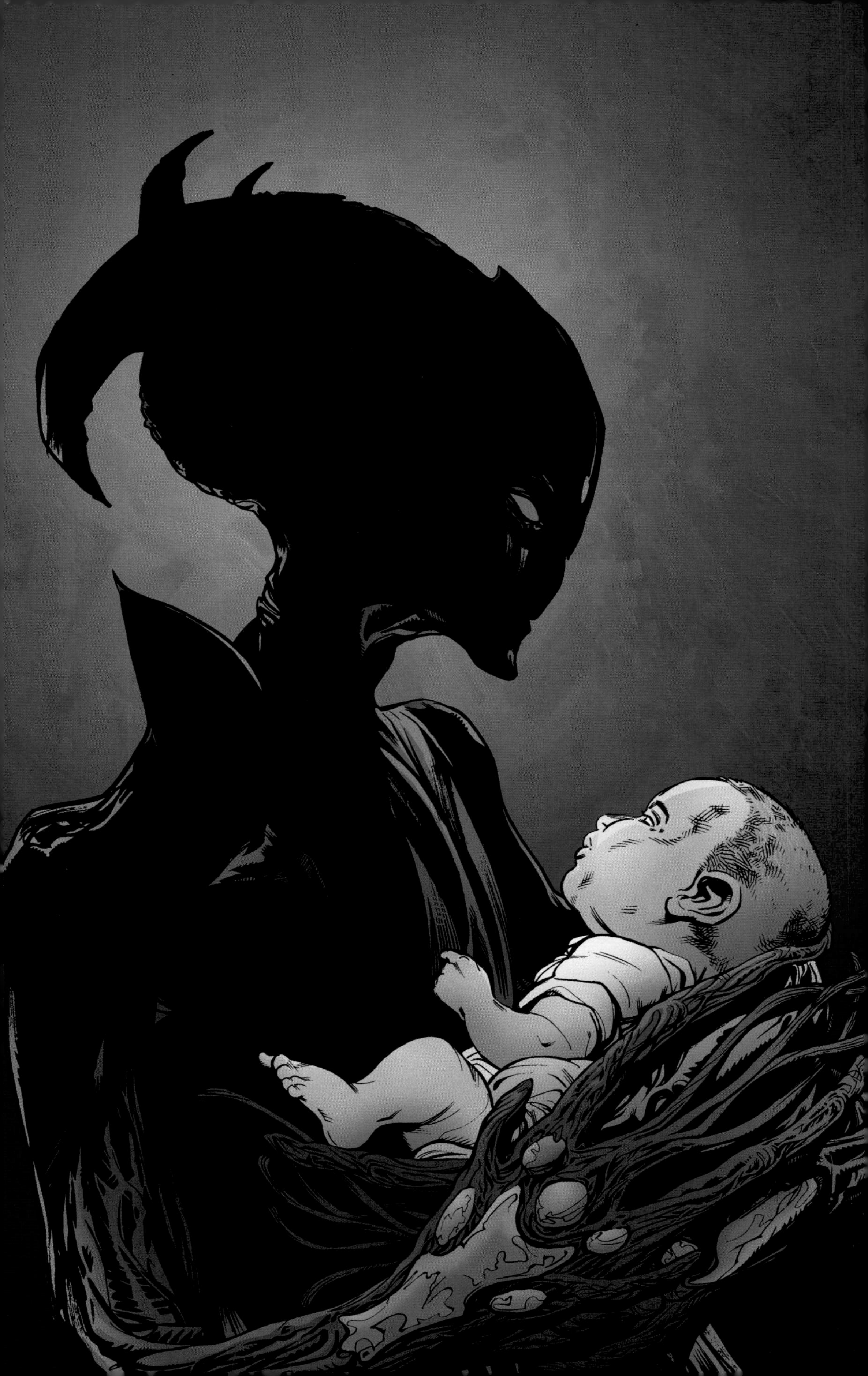

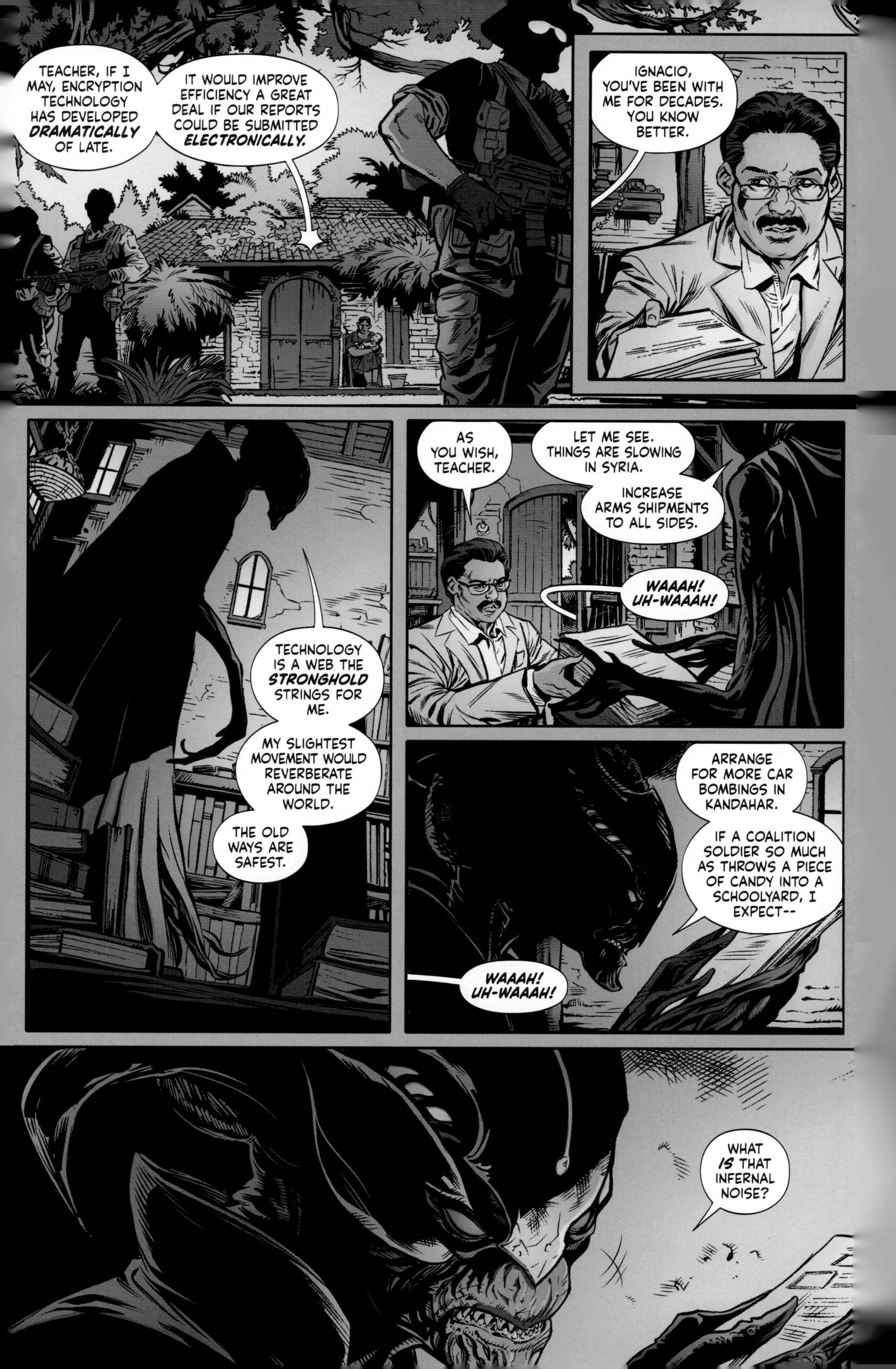
TEACHER, IF I MAY, ENCRYPTION TECHNOLOGY HAS DEVELOPED *DRAMATICALLY* OF LATE.
IT WOULD IMPROVE EFFICIENCY A GREAT DEAL IF OUR REPORTS COULD BE SUBMITTED *ELECTRONICALLY.*
IGNACIO, YOU'VE BEEN WITH ME FOR DECADES. YOU KNOW BETTER.
TECHNOLOGY IS A WEB THE *STRONGHOLD* STRINGS FOR ME.
MY SLIGHTEST MOVEMENT WOULD REVERBERATE AROUND THE WORLD.
THE OLD WAYS ARE SAFEST.
AS YOU WISH, TEACHER.
LET ME SEE. THINGS ARE SLOWING IN SYRIA.
INCREASE ARMS SHIPMENTS TO ALL SIDES.
WAAAH! UH-WAAAH!
ARRANGE FOR MORE CAR BOMBINGS IN KANDAHAR.
IF A COALITION SOLDIER SO MUCH AS THROWS A PIECE OF CANDY INTO A SCHOOLYARD, I EXPECT--
WAAAH! UH-WAAAH!
WHAT *IS* THAT INFERNAL NOISE?

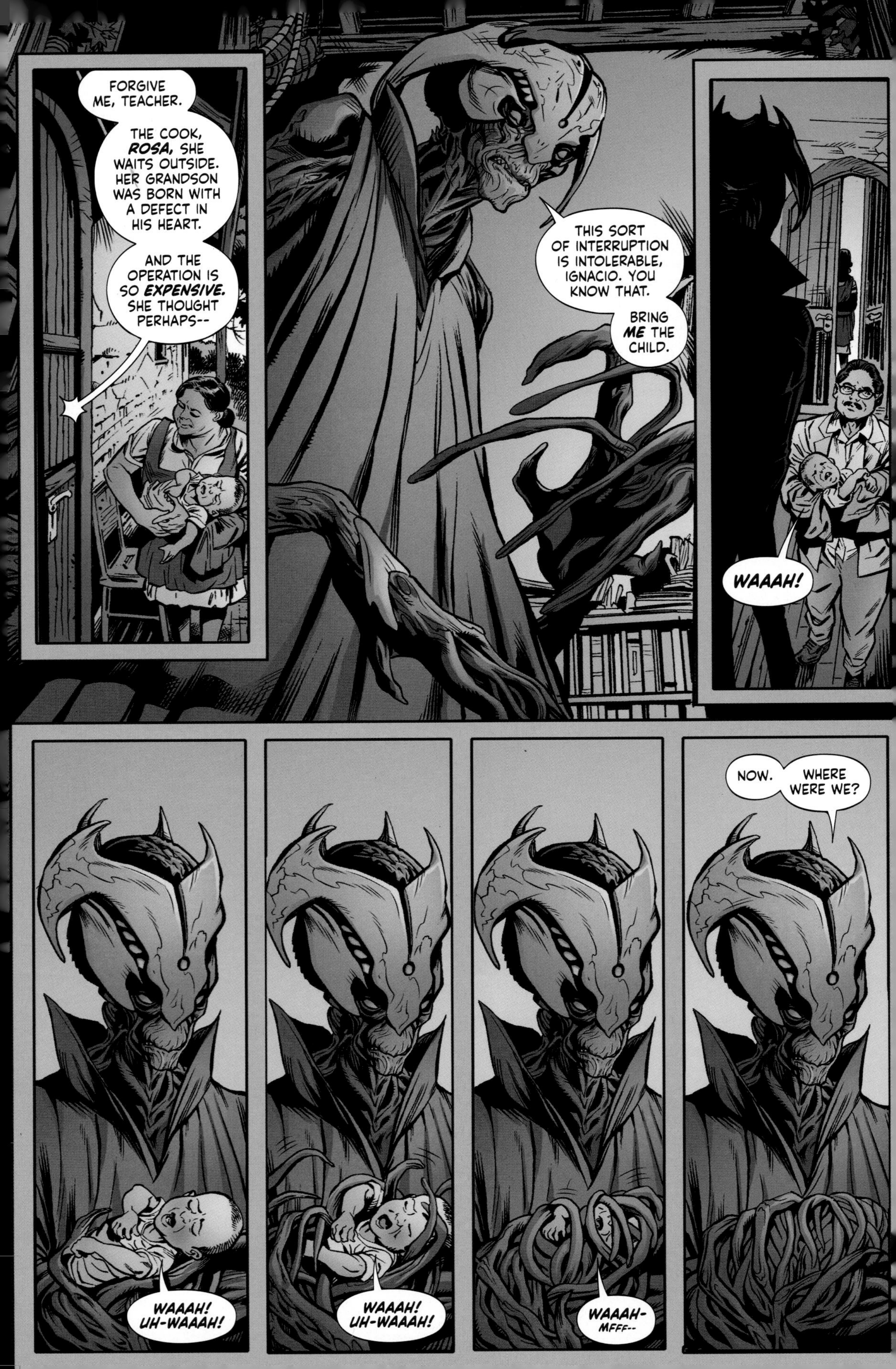
FORGIVE ME, TEACHER.
THE COOK, ROSA, SHE WAITS OUTSIDE. HER GRANDSON WAS BORN WITH A DEFECT IN HIS HEART.
AND THE OPERATION IS SO EXPENSIVE. SHE THOUGHT PERHAPS--
THIS SORT OF INTERRUPTION IS INTOLERABLE, IGNACIO. YOU KNOW THAT.
BRING ME THE CHILD.
WAAAH!
WAAAH! UH-WAAAH!
WAAAH! UH-WAAAH!
WAAAH-MFFF--
NOW.
WHERE WERE WE?

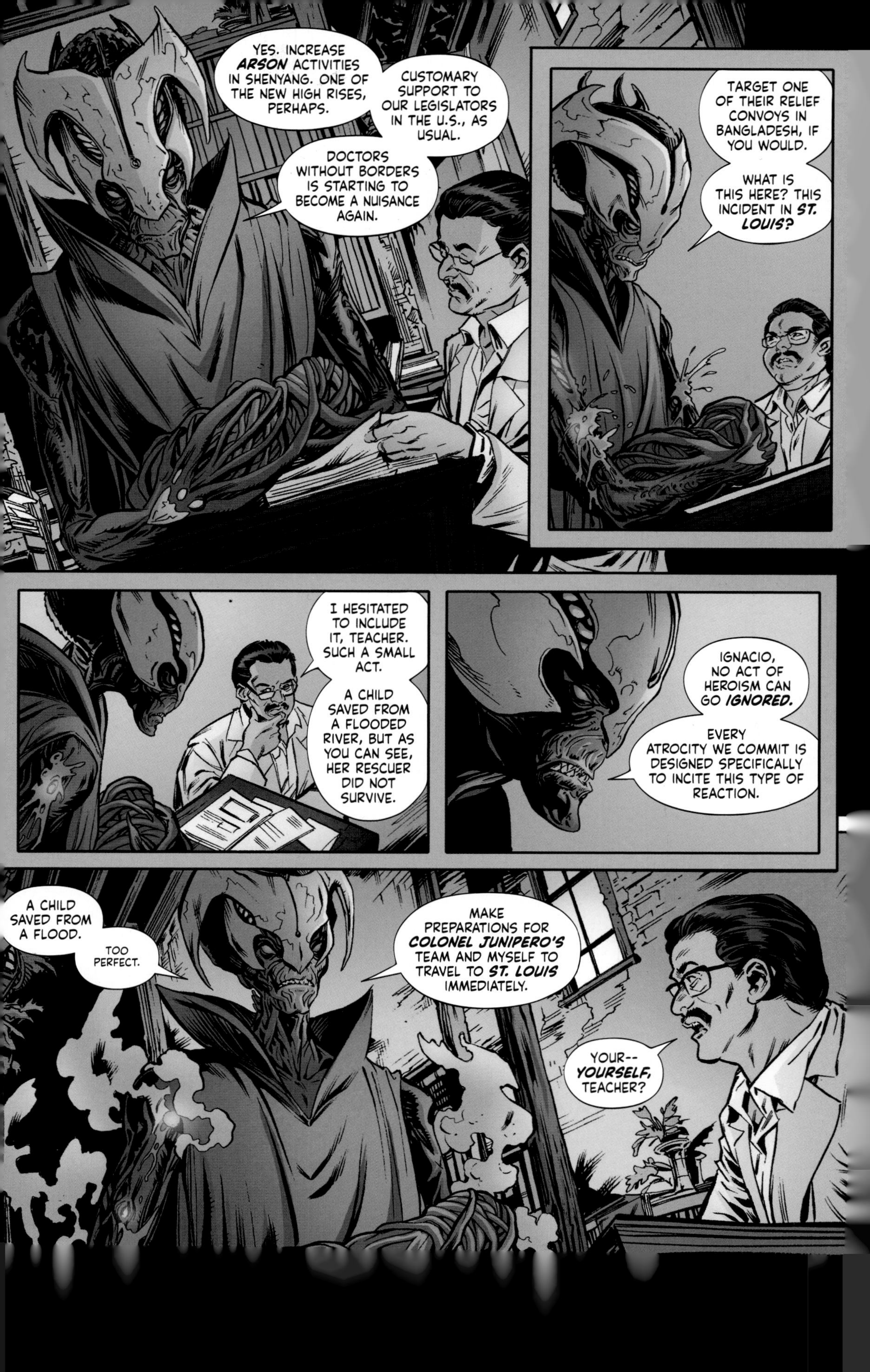
YES. INCREASE ARSON ACTIVITIES IN SHENYANG. ONE OF THE NEW HIGH RISES, PERHAPS.
CUSTOMARY SUPPORT TO OUR LEGISLATORS IN THE U.S., AS USUAL.
DOCTORS WITHOUT BORDERS IS STARTING TO BECOME A NUISANCE AGAIN.
TARGET ONE OF THEIR RELIEF CONVOYS IN BANGLADESH, IF YOU WOULD.
WHAT IS THIS HERE? THIS INCIDENT IN ST. LOUIS?
I HESITATED TO INCLUDE IT, TEACHER. SUCH A SMALL ACT.
A CHILD SAVED FROM A FLOODED RIVER, BUT AS YOU CAN SEE, HER RESCUER DID NOT SURVIVE.
IGNACIO, NO ACT OF HEROISM CAN GO IGNORED.
EVERY ATROCITY WE COMMIT IS DESIGNED SPECIFICALLY TO INCITE THIS TYPE OF REACTION.
A CHILD SAVED FROM A FLOOD.
TOO PERFECT.
MAKE PREPARATIONS FOR COLONEL JUNIPERO'S TEAM AND MYSELF TO TRAVEL TO ST. LOUIS IMMEDIATELY.
YOUR-- YOURSELF, TEACHER?

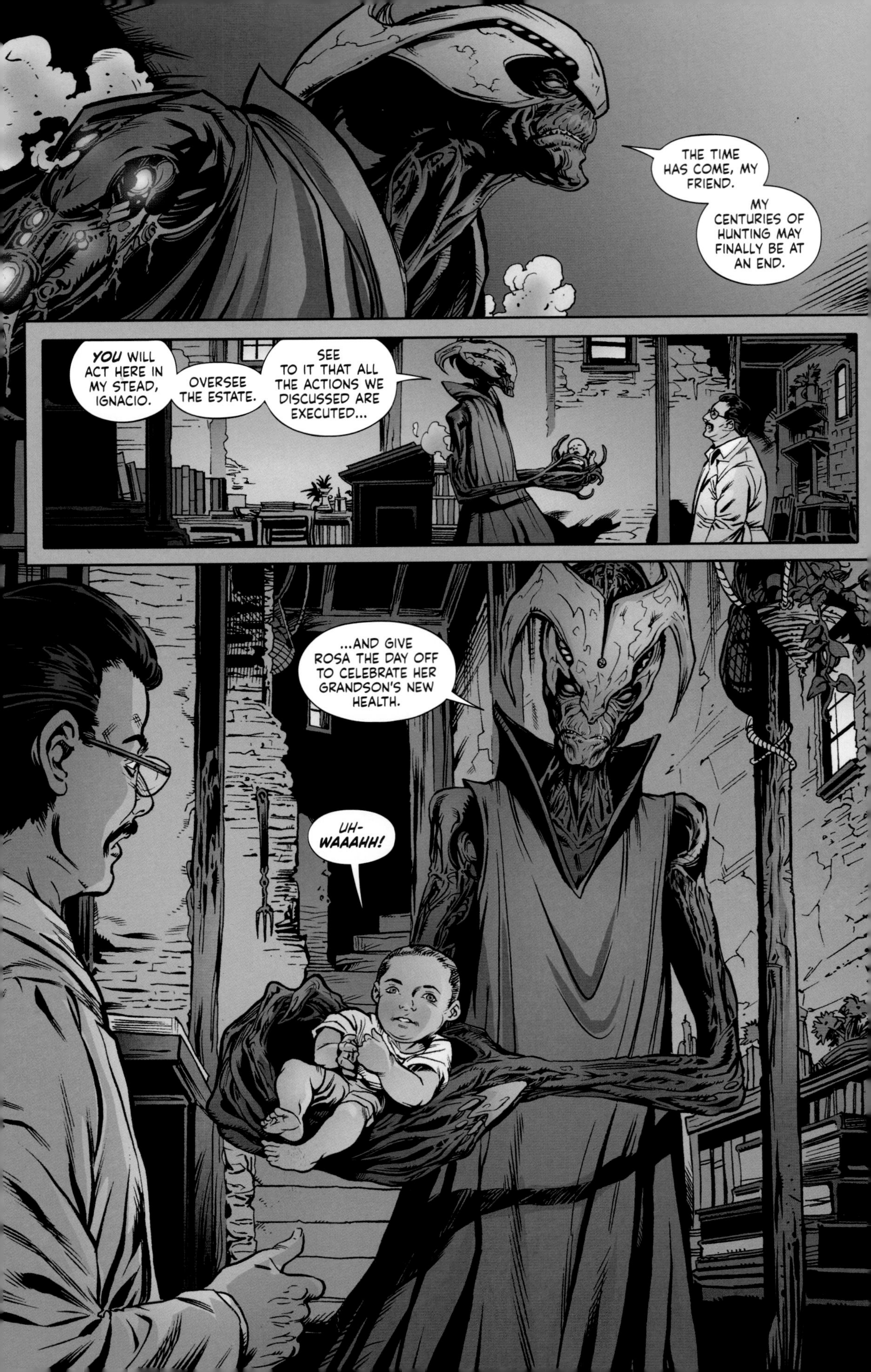
THE TIME HAS COME, MY FRIEND.
MY CENTURIES OF HUNTING MAY FINALLY BE AT AN END.
YOU WILL ACT HERE IN MY STEAD, IGNACIO.
OVERSEE THE ESTATE.
SEE TO IT THAT ALL THE ACTIONS WE DISCUSSED ARE EXECUTED...
...AND GIVE ROSA THE DAY OFF TO CELEBRATE HER GRANDSON'S NEW HEALTH.
UH-WAAAHH!

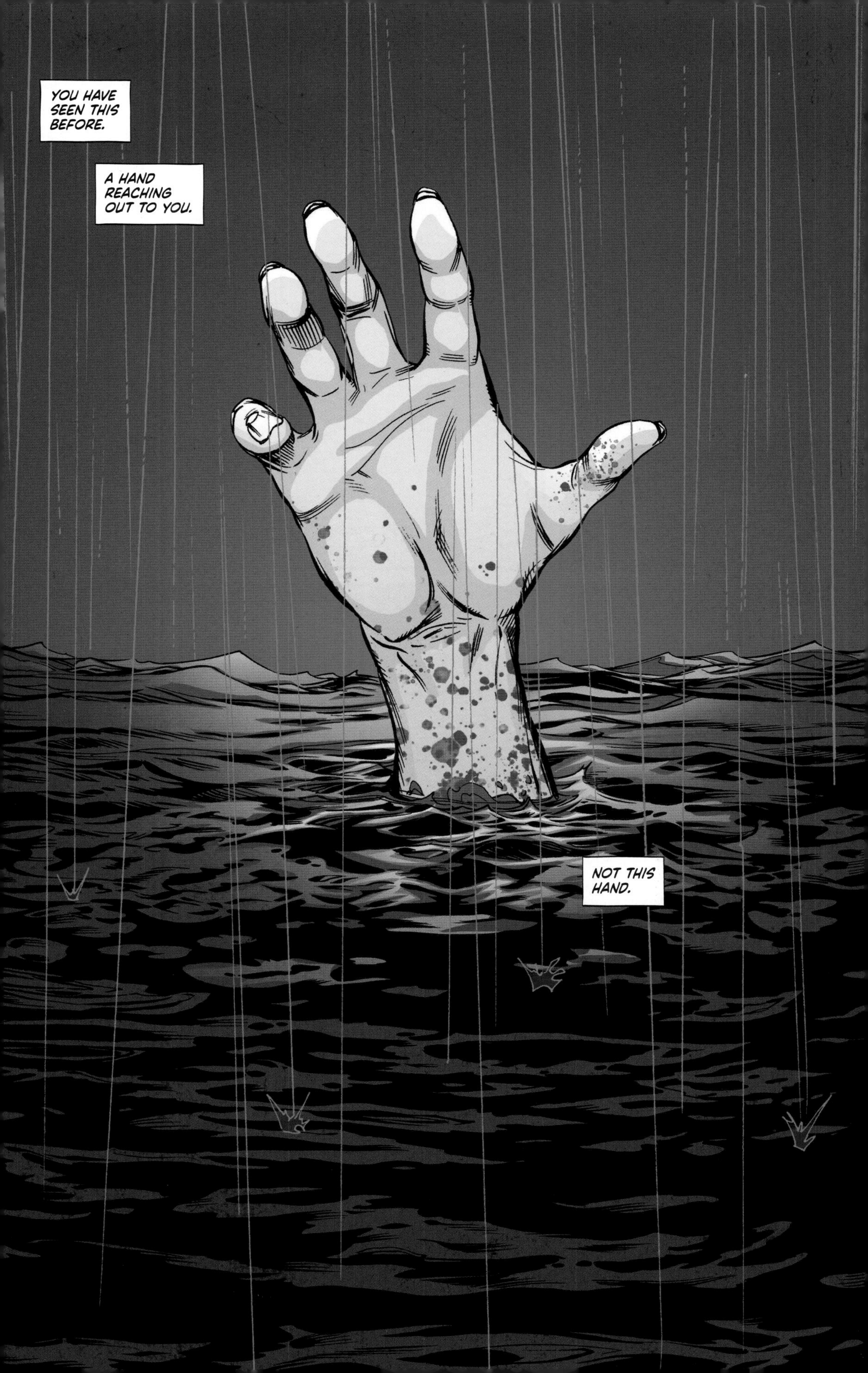
YOU HAVE SEEN THIS BEFORE.
A HAND REACHING OUT TO YOU.
NOT THIS HAND.

A FLOOD SWEEPS IT AWAY.

NOT THIS FLOOD.

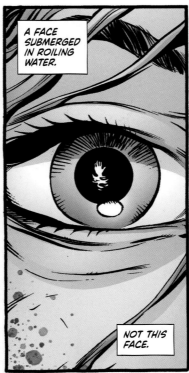

A FACE SUBMERGED IN ROILING WATER.

NOT THIS FACE.

CLAIRE.

A WOMAN YOU BARELY KNOW. A WOMAN YOU SHOULD NOT CARE FOR SO DEEPLY.

IT'S *HER* HAND HELD OUT TO YOU, *HER* FACE SWEPT AWAY IN THE WATER.

NO.

NOT WATER.

IT *IS* A FLOOD, JUST LIKE THE ONE YOU RESCUED THAT LITTLE GIRL FROM LAST WEEK.

BUT IT IS *NOT WATER.*

IT'S A RIVER OF *BLOOD* CARRYING CLAIRE AWAY FROM YOU.

AND IF YOU TAKE HER HAND--

--IT WILL SWALLOW YOU, TOO.

--SAID THIS IS THE END OF THE LINE, MISTER.

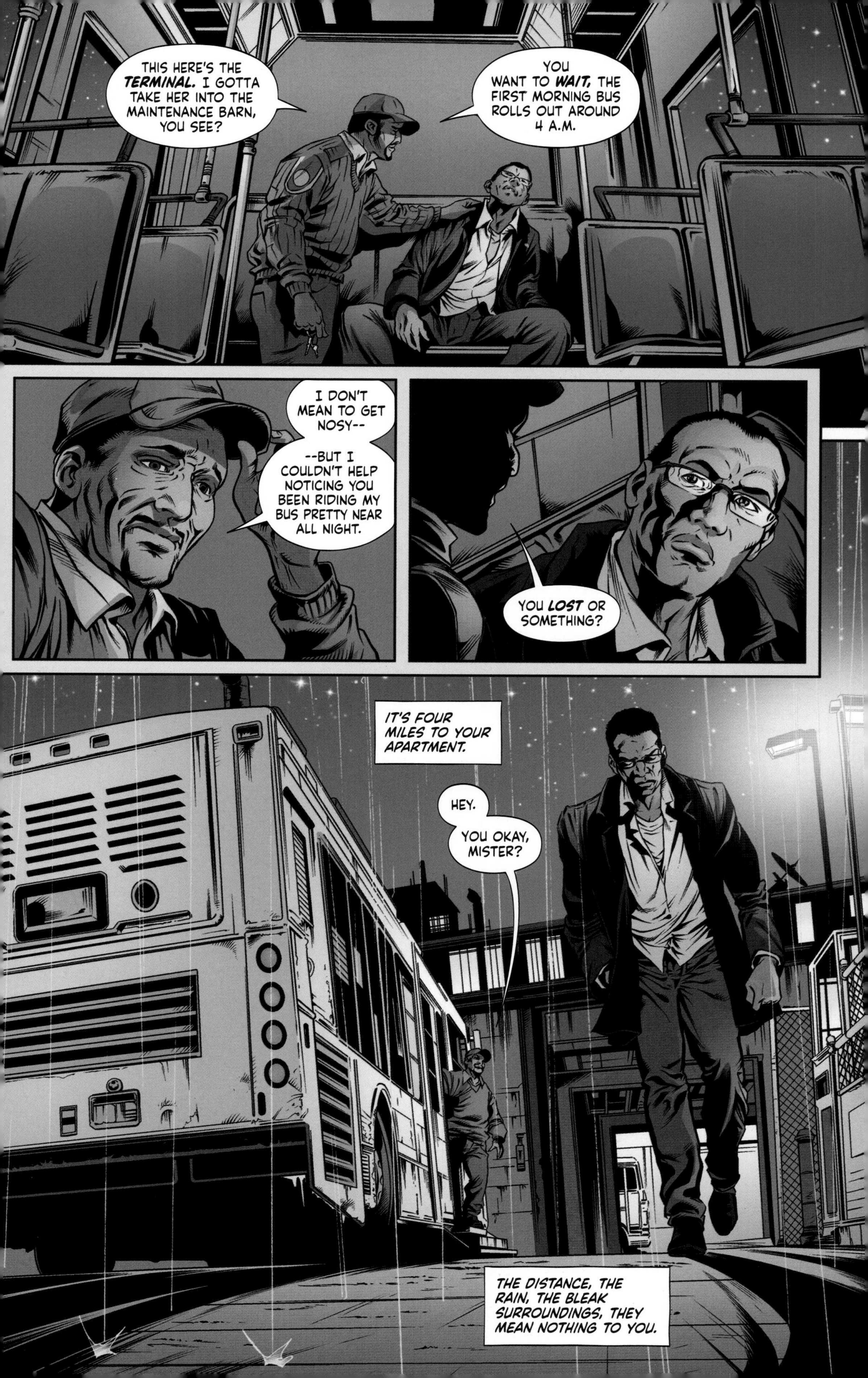
THIS HERE'S THE TERMINAL. I GOTTA TAKE HER INTO THE MAINTENANCE BARN, YOU SEE?
YOU WANT TO WAIT, THE FIRST MORNING BUS ROLLS OUT AROUND 4 A.M.
I DON'T MEAN TO GET NOSY--
--BUT I COULDN'T HELP NOTICING YOU BEEN RIDING MY BUS PRETTY NEAR ALL NIGHT.
YOU LOST OR SOMETHING?
IT'S FOUR MILES TO YOUR APARTMENT.
HEY.
YOU OKAY, MISTER?
THE DISTANCE, THE RAIN, THE BLEAK SURROUNDINGS, THEY MEAN NOTHING TO YOU.

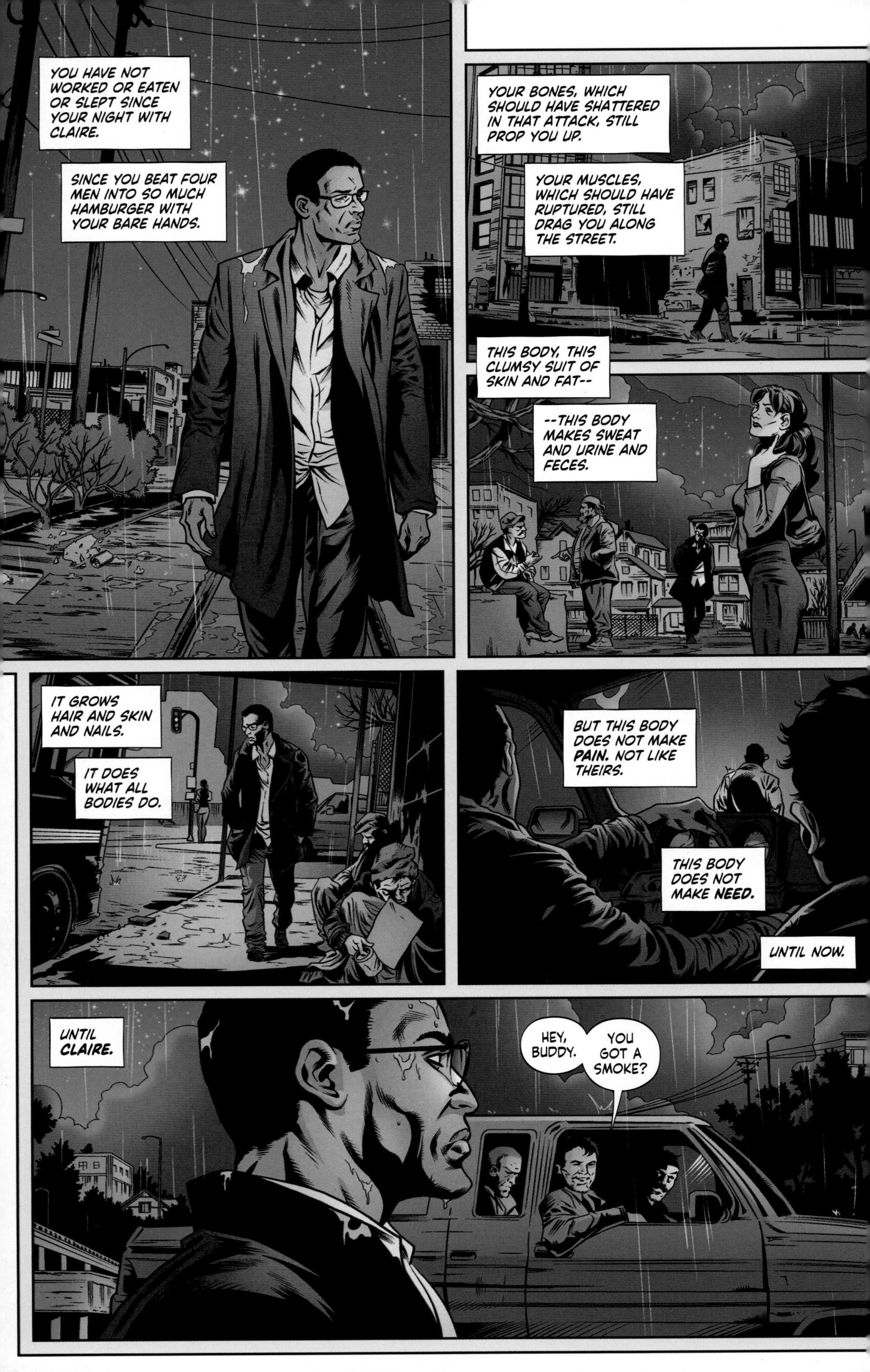
YOU HAVE NOT WORKED OR EATEN OR SLEPT SINCE YOUR NIGHT WITH CLAIRE.
SINCE YOU BEAT FOUR MEN INTO SO MUCH HAMBURGER WITH YOUR BARE HANDS.
YOUR BONES, WHICH SHOULD HAVE SHATTERED IN THAT ATTACK, STILL PROP YOU UP.
YOUR MUSCLES, WHICH SHOULD HAVE RUPTURED, STILL DRAG YOU ALONG THE STREET.
THIS BODY, THIS CLUMSY SUIT OF SKIN AND FAT--
--THIS BODY MAKES SWEAT AND URINE AND FECES.
IT GROWS HAIR AND SKIN AND NAILS.
IT DOES WHAT ALL BODIES DO.
BUT THIS BODY DOES NOT MAKE PAIN. NOT LIKE THEIRS.
THIS BODY DOES NOT MAKE NEED.
UNTIL NOW.
UNTIL CLAIRE.
HEY, BUDDY.
YOU GOT A SMOKE?

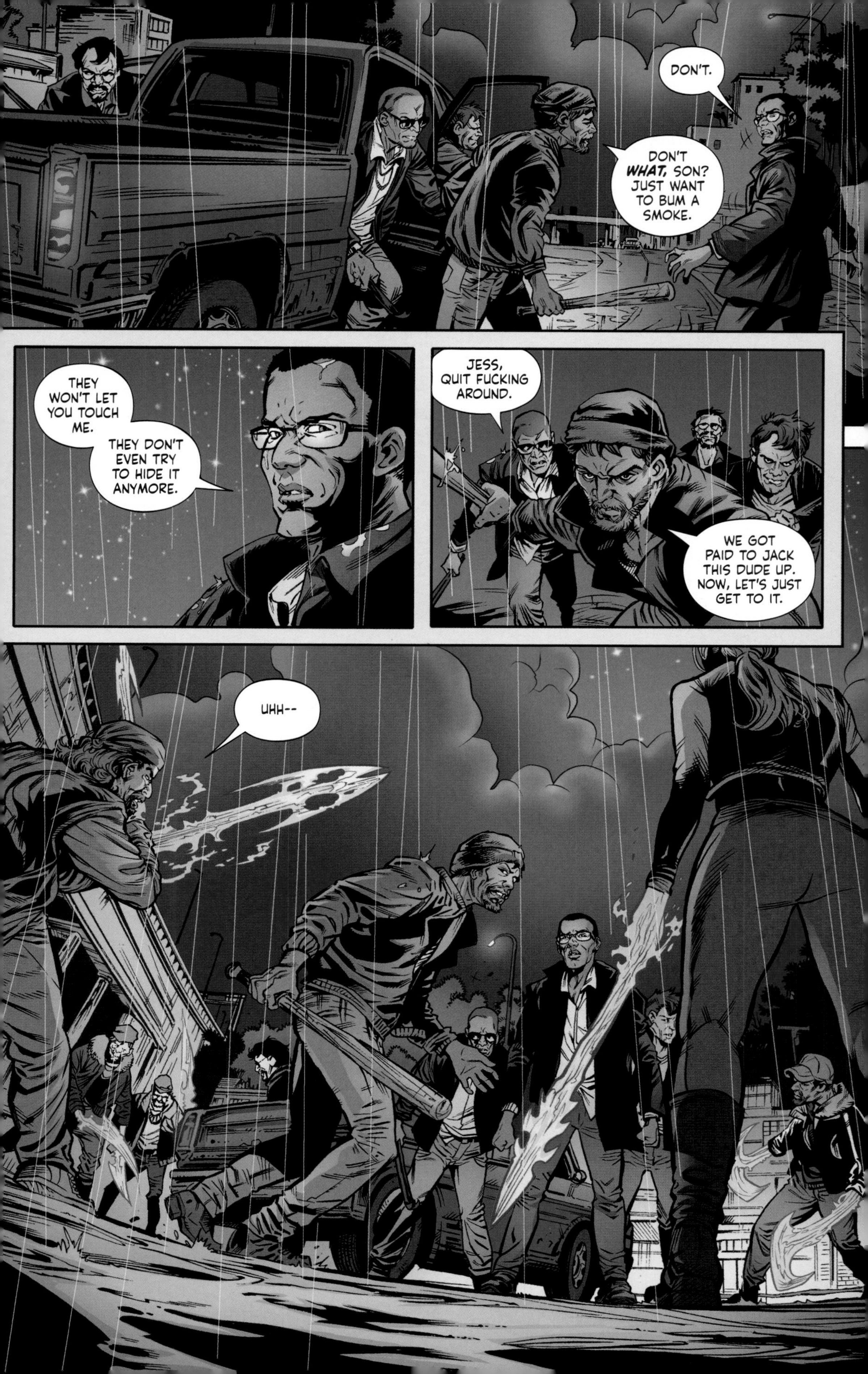
DON'T.
DON'T WHAT, SON? JUST WANT TO BUM A SMOKE.
THEY WON'T LET YOU TOUCH ME.
THEY DON'T EVEN TRY TO HIDE IT ANYMORE.
JESS, QUIT FUCKING AROUND.
WE GOT PAID TO JACK THIS DUDE UP. NOW, LET'S JUST GET TO IT.
UHH--

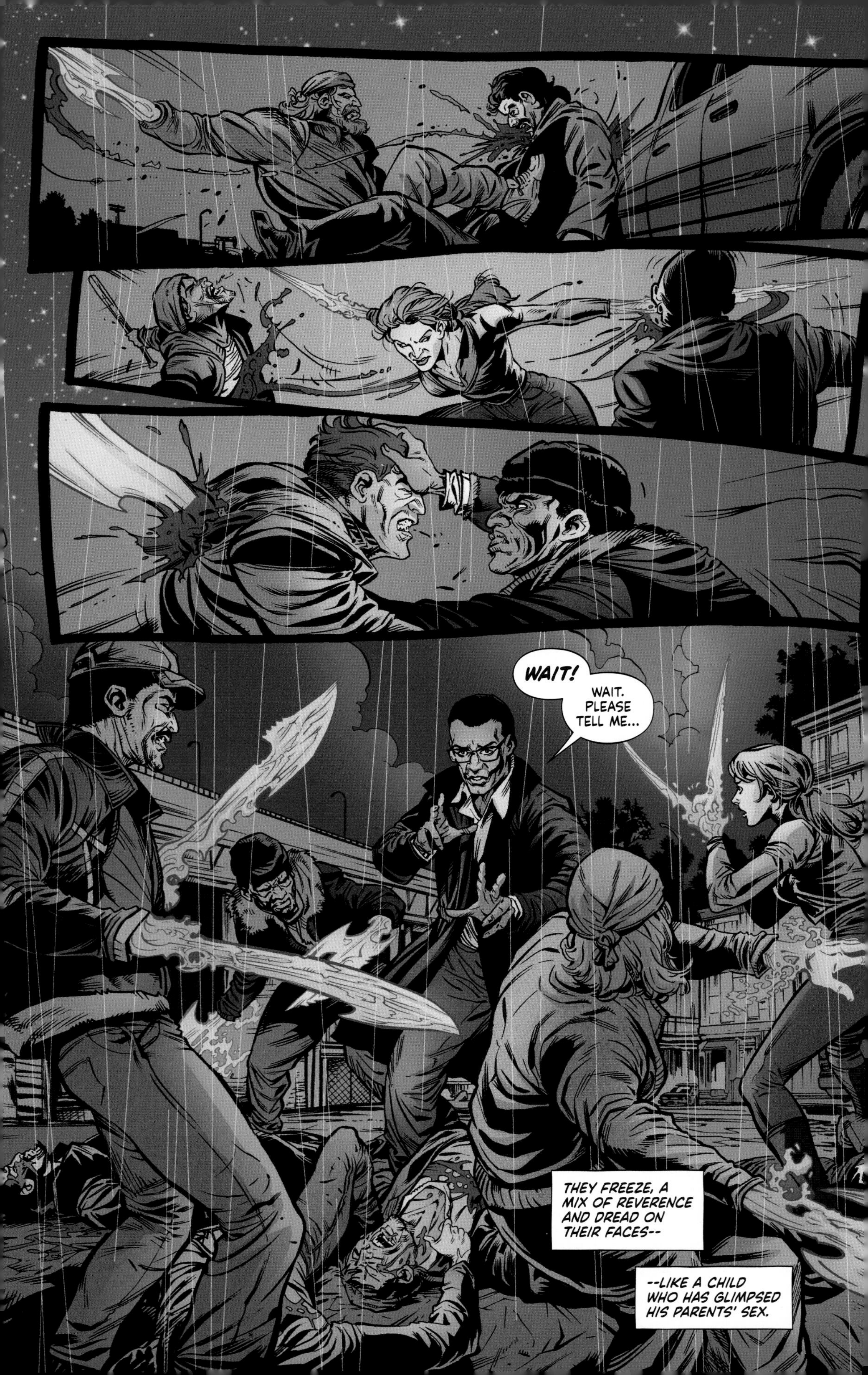
WAIT!
WAIT. PLEASE TELL ME...
THEY FREEZE, A MIX OF REVERENCE AND DREAD ON THEIR FACES--
--LIKE A CHILD WHO HAS GLIMPSED HIS PARENTS' SEX.

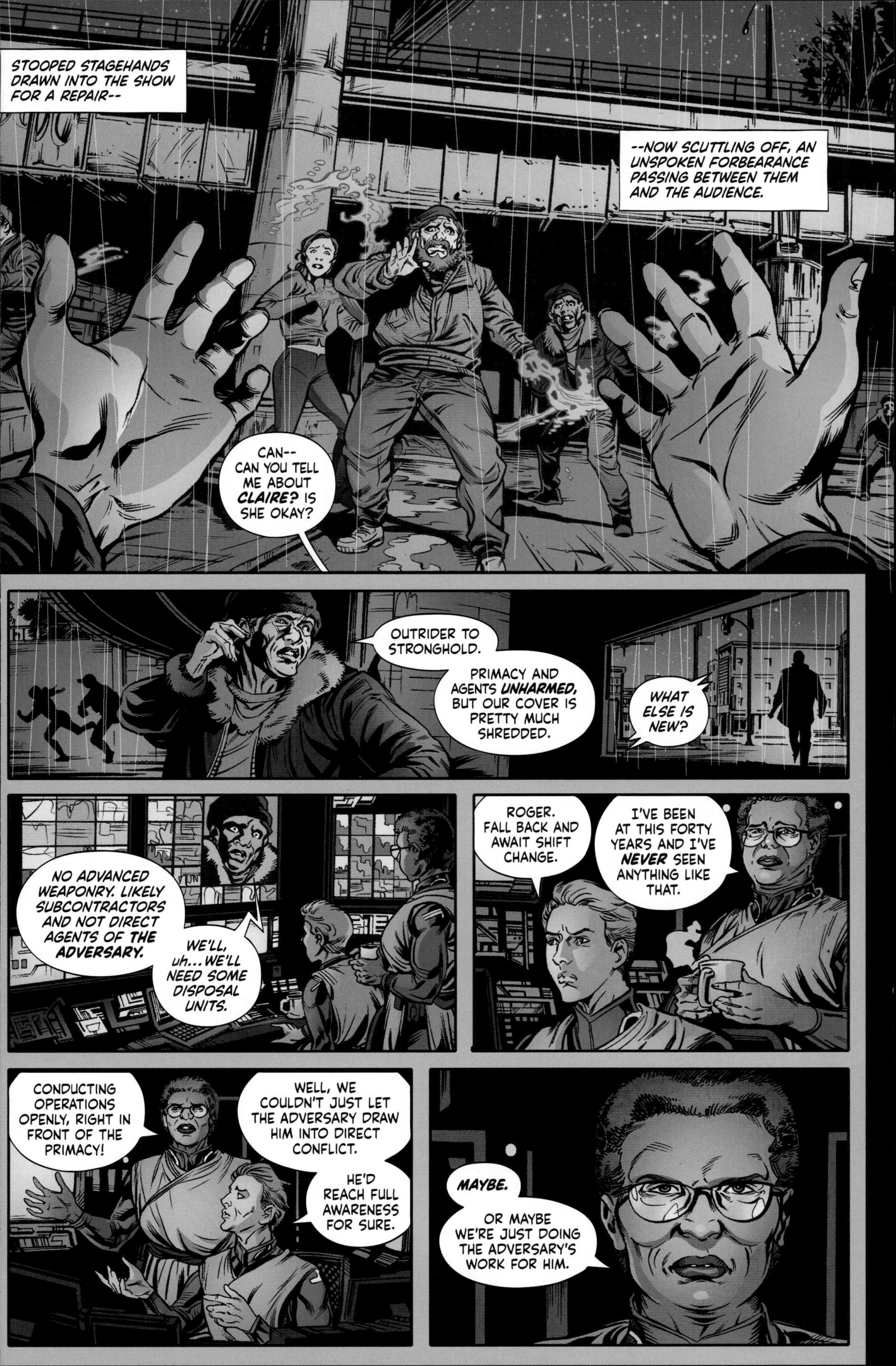
STOOPED STAGEHANDS DRAWN INTO THE SHOW FOR A REPAIR--
--NOW SCUTTLING OFF, AN UNSPOKEN FORBEARANCE PASSING BETWEEN THEM AND THE AUDIENCE.
CAN-- CAN YOU TELL ME ABOUT CLAIRE? IS SHE OKAY?
OUTRIDER TO STRONGHOLD.
PRIMACY AND AGENTS UNHARMED, BUT OUR COVER IS PRETTY MUCH SHREDDED.
WHAT ELSE IS NEW?
NO ADVANCED WEAPONRY. LIKELY SUBCONTRACTORS AND NOT DIRECT AGENTS OF THE ADVERSARY.
WE'LL, uh... WE'LL NEED SOME DISPOSAL UNITS.
ROGER. FALL BACK AND AWAIT SHIFT CHANGE.
I'VE BEEN AT THIS FORTY YEARS AND I'VE NEVER SEEN ANYTHING LIKE THAT.
CONDUCTING OPERATIONS OPENLY, RIGHT IN FRONT OF THE PRIMACY!
WELL, WE COULDN'T JUST LET THE ADVERSARY DRAW HIM INTO DIRECT CONFLICT.
HE'D REACH FULL AWARENESS FOR SURE.
MAYBE.
OR MAYBE WE'RE JUST DOING THE ADVERSARY'S WORK FOR HIM.

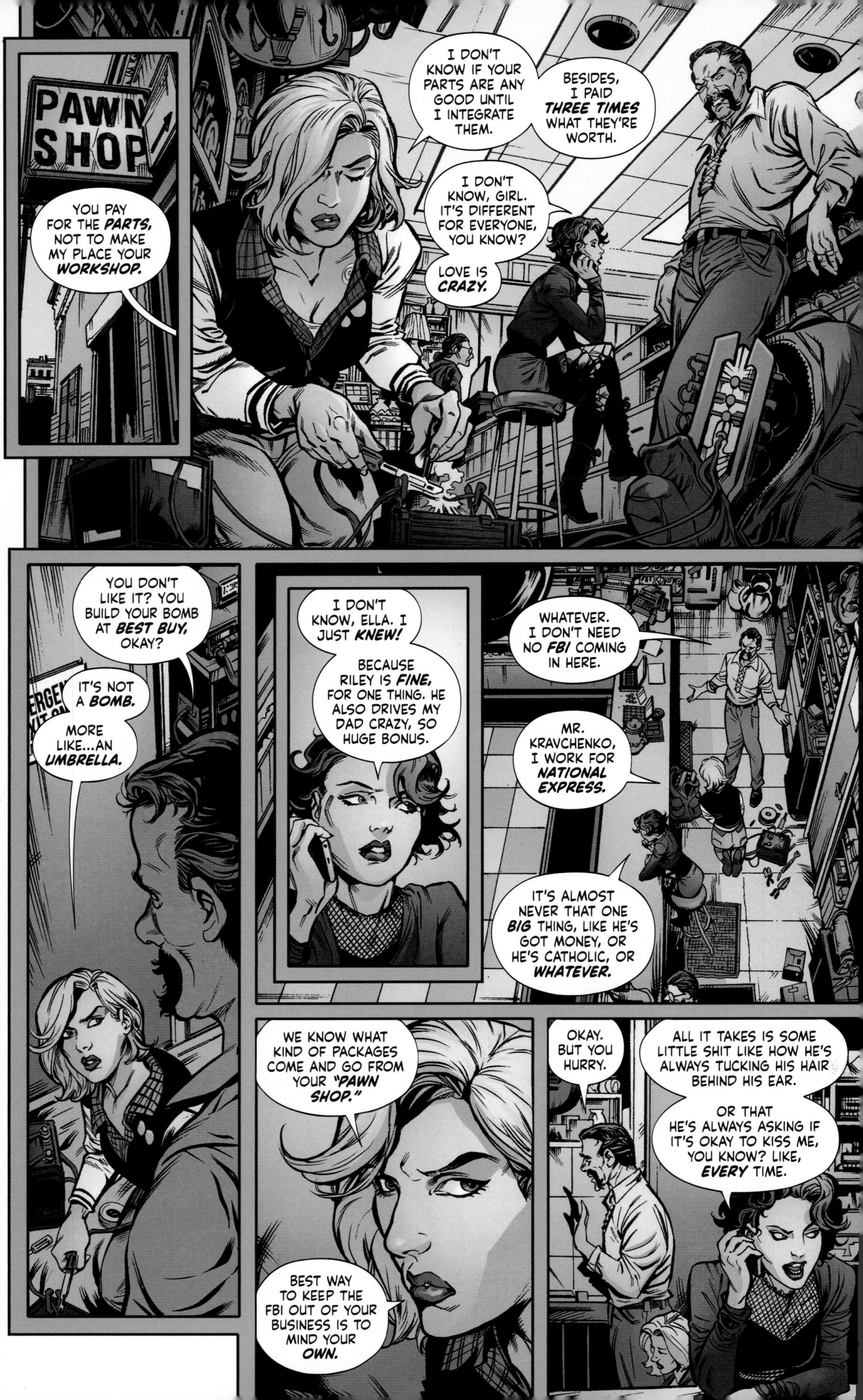
PAWN SHOP
YOU PAY FOR THE PARTS, NOT TO MAKE MY PLACE YOUR WORKSHOP.
I DON'T KNOW IF YOUR PARTS ARE ANY GOOD UNTIL I INTEGRATE THEM.
BESIDES, I PAID THREE TIMES WHAT THEY'RE WORTH.
I DON'T KNOW, GIRL. IT'S DIFFERENT FOR EVERYONE, YOU KNOW?
LOVE IS CRAZY.
YOU DON'T LIKE IT? YOU BUILD YOUR BOMB AT BEST BUY, OKAY?
IT'S NOT A BOMB.
MORE LIKE...AN UMBRELLA.
I DON'T KNOW, ELLA. I JUST KNEW!
BECAUSE RILEY IS FINE, FOR ONE THING. HE ALSO DRIVES MY DAD CRAZY, SO HUGE BONUS.
WHATEVER. I DON'T NEED NO FBI COMING IN HERE.
MR. KRAVCHENKO, I WORK FOR NATIONAL EXPRESS.
IT'S ALMOST NEVER THAT ONE BIG THING, LIKE HE'S GOT MONEY, OR HE'S CATHOLIC, OR WHATEVER.
WE KNOW WHAT KIND OF PACKAGES COME AND GO FROM YOUR "PAWN SHOP."
BEST WAY TO KEEP THE FBI OUT OF YOUR BUSINESS IS TO MIND YOUR OWN.
OKAY. BUT YOU HURRY.
ALL IT TAKES IS SOME LITTLE SHIT LIKE HOW HE'S ALWAYS TUCKING HIS HAIR BEHIND HIS EAR.
OR THAT HE'S ALWAYS ASKING IF IT'S OKAY TO KISS ME, YOU KNOW? LIKE, EVERY TIME.

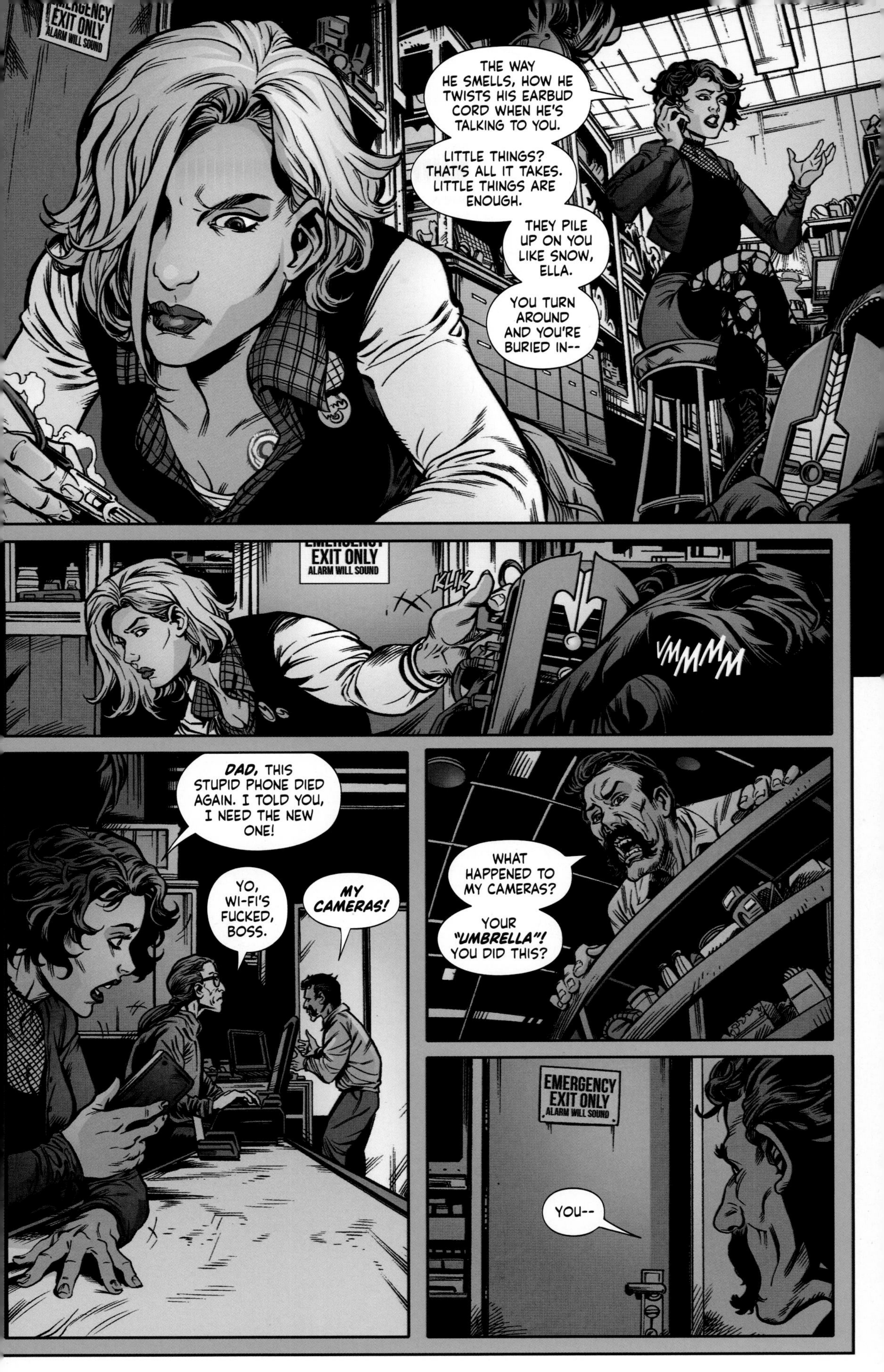
EMERGENCY EXIT ONLY ALARM WILL SOUND
THE WAY HE SMELLS, HOW HE TWISTS HIS EARBUD CORD WHEN HE'S TALKING TO YOU.
LITTLE THINGS? THAT'S ALL IT TAKES. LITTLE THINGS ARE ENOUGH.
THEY PILE UP ON YOU LIKE SNOW, ELLA.
YOU TURN AROUND AND YOU'RE BURIED IN--
EXIT ONLY ALARM WILL SOUND
KLIK
VMMMM
DAD, THIS STUPID PHONE DIED AGAIN. I TOLD YOU, I NEED THE NEW ONE!
YO, WI-FI'S FUCKED, BOSS.
MY CAMERAS!
WHAT HAPPENED TO MY CAMERAS?
YOUR "UMBRELLA"! YOU DID THIS?
EMERGENCY EXIT ONLY ALARM WILL SOUND
YOU--

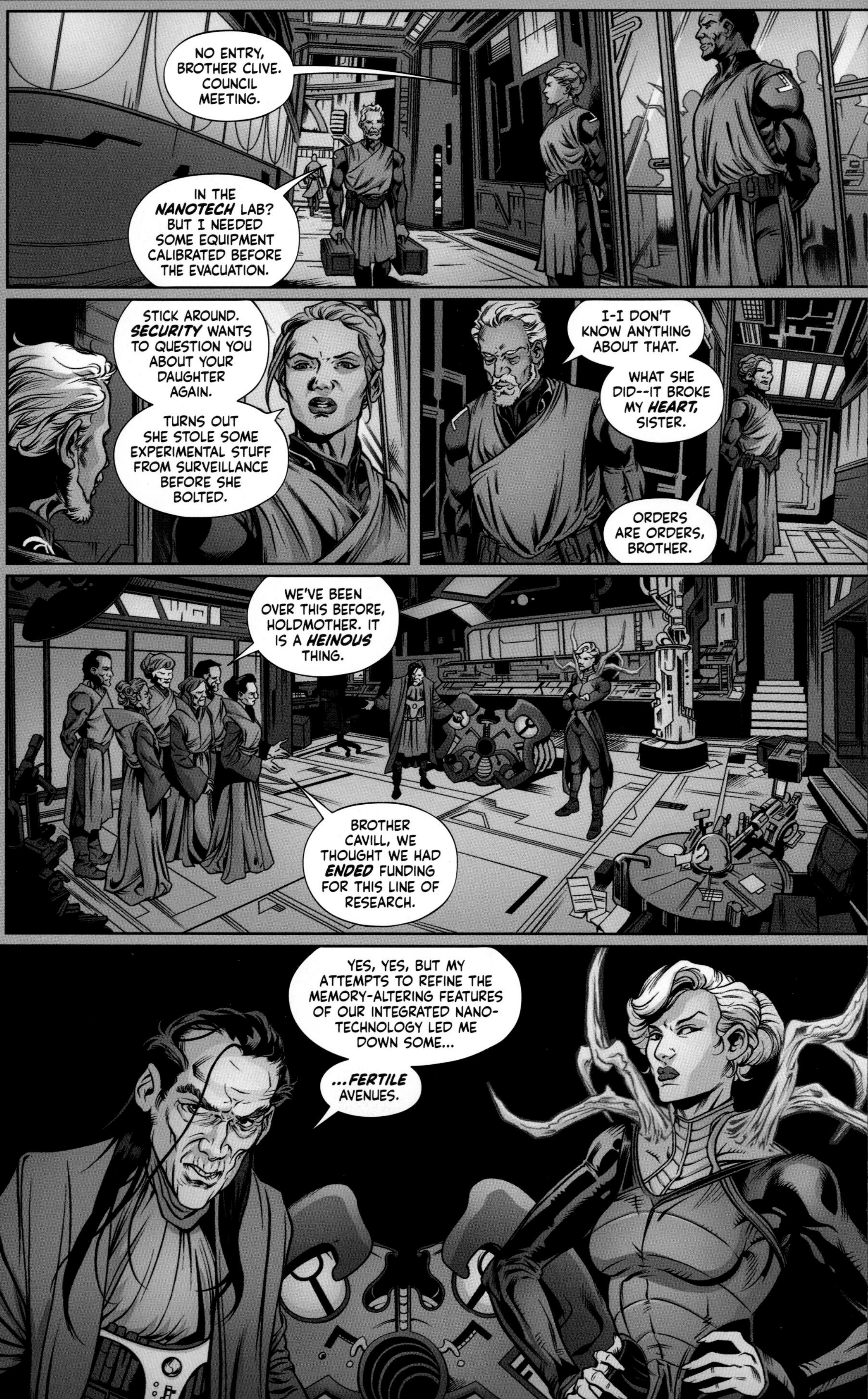
NO ENTRY, BROTHER CLIVE. COUNCIL MEETING.
IN THE NANOTECH LAB? BUT I NEEDED SOME EQUIPMENT CALIBRATED BEFORE THE EVACUATION.
STICK AROUND. SECURITY WANTS TO QUESTION YOU ABOUT YOUR DAUGHTER AGAIN.
TURNS OUT SHE STOLE SOME EXPERIMENTAL STUFF FROM SURVEILLANCE BEFORE SHE BOLTED.
I-I DON'T KNOW ANYTHING ABOUT THAT.
WHAT SHE DID--IT BROKE MY HEART, SISTER.
ORDERS ARE ORDERS, BROTHER.
WE'VE BEEN OVER THIS BEFORE, HOLDMOTHER. IT IS A HEINOUS THING.
BROTHER CAVILL, WE THOUGHT WE HAD ENDED FUNDING FOR THIS LINE OF RESEARCH.
YES, YES, BUT MY ATTEMPTS TO REFINE THE MEMORY-ALTERING FEATURES OF OUR INTEGRATED NANO-TECHNOLOGY LED ME DOWN SOME...
...FERTILE AVENUES.

WE'VE TRIED TECHNOLOGICAL SOLUTIONS *BEFORE*. IT IS NEVER WORTH THE RISK.

WE'VE SPENT *DECADES* BUILDING THIS LIFE FOR THE PRIMACY.

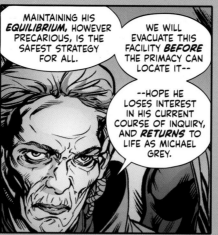

MAINTAINING HIS *EQUILIBRIUM*, HOWEVER PRECARIOUS, IS THE SAFEST STRATEGY FOR ALL.

WE WILL EVACUATE THIS FACILITY *BEFORE* THE PRIMACY CAN LOCATE IT--

--HOPE HE LOSES INTEREST IN HIS CURRENT COURSE OF INQUIRY, AND *RETURNS* TO LIFE AS MICHAEL GREY.

"*LOSES INTEREST IN HIS CURRENT COURSE OF INQUIRY*"?

CAN YOU *HEAR* YOURSELVES?

OUR *GOD* WANDERS THE STREET LIKE A MADMAN, AND YOU WANT TO *HIDE* AND HOPE IT *GOES AWAY*?

DO YOU REALIZE WHAT WILL HAPPEN SHOULD THE PRIMACY *REGAIN* HIS AWARENESS AND REALIZE *OUR* COMPLICITY?

CAN YOU *IMAGINE* HIS WRATH?

HOLDMOTHER, YOU SPEAK *BLASPHEMY*.

I SPEAK THE *TRUTH*!

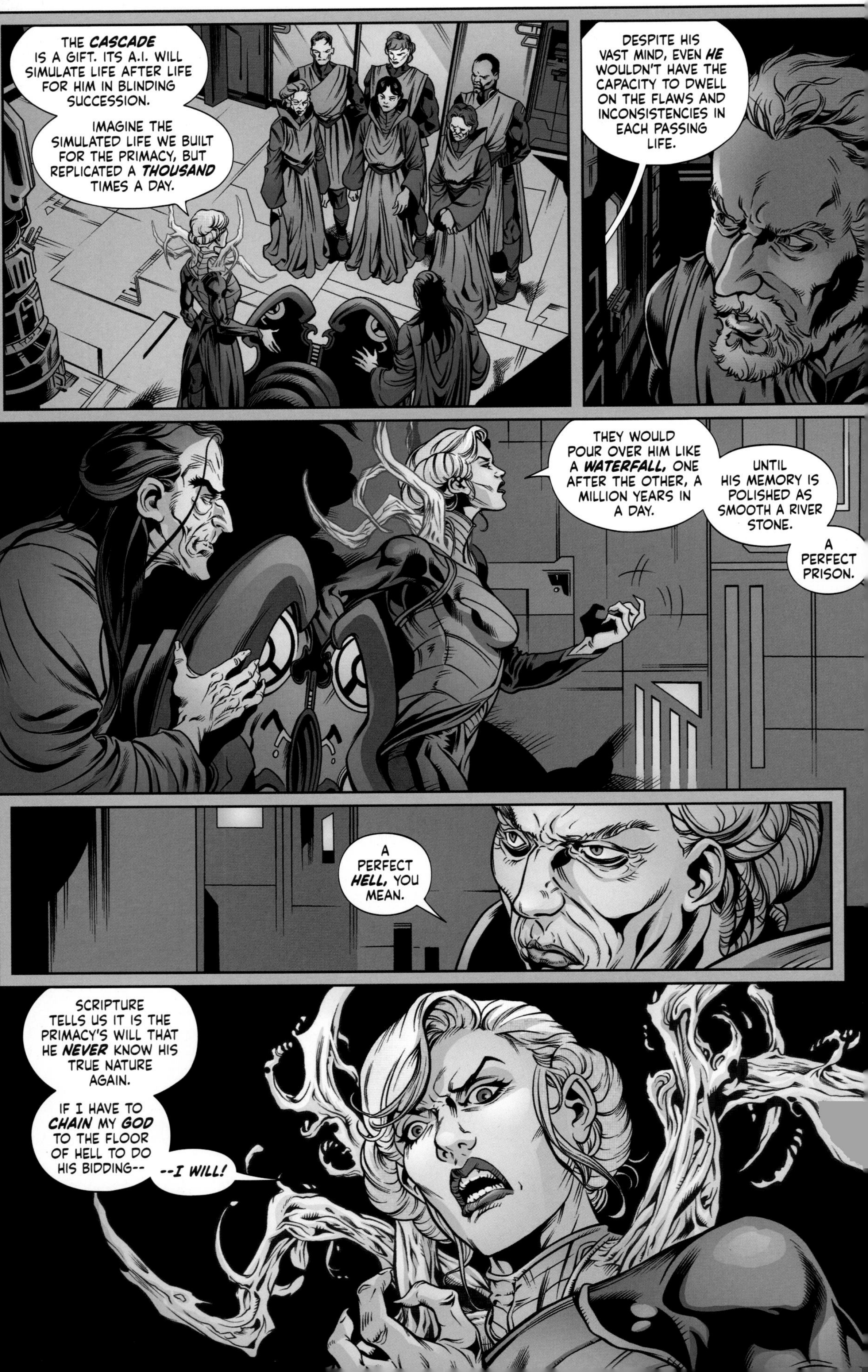
THE CASCADE IS A GIFT. ITS A.I. WILL SIMULATE LIFE AFTER LIFE FOR HIM IN BLINDING SUCCESSION.
IMAGINE THE SIMULATED LIFE WE BUILT FOR THE PRIMACY, BUT REPLICATED A THOUSAND TIMES A DAY.
DESPITE HIS VAST MIND, EVEN HE WOULDN'T HAVE THE CAPACITY TO DWELL ON THE FLAWS AND INCONSISTENCIES IN EACH PASSING LIFE.
THEY WOULD POUR OVER HIM LIKE A WATERFALL, ONE AFTER THE OTHER, A MILLION YEARS IN A DAY.
UNTIL HIS MEMORY IS POLISHED AS SMOOTH A RIVER STONE.
A PERFECT PRISON.
A PERFECT HELL, YOU MEAN.
SCRIPTURE TELLS US IT IS THE PRIMACY'S WILL THAT HE NEVER KNOW HIS TRUE NATURE AGAIN.
IF I HAVE TO CHAIN MY GOD TO THE FLOOR OF HELL TO DO HIS BIDDING--
--I WILL!

WHAT-- WHAT *IS* THIS MADNESS?

ELDER, DID YOU THINK BROTHER CAVILL WOULD PERFECT HIS MASTERPIECE WITHOUT FIRST PRODUCING A NUMBER OF *PROTOTYPES?*

I WASTED ALL THAT TIME *TELLING* YOU WHAT THE CASCADE COULD DO--

--WHEN I SIMPLY COULD HAVE *SHOWN* YOU.

WHAT SORT OF *LIVES* SHALL I PROGRAM FOR THEM, HOLDMOTHER?

SOMETHING *PLEASANT.*

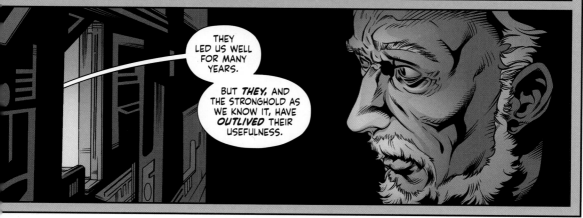

THEY LED US WELL FOR MANY YEARS.

BUT *THEY,* AND THE STRONGHOLD AS WE KNOW IT, HAVE *OUTLIVED* THEIR USEFULNESS.

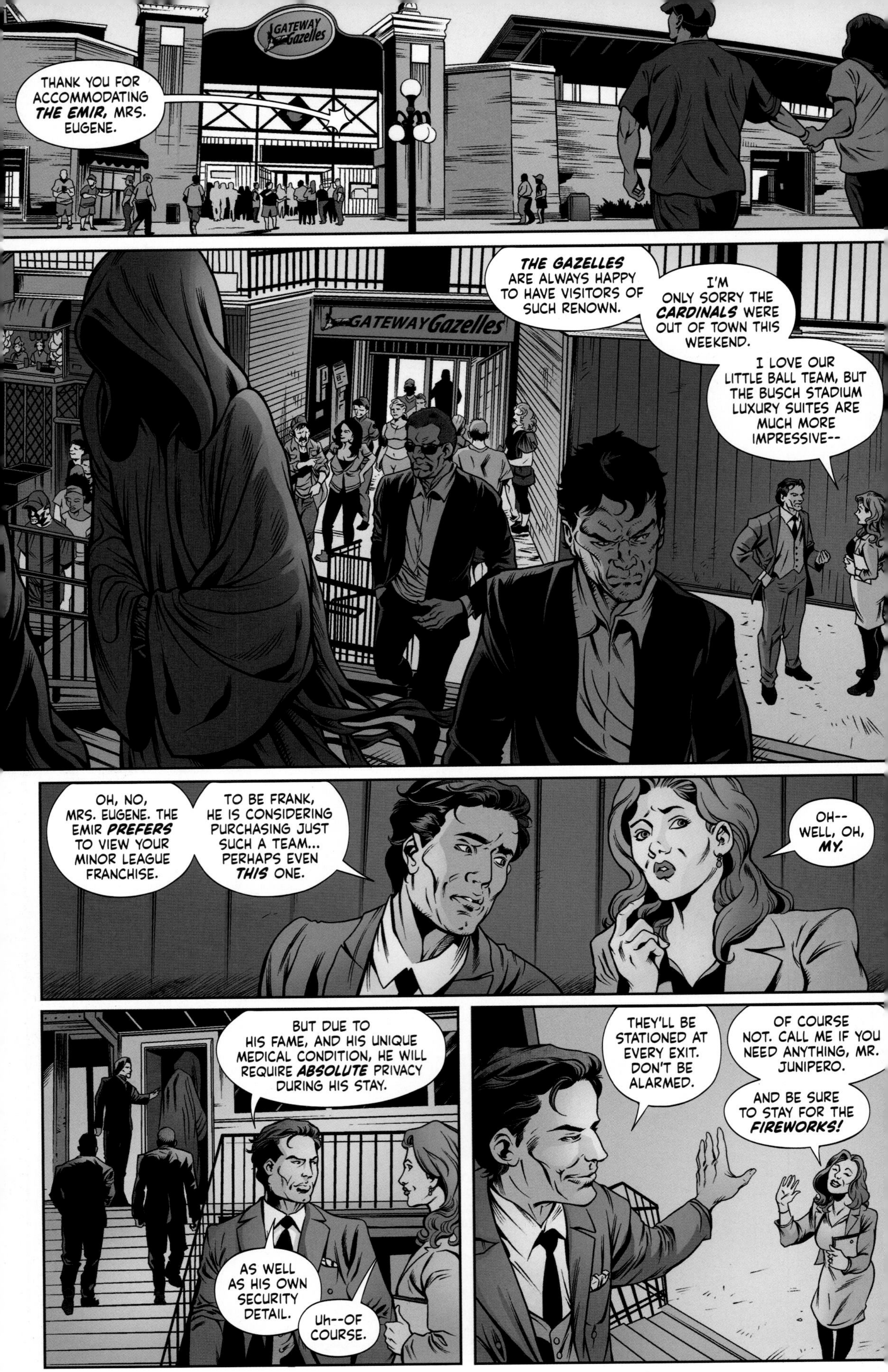
GATEWAY Gazelles
THANK YOU FOR ACCOMMODATING THE EMIR, MRS. EUGENE.
GATEWAY Gazelles
THE GAZELLES ARE ALWAYS HAPPY TO HAVE VISITORS OF SUCH RENOWN.
I'M ONLY SORRY THE CARDINALS WERE OUT OF TOWN THIS WEEKEND.
I LOVE OUR LITTLE BALL TEAM, BUT THE BUSCH STADIUM LUXURY SUITES ARE MUCH MORE IMPRESSIVE--
OH, NO, MRS. EUGENE. THE EMIR PREFERS TO VIEW YOUR MINOR LEAGUE FRANCHISE.
TO BE FRANK, HE IS CONSIDERING PURCHASING JUST SUCH A TEAM... PERHAPS EVEN THIS ONE.
OH-- WELL, OH, MY.
BUT DUE TO HIS FAME, AND HIS UNIQUE MEDICAL CONDITION, HE WILL REQUIRE ABSOLUTE PRIVACY DURING HIS STAY.
AS WELL AS HIS OWN SECURITY DETAIL.
Uh--OF COURSE.
THEY'LL BE STATIONED AT EVERY EXIT. DON'T BE ALARMED.
OF COURSE NOT. CALL ME IF YOU NEED ANYTHING, MR. JUNIPERO.
AND BE SURE TO STAY FOR THE FIREWORKS!

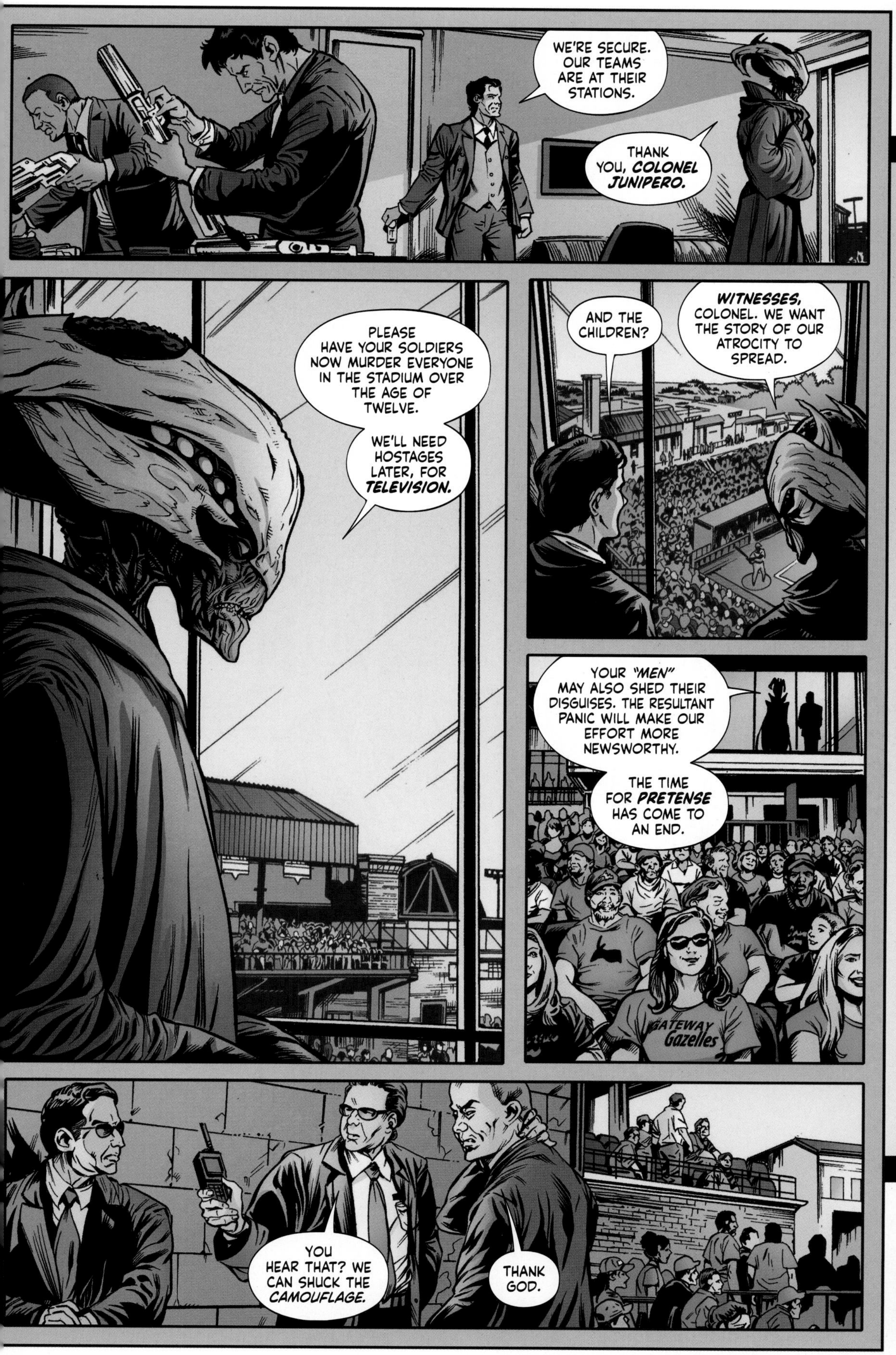
WE'RE SECURE. OUR TEAMS ARE AT THEIR STATIONS.
THANK YOU, COLONEL JUNIPERO.
PLEASE HAVE YOUR SOLDIERS NOW MURDER EVERYONE IN THE STADIUM OVER THE AGE OF TWELVE.
WE'LL NEED HOSTAGES LATER, FOR TELEVISION.
AND THE CHILDREN?
WITNESSES, COLONEL. WE WANT THE STORY OF OUR ATROCITY TO SPREAD.
YOUR "MEN" MAY ALSO SHED THEIR DISGUISES. THE RESULTANT PANIC WILL MAKE OUR EFFORT MORE NEWSWORTHY.
THE TIME FOR PRETENSE HAS COME TO AN END.
GATEWAY Gazelles
YOU HEAR THAT? WE CAN SHUCK THE CAMOUFLAGE.
THANK GOD.

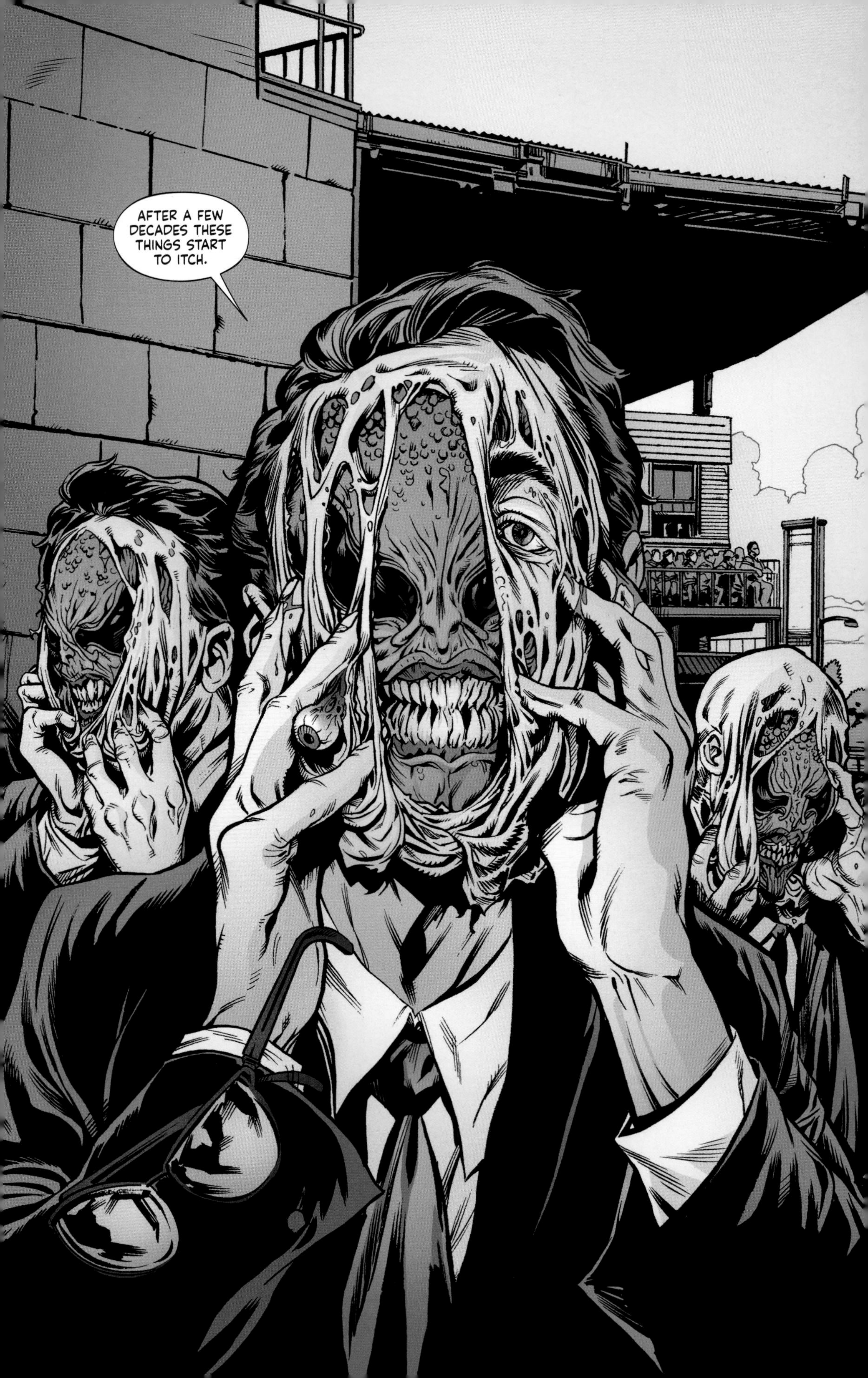
AFTER A FEW DECADES THESE THINGS START TO ITCH.

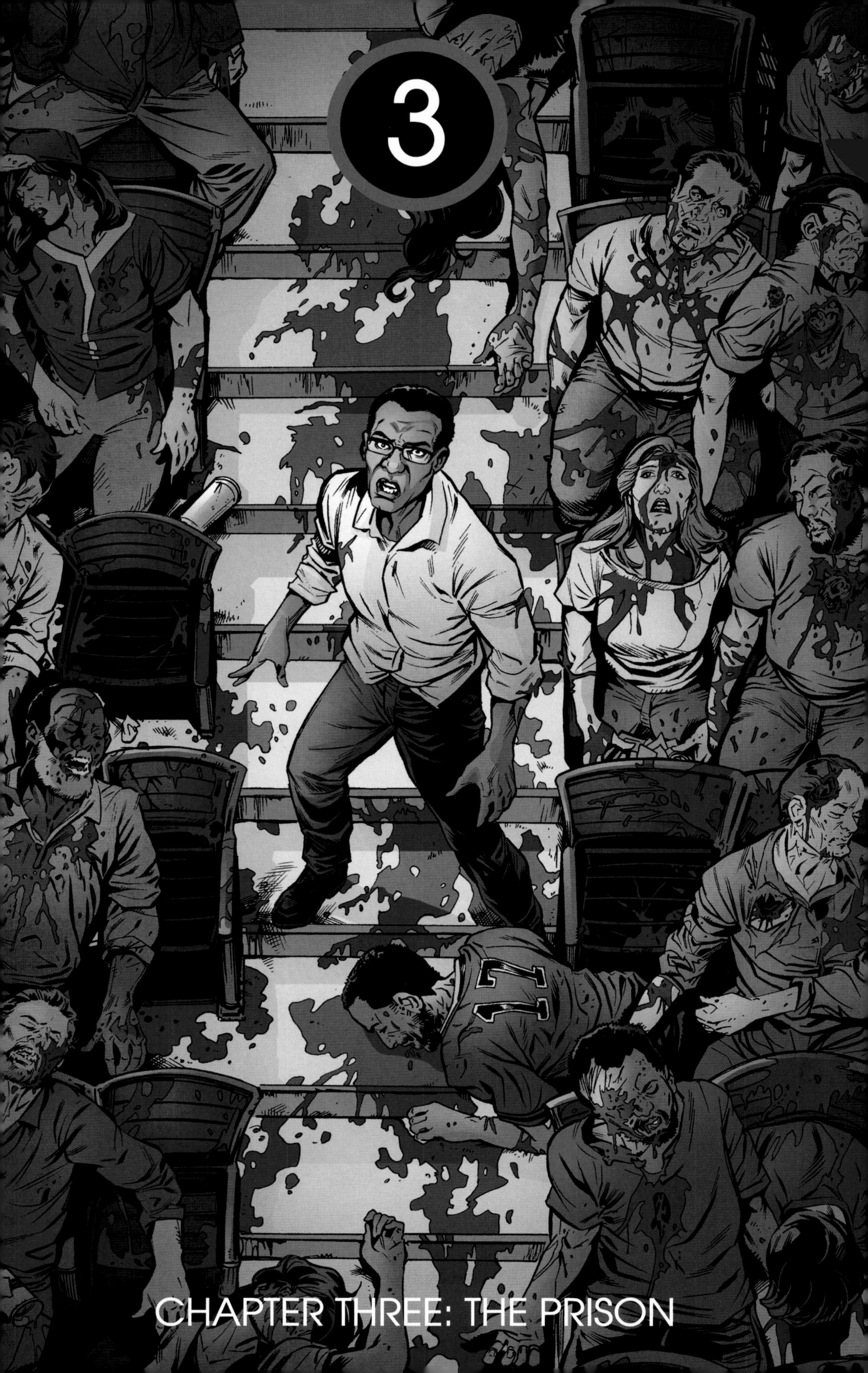

3

CHAPTER THREE: THE PRISON

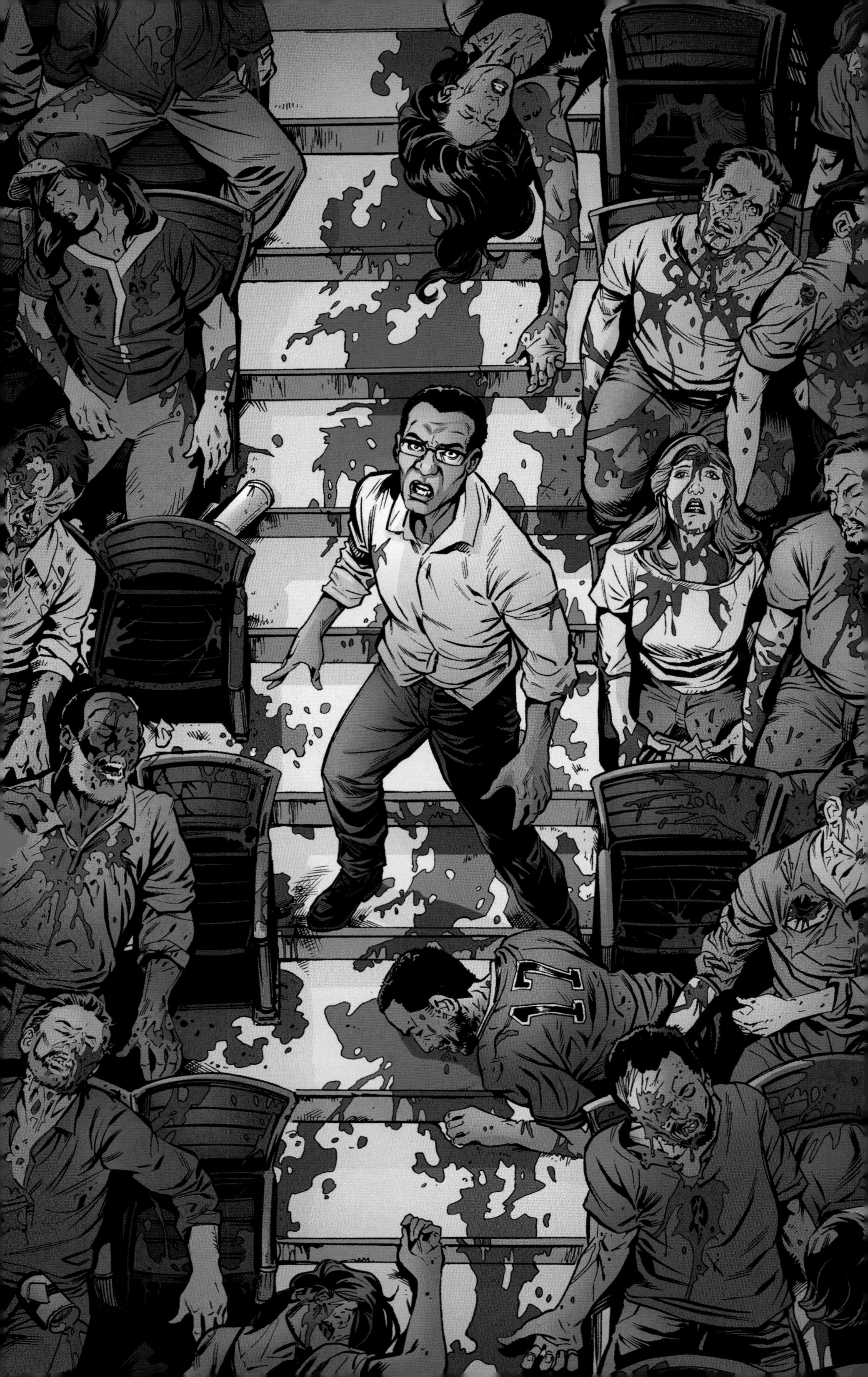

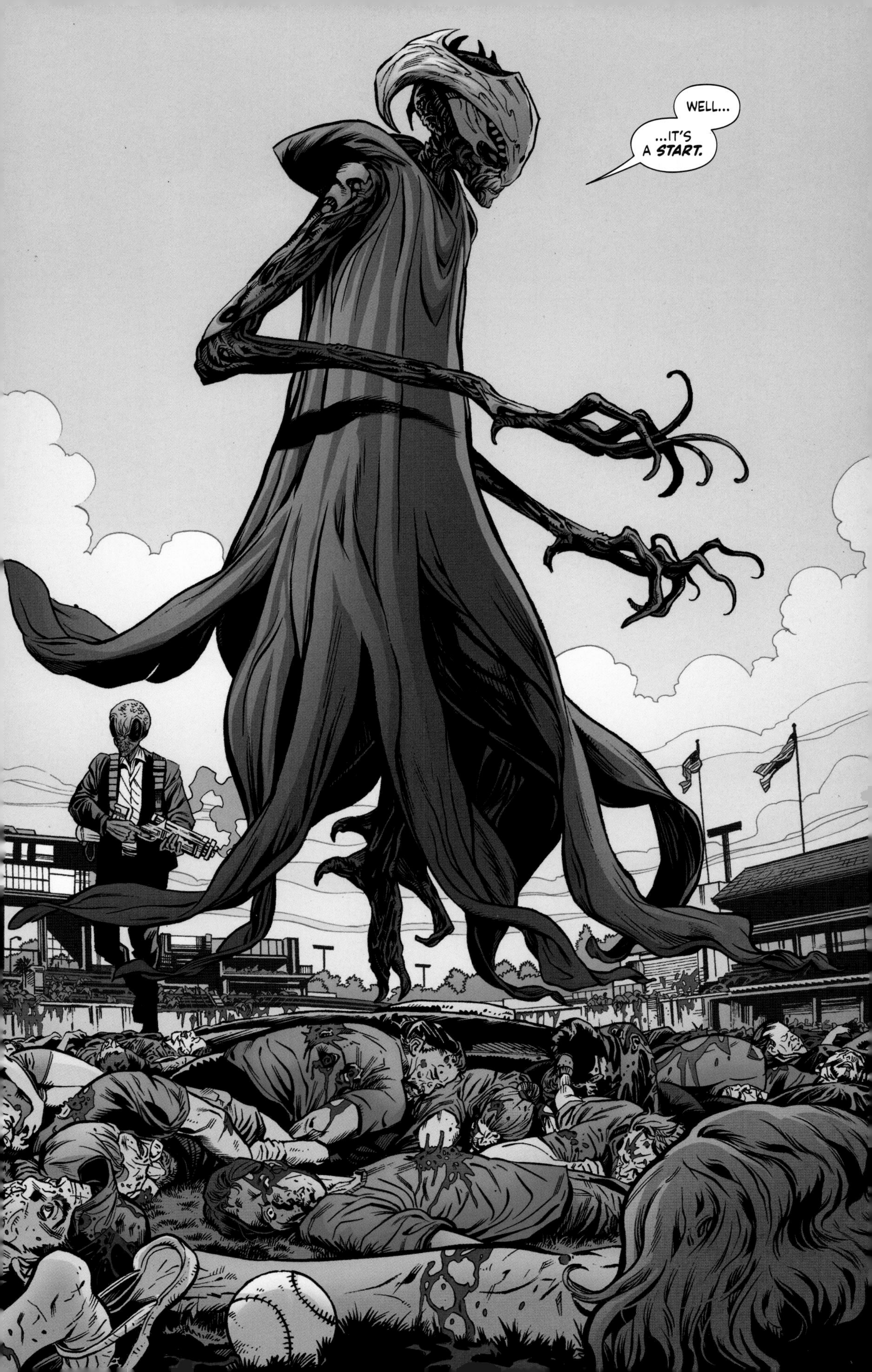
WELL...
...IT'S A START.

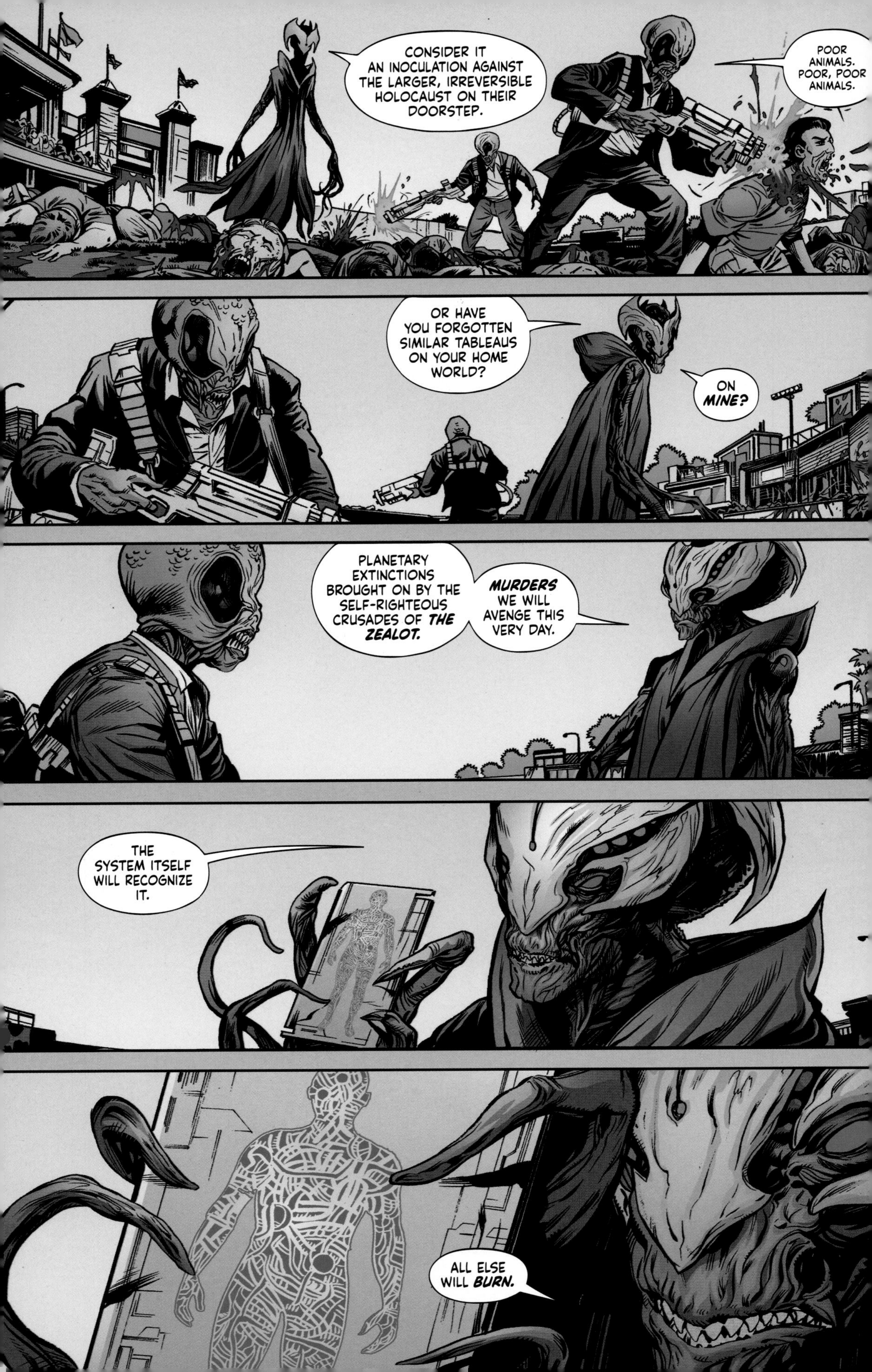
CONSIDER IT AN INOCULATION AGAINST THE LARGER, IRREVERSIBLE HOLOCAUST ON THEIR DOORSTEP.
POOR ANIMALS. POOR, POOR ANIMALS.
OR HAVE YOU FORGOTTEN SIMILAR TABLEAUS ON YOUR HOME WORLD?
ON MINE?
PLANETARY EXTINCTIONS BROUGHT ON BY THE SELF-RIGHTEOUS CRUSADES OF THE ZEALOT.
MURDERS WE WILL AVENGE THIS VERY DAY.
THE SYSTEM ITSELF WILL RECOGNIZE IT.
ALL ELSE WILL BURN.

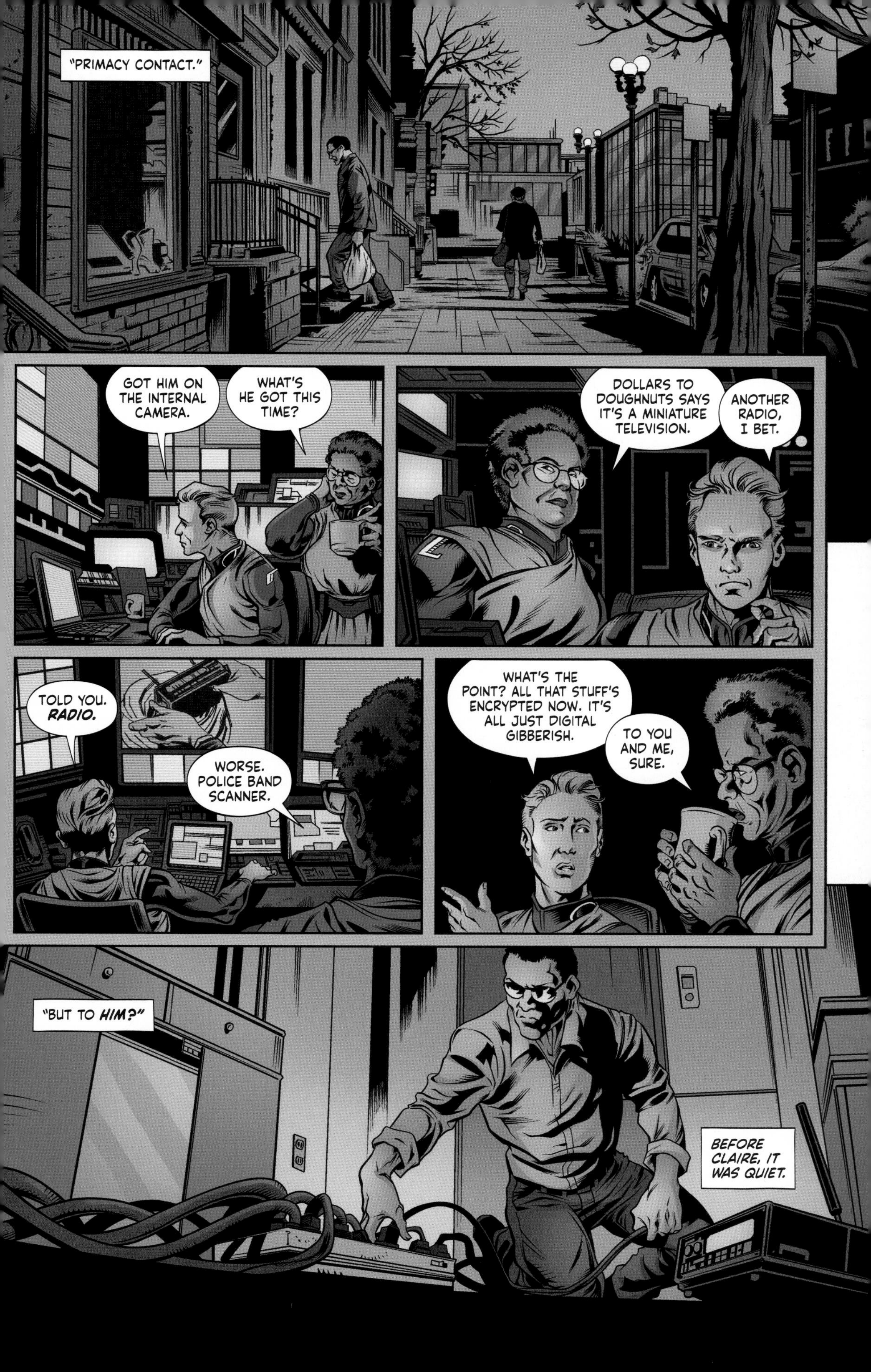

"PRIMACY CONTACT."
GOT HIM ON THE INTERNAL CAMERA.
WHAT'S HE GOT THIS TIME?
DOLLARS TO DOUGHNUTS SAYS IT'S A MINIATURE TELEVISION.
ANOTHER RADIO, I BET.
TOLD YOU. *RADIO.*
WORSE. POLICE BAND SCANNER.
WHAT'S THE POINT? ALL THAT STUFF'S ENCRYPTED NOW. IT'S ALL JUST DIGITAL GIBBERISH.
TO YOU AND ME, SURE.
"BUT TO *HIM?*"
BEFORE CLAIRE, IT WAS QUIET.

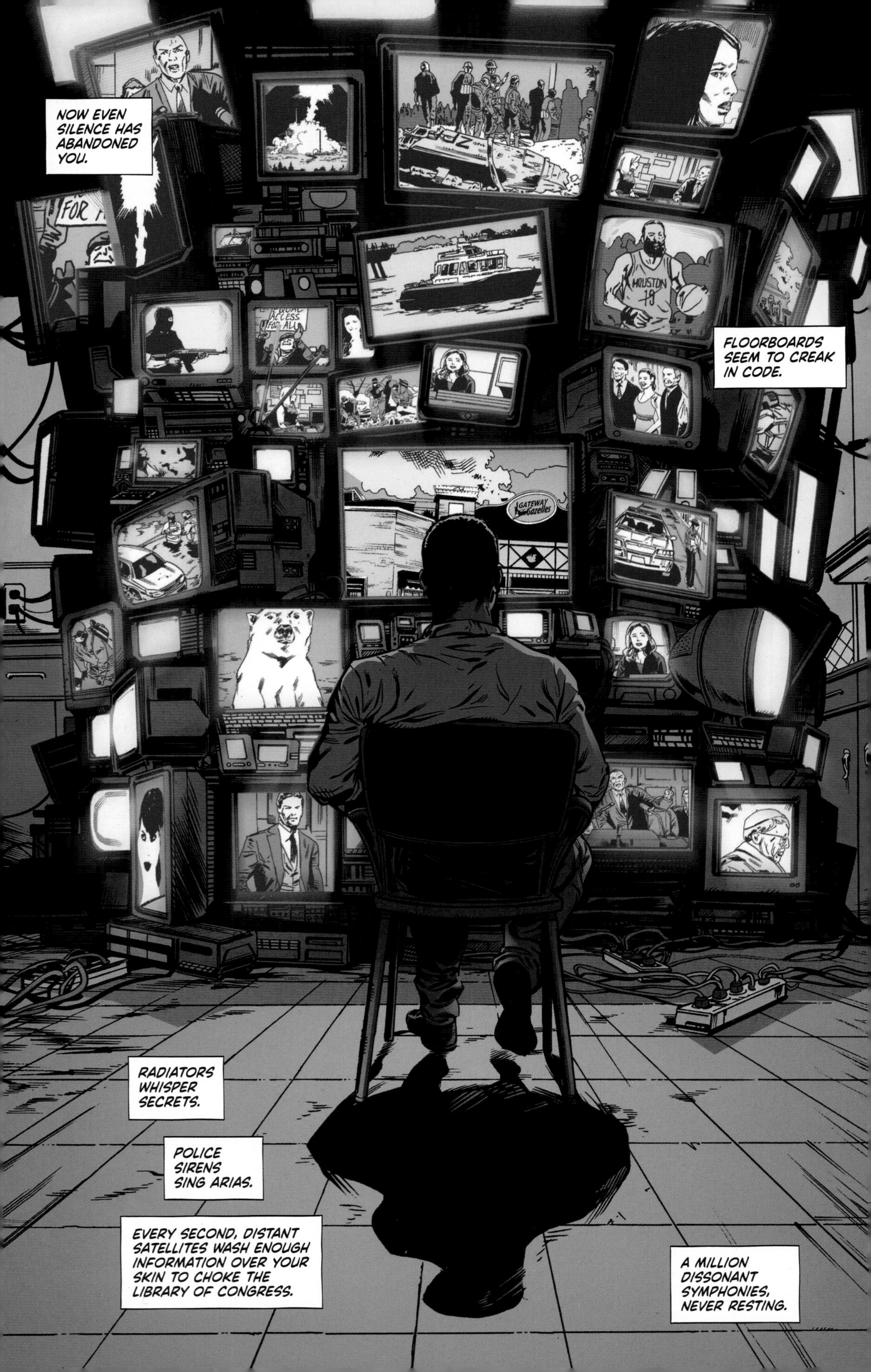
NOW EVEN SILENCE HAS ABANDONED YOU.
FLOORBOARDS SEEM TO CREAK IN CODE.
RADIATORS WHISPER SECRETS.
POLICE SIRENS SING ARIAS.
EVERY SECOND, DISTANT SATELLITES WASH ENOUGH INFORMATION OVER YOUR SKIN TO CHOKE THE LIBRARY OF CONGRESS.
A MILLION DISSONANT SYMPHONIES, NEVER RESTING.

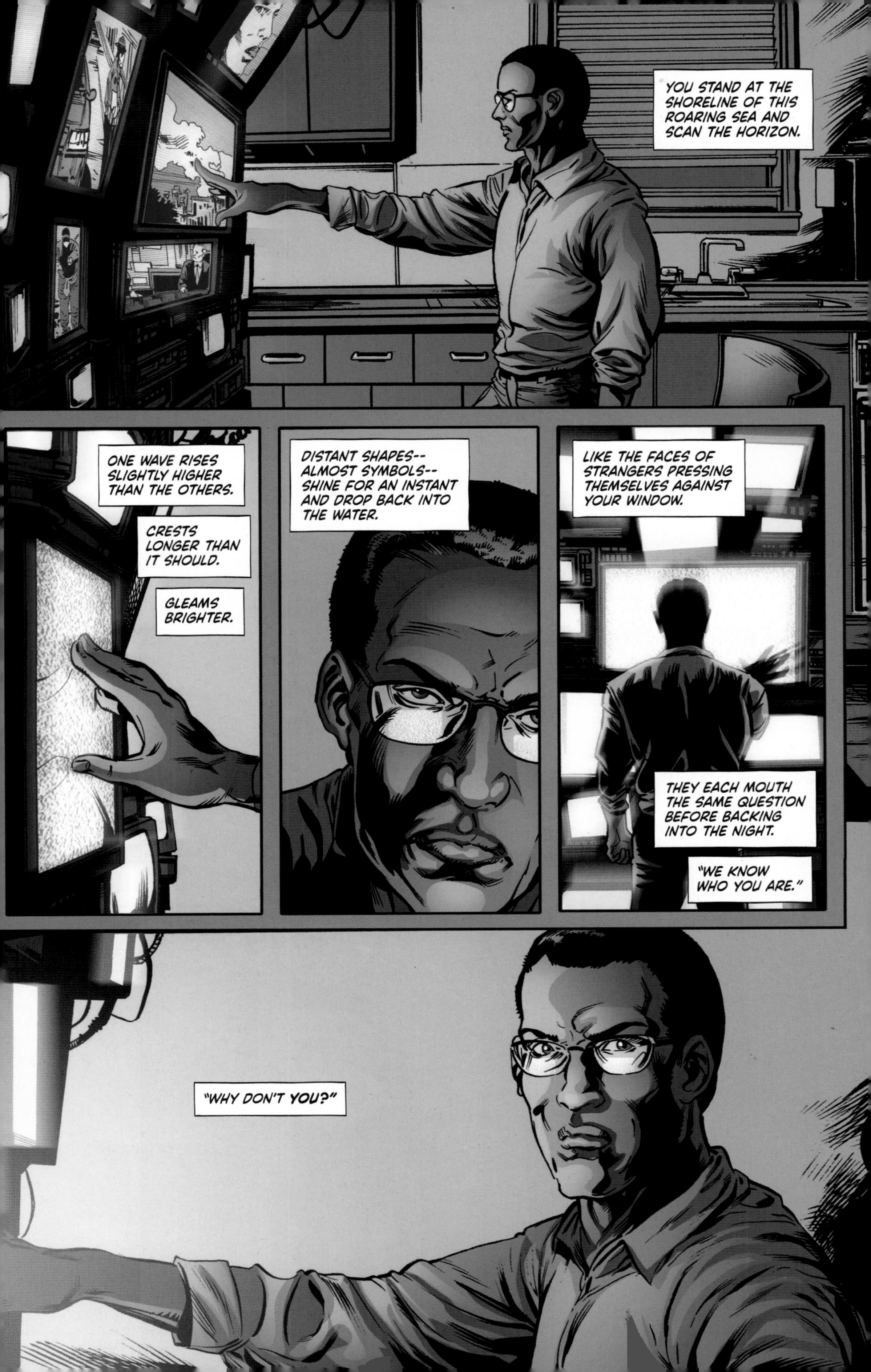
YOU STAND AT THE SHORELINE OF THIS ROARING SEA AND SCAN THE HORIZON.
ONE WAVE RISES SLIGHTLY HIGHER THAN THE OTHERS.
CRESTS LONGER THAN IT SHOULD.
GLEAMS BRIGHTER.
DISTANT SHAPES-- ALMOST SYMBOLS-- SHINE FOR AN INSTANT AND DROP BACK INTO THE WATER.
LIKE THE FACES OF STRANGERS PRESSING THEMSELVES AGAINST YOUR WINDOW.
THEY EACH MOUTH THE SAME QUESTION BEFORE BACKING INTO THE NIGHT.
"WE KNOW WHO YOU ARE."
"WHY DON'T YOU?"

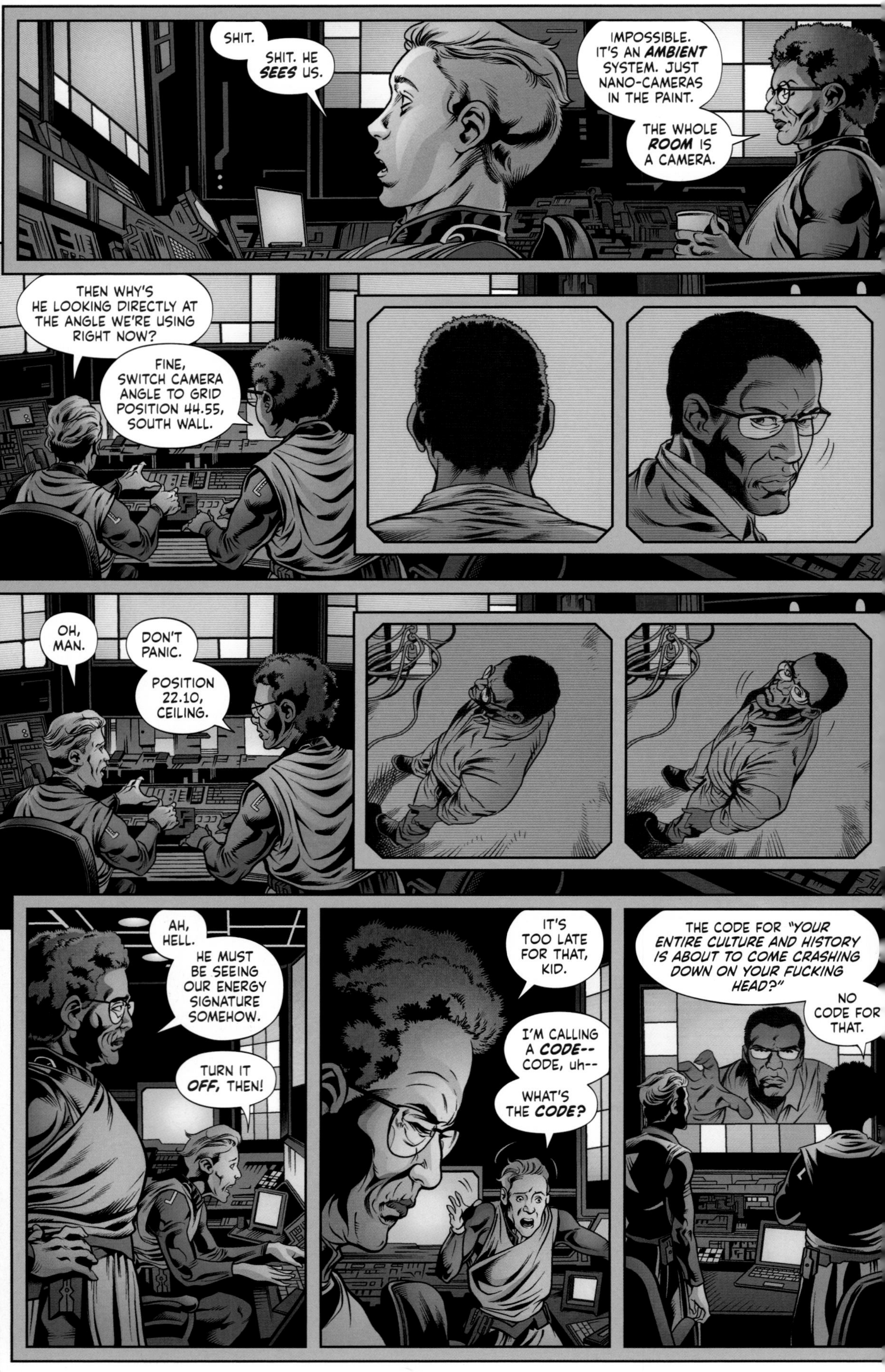
SHIT.
SHIT. HE SEES US.
IMPOSSIBLE. IT'S AN AMBIENT SYSTEM. JUST NANO-CAMERAS IN THE PAINT.
THE WHOLE ROOM IS A CAMERA.
THEN WHY'S HE LOOKING DIRECTLY AT THE ANGLE WE'RE USING RIGHT NOW?
FINE, SWITCH CAMERA ANGLE TO GRID POSITION 44.55, SOUTH WALL.
OH, MAN.
DON'T PANIC.
POSITION 22.10, CEILING.
AH, HELL.
HE MUST BE SEEING OUR ENERGY SIGNATURE SOMEHOW.
TURN IT OFF, THEN!
IT'S TOO LATE FOR THAT, KID.
I'M CALLING A CODE-- CODE, uh--
WHAT'S THE CODE?
THE CODE FOR "YOUR ENTIRE CULTURE AND HISTORY IS ABOUT TO COME CRASHING DOWN ON YOUR FUCKING HEAD?"
NO CODE FOR THAT.

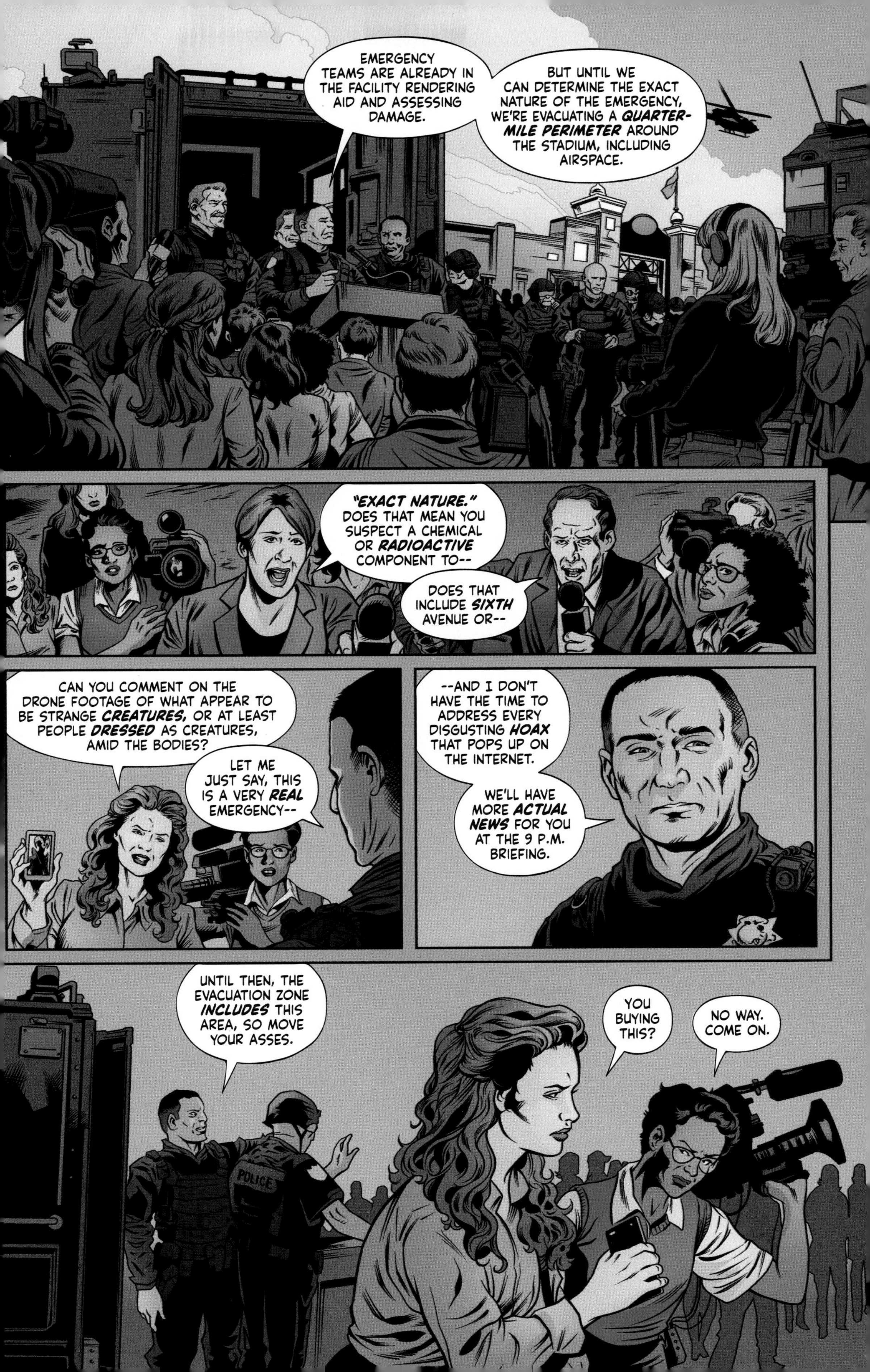
EMERGENCY TEAMS ARE ALREADY IN THE FACILITY RENDERING AID AND ASSESSING DAMAGE.
BUT UNTIL WE CAN DETERMINE THE EXACT NATURE OF THE EMERGENCY, WE'RE EVACUATING A QUARTER-MILE PERIMETER AROUND THE STADIUM, INCLUDING AIRSPACE.
"EXACT NATURE." DOES THAT MEAN YOU SUSPECT A CHEMICAL OR RADIOACTIVE COMPONENT TO--
DOES THAT INCLUDE SIXTH AVENUE OR--
CAN YOU COMMENT ON THE DRONE FOOTAGE OF WHAT APPEAR TO BE STRANGE CREATURES, OR AT LEAST PEOPLE DRESSED AS CREATURES, AMID THE BODIES?
LET ME JUST SAY, THIS IS A VERY REAL EMERGENCY--
--AND I DON'T HAVE THE TIME TO ADDRESS EVERY DISGUSTING HOAX THAT POPS UP ON THE INTERNET.
WE'LL HAVE MORE ACTUAL NEWS FOR YOU AT THE 9 P.M. BRIEFING.
UNTIL THEN, THE EVACUATION ZONE INCLUDES THIS AREA, SO MOVE YOUR ASSES.
POLICE
YOU BUYING THIS?
NO WAY. COME ON.

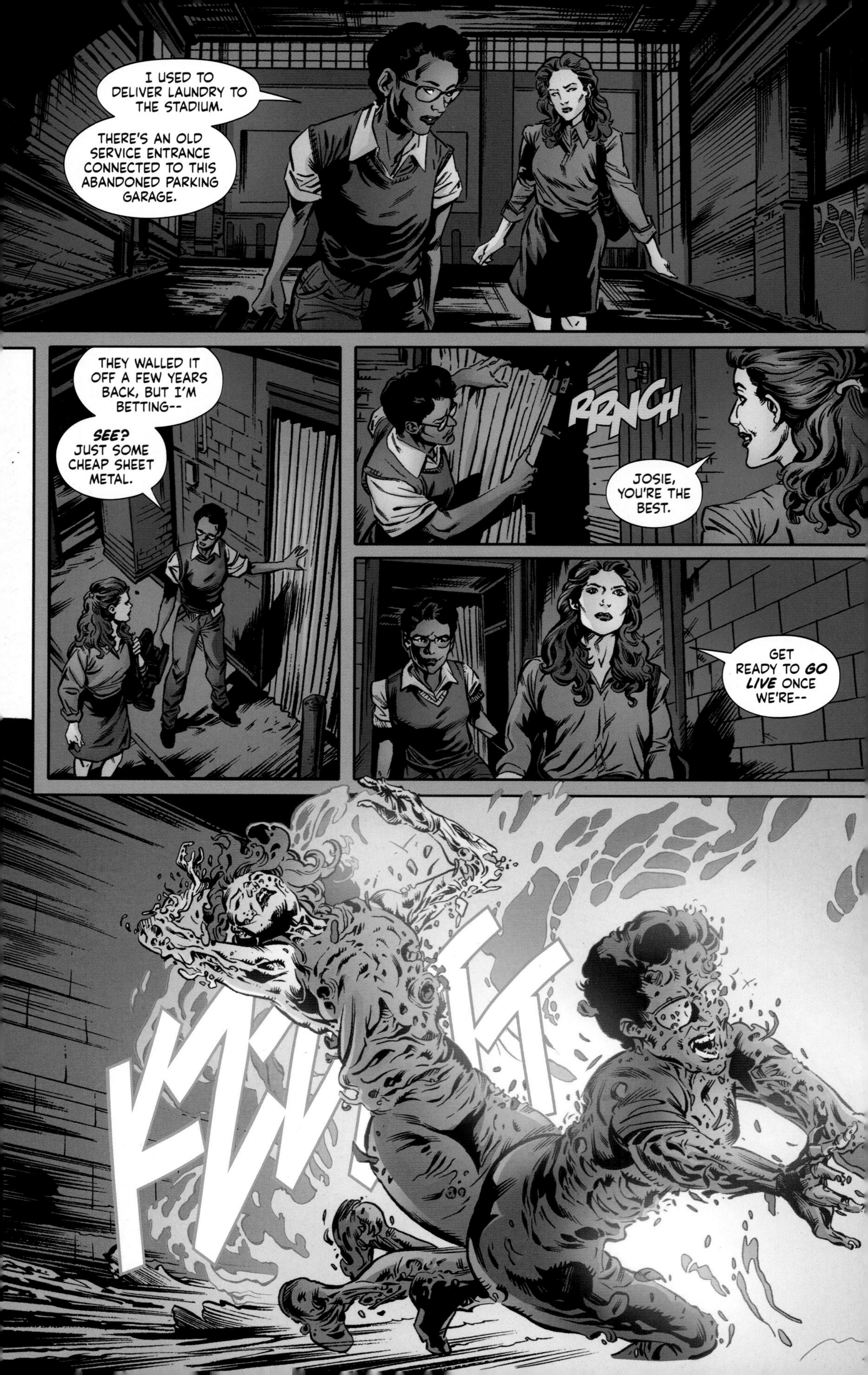

I USED TO DELIVER LAUNDRY TO THE STADIUM.
THERE'S AN OLD SERVICE ENTRANCE CONNECTED TO THIS ABANDONED PARKING GARAGE.
THEY WALLED IT OFF A FEW YEARS BACK, BUT I'M BETTING--
SEE? JUST SOME CHEAP SHEET METAL.
RRNCH
JOSIE, YOU'RE THE BEST.
GET READY TO GO LIVE ONCE WE'RE--

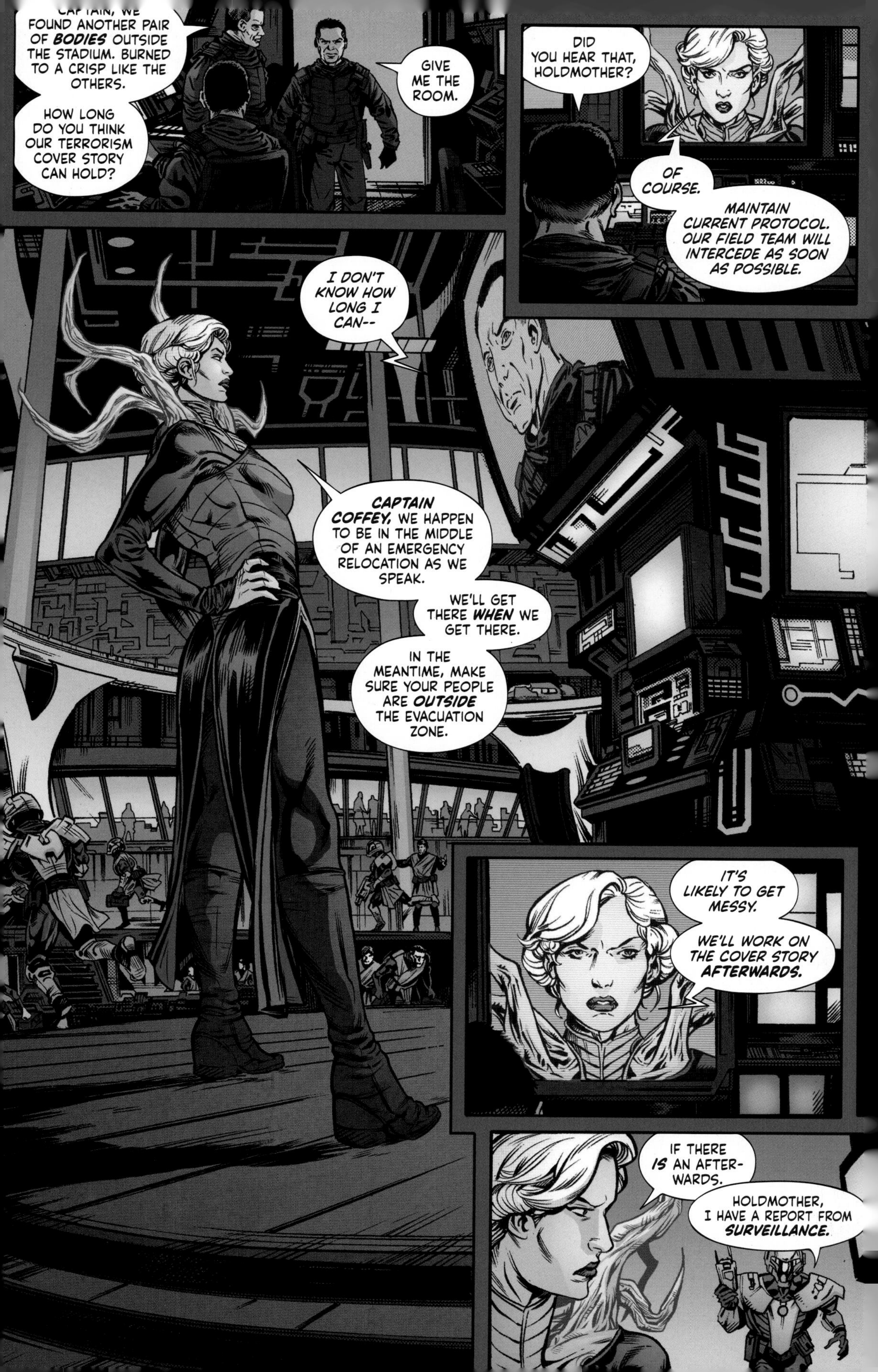
CAPTAIN, WE FOUND ANOTHER PAIR OF BODIES OUTSIDE THE STADIUM. BURNED TO A CRISP LIKE THE OTHERS.
HOW LONG DO YOU THINK OUR TERRORISM COVER STORY CAN HOLD?
GIVE ME THE ROOM.
DID YOU HEAR THAT, HOLDMOTHER?
OF COURSE.
MAINTAIN CURRENT PROTOCOL. OUR FIELD TEAM WILL INTERCEDE AS SOON AS POSSIBLE.
I DON'T KNOW HOW LONG I CAN--
CAPTAIN COFFEY, WE HAPPEN TO BE IN THE MIDDLE OF AN EMERGENCY RELOCATION AS WE SPEAK.
WE'LL GET THERE WHEN WE GET THERE.
IN THE MEANTIME, MAKE SURE YOUR PEOPLE ARE OUTSIDE THE EVACUATION ZONE.
IT'S LIKELY TO GET MESSY.
WE'LL WORK ON THE COVER STORY AFTERWARDS.
IF THERE IS AN AFTER-WARDS.
HOLDMOTHER, I HAVE A REPORT FROM SURVEILLANCE.

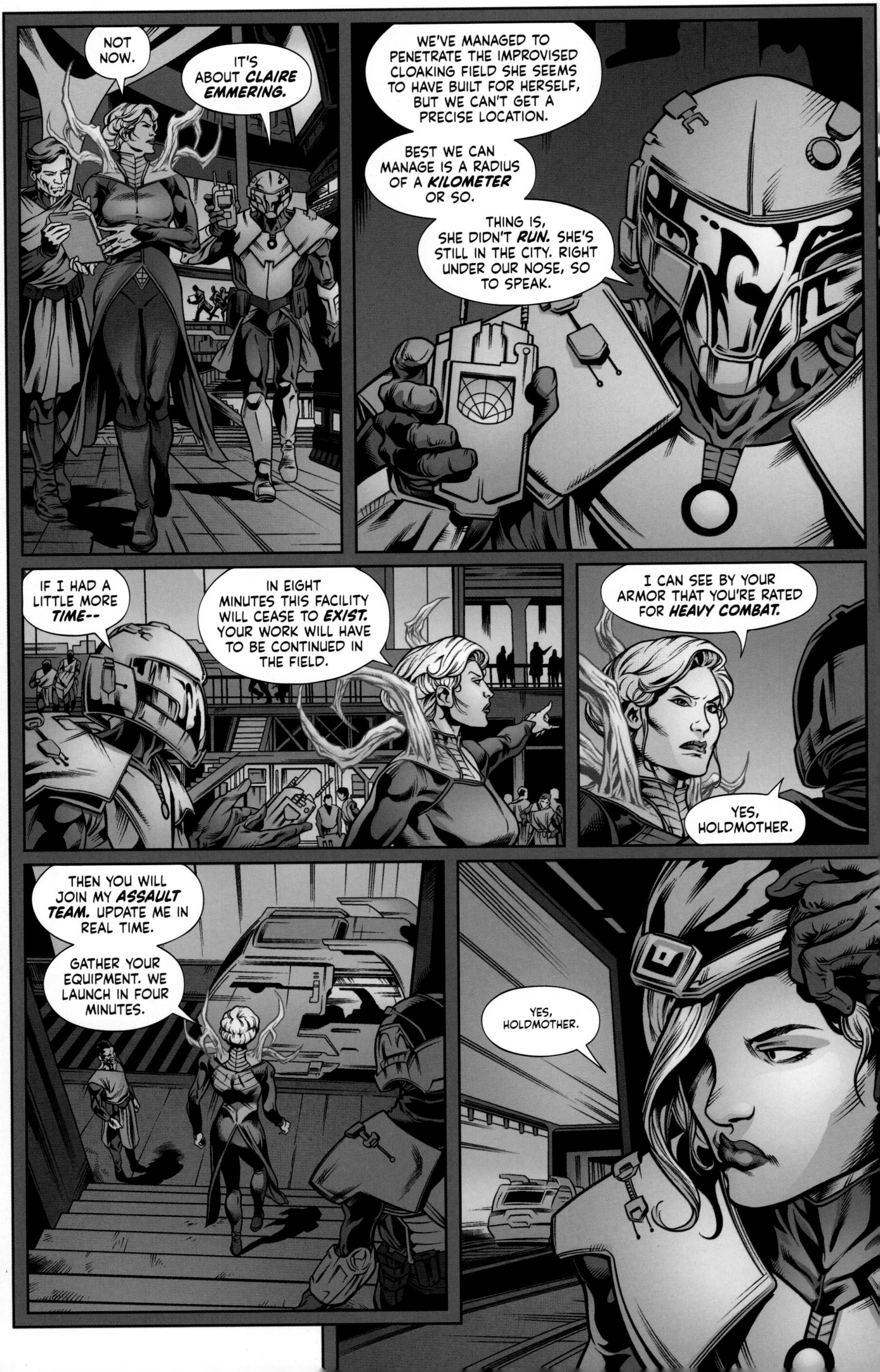
NOT NOW.
IT'S ABOUT CLAIRE EMMERING.
WE'VE MANAGED TO PENETRATE THE IMPROVISED CLOAKING FIELD SHE SEEMS TO HAVE BUILT FOR HERSELF, BUT WE CAN'T GET A PRECISE LOCATION.
BEST WE CAN MANAGE IS A RADIUS OF A KILOMETER OR SO.
THING IS, SHE DIDN'T RUN. SHE'S STILL IN THE CITY. RIGHT UNDER OUR NOSE, SO TO SPEAK.
IF I HAD A LITTLE MORE TIME--
IN EIGHT MINUTES THIS FACILITY WILL CEASE TO EXIST. YOUR WORK WILL HAVE TO BE CONTINUED IN THE FIELD.
I CAN SEE BY YOUR ARMOR THAT YOU'RE RATED FOR HEAVY COMBAT.
YES, HOLDMOTHER.
THEN YOU WILL JOIN MY ASSAULT TEAM. UPDATE ME IN REAL TIME.
GATHER YOUR EQUIPMENT. WE LAUNCH IN FOUR MINUTES.
YES, HOLDMOTHER.

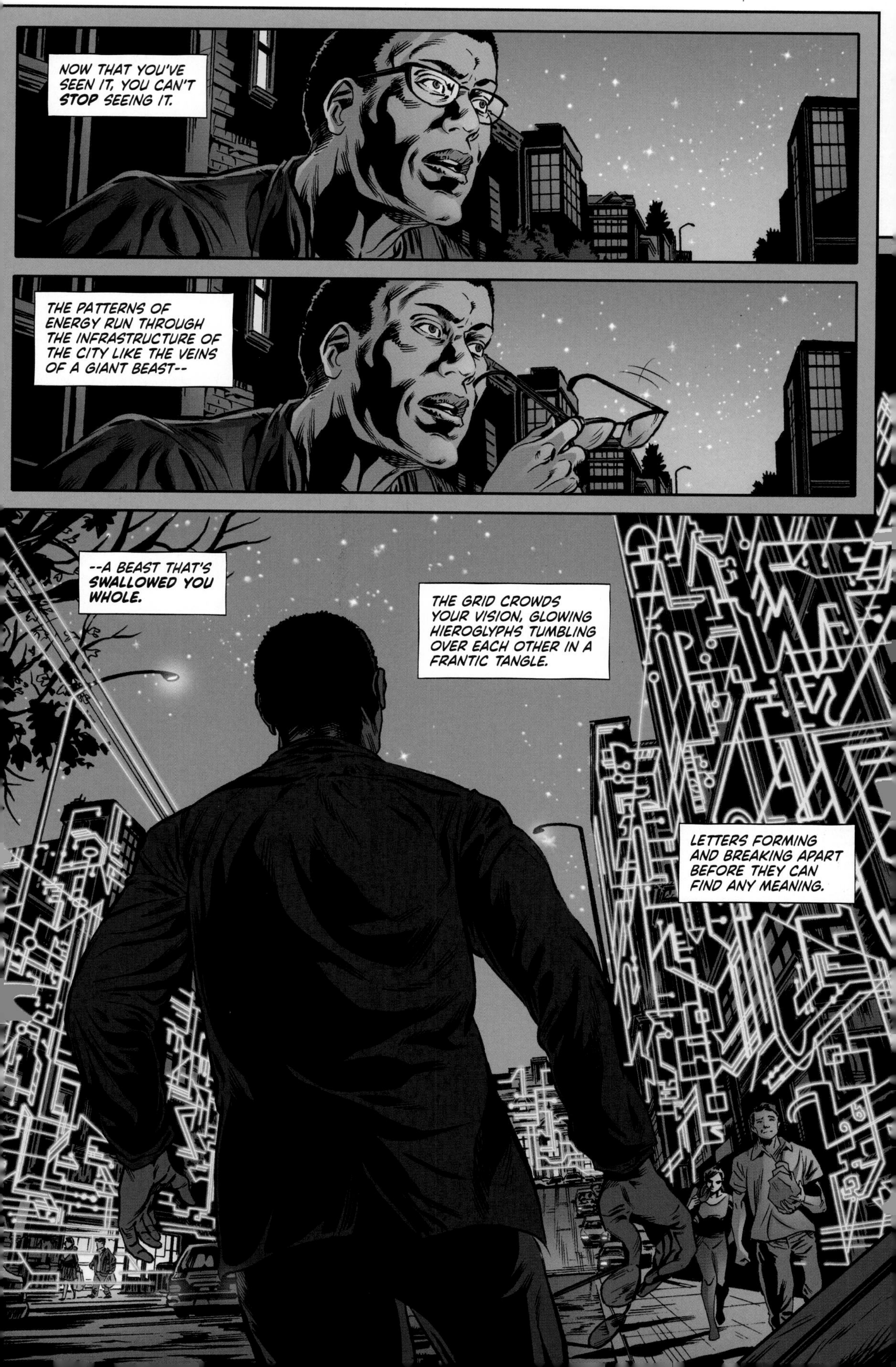
NOW THAT YOU'VE SEEN IT, YOU CAN'T STOP SEEING IT.
THE PATTERNS OF ENERGY RUN THROUGH THE INFRASTRUCTURE OF THE CITY LIKE THE VEINS OF A GIANT BEAST--
--A BEAST THAT'S SWALLOWED YOU WHOLE.
THE GRID CROWDS YOUR VISION, GLOWING HIEROGLYPHS TUMBLING OVER EACH OTHER IN A FRANTIC TANGLE.
LETTERS FORMING AND BREAKING APART BEFORE THEY CAN FIND ANY MEANING.

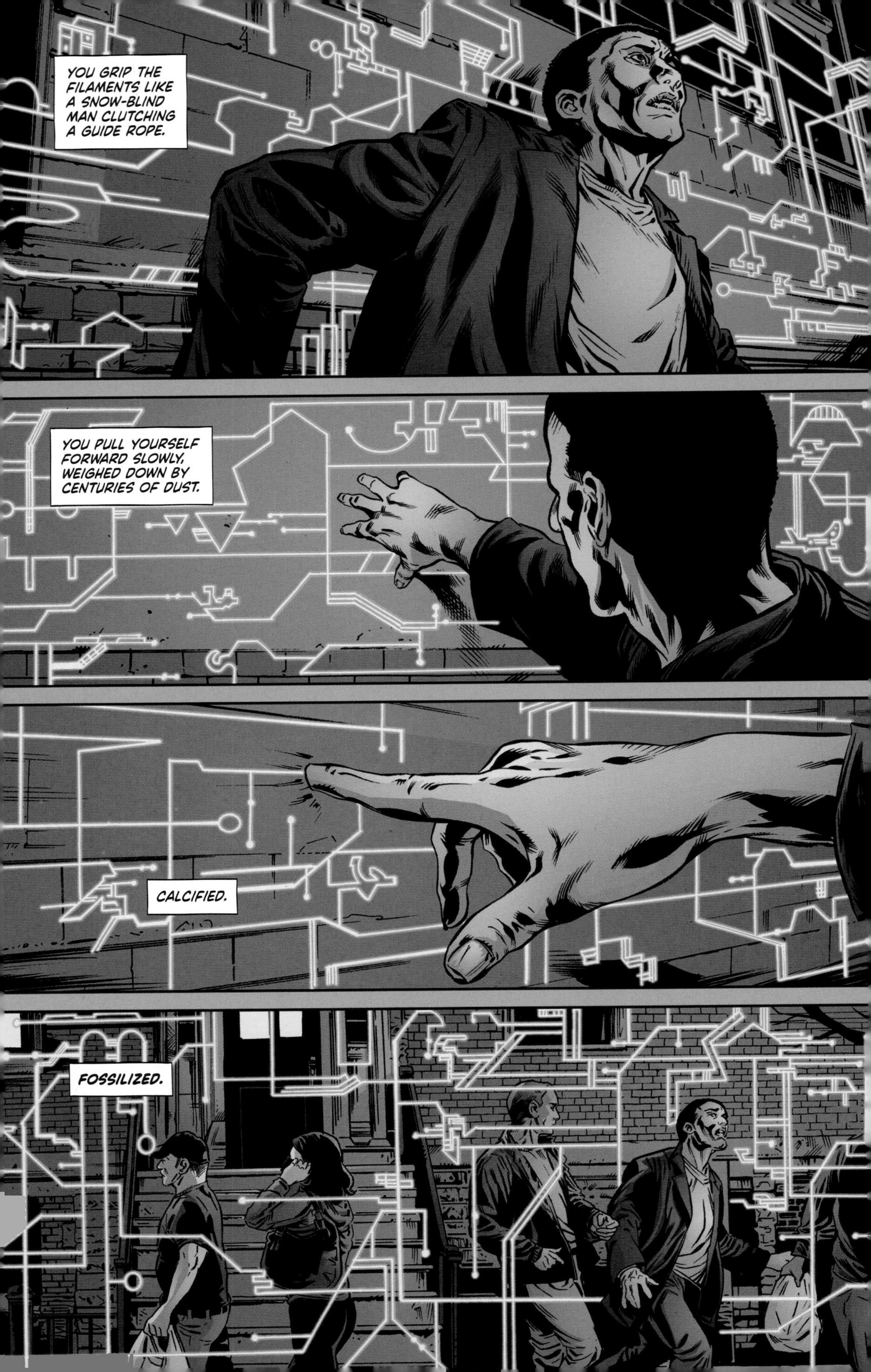
YOU GRIP THE FILAMENTS LIKE A SNOW-BLIND MAN CLUTCHING A GUIDE ROPE.
YOU PULL YOURSELF FORWARD SLOWLY, WEIGHED DOWN BY CENTURIES OF DUST.
CALCIFIED.
FOSSILIZED.

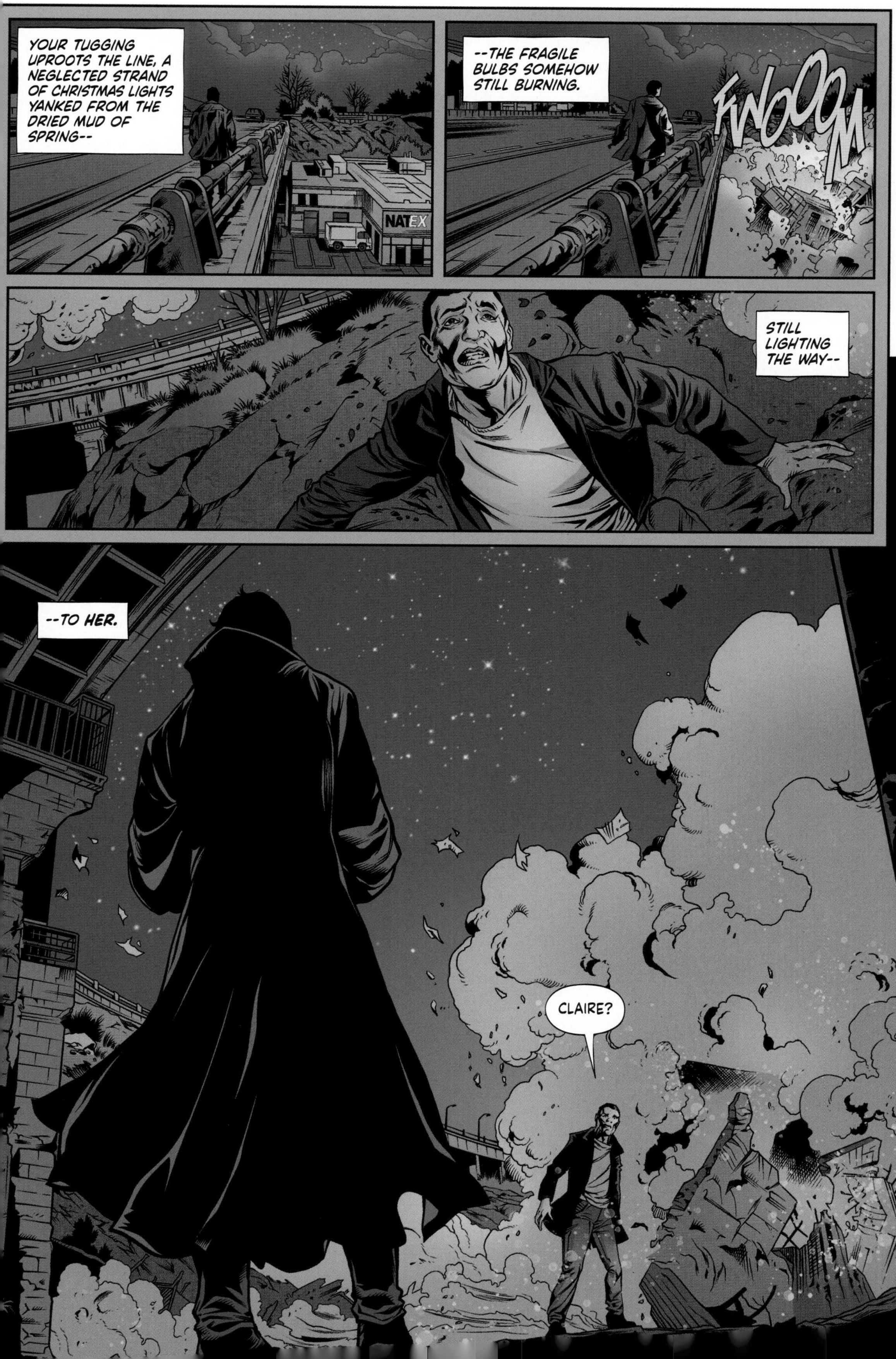
YOUR TUGGING UPROOTS THE LINE, A NEGLECTED STRAND OF CHRISTMAS LIGHTS YANKED FROM THE DRIED MUD OF SPRING--
NATEX
--THE FRAGILE BULBS SOMEHOW STILL BURNING.
FWOOOM
STILL LIGHTING THE WAY--
--TO HER.
CLAIRE?

I DIDN'T THINK THE FAMILY RESEMBLANCE WAS THAT STRONG.

YOU'RE LOOKING FOR MY *DAUGHTER*.

FROM THAT *PLACE*, AREN'T YOU?

THE STRONGHOLD.

YES. WELL, UNTIL ABOUT FIFTEEN MINUTES AGO.

YOU DON'T REMEMBER ME, DO YOU? HOW COULD YOU?

I'M AN OLD MAN NOW...

...WHILE YOU HAVEN'T CHANGED AT ALL.

I'M SORRY, I DON'T KNOW--

WHEN WE BEGAN THE ST. LOUIS OPERATION, I WAS YOUR OPTOMETRIST.

I--I DON'T NEED GLASSES ANYMORE.

YOU NEVER DID. IT WAS PART OF OUR RUSE TO KEEP YOU FROM TRULY SEEING THE WORLD.

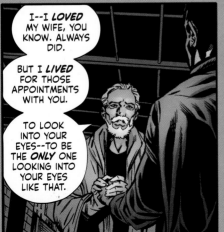

I--I *LOVED* MY WIFE, YOU KNOW. ALWAYS DID.

BUT I *LIVED* FOR THOSE APPOINTMENTS WITH YOU.

TO LOOK INTO YOUR EYES--TO BE THE *ONLY* ONE LOOKING INTO YOUR EYES LIKE THAT.

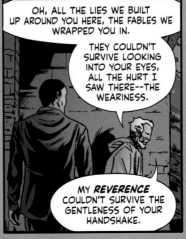

OH, ALL THE LIES WE BUILT UP AROUND YOU HERE, THE FABLES WE WRAPPED YOU IN.

THEY COULDN'T SURVIVE LOOKING INTO YOUR EYES, ALL THE HURT I SAW THERE--THE WEARINESS.

MY *REVERENCE* COULDN'T SURVIVE THE GENTLENESS OF YOUR HANDSHAKE.

IT WAS *REPLACED* BY...SOMETHING ELSE.

WHAT **ABOUT** CLAIRE?

CLAIRE. YES, JUST LIKE HER OLD MAN.

IF I KNOW MY DAUGHTER, SHE'S BEEN WATCHING YOU FROM THE SHADOWS, STAYING OUT OF THE STRONGHOLD'S REACH.

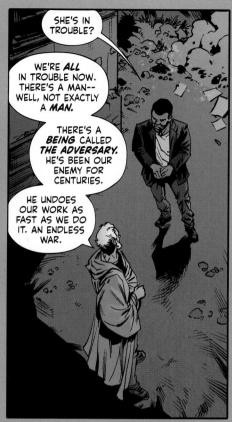

SHE'S IN TROUBLE?

WE'RE **ALL** IN TROUBLE NOW. THERE'S A MAN-- WELL, NOT EXACTLY A **MAN.**

THERE'S A **BEING** CALLED **THE ADVERSARY.** HE'S BEEN OUR ENEMY FOR CENTURIES.

HE UNDOES OUR WORK AS FAST AS WE DO IT. AN ENDLESS WAR.

THAT WAR KILLED MY **WIFE...** CLAIRE'S MOTHER.

AND NOW HE'S TRYING TO DRAW YOU INTO IT BY PERPETUATING A TERRIBLE CRIME. IT'S ON THE NEWS BY NOW.

OUR LEADERS ARE RESPONDING TO THE ATTACK, HOPING THEY CAN CONTAIN IT BEFORE YOU LEARN OF IT.

BUT IT'S TOO LATE FOR THAT. YOU WANT TO KNOW IT **ALL** NOW. I SEE IT IN THOSE EYES.

WHEN YOU GO THERE, I HAVE A **FAVOR** TO ASK.

I VERY MUCH HOPE THAT YOU MIGHT USE THOSE GENTLE HANDS OF YOURS TO **KILL** THE ADVERSARY.

I DON'T-- I DON'T UNDER-STAND ANY OF THIS.

YOU WILL. GOD HELP US, YOU *WILL*.

BUT SOON, *I* WILL REMEMBER NONE OF IT.

I HAVE MANAGED TO EXTRACT THE BRAND BURNED INTO ALL STRONGHOLD MEMBERS AT BIRTH.

WITHOUT ITS PROPERTIES, ALL MEMORIES OF THE STRONGHOLD... AND *YOU*, WILL FADE.

EVEN, I'M AFRAID, THOSE OF MY *DAUGHTER*.

IT'S THE ONLY WAY TO PROTECT HER, SEE?

IF THE STRONGHOLD *CAPTURES* ME--WELL, THEY CAN'T *EXTRACT* INFORMATION I NO LONGER RECALL.

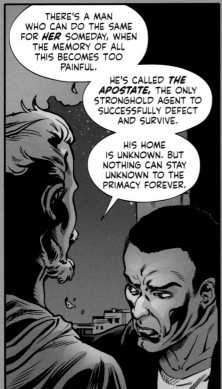

THERE'S A MAN WHO CAN DO THE SAME FOR *HER* SOMEDAY, WHEN THE MEMORY OF ALL THIS BECOMES TOO PAINFUL.

HE'S CALLED *THE APOSTATE*, THE ONLY STRONGHOLD AGENT TO SUCCESSFULLY DEFECT AND SURVIVE.

HIS HOME IS UNKNOWN. BUT NOTHING CAN STAY UNKNOWN TO THE PRIMACY FOREVER.

PLEASE, WHEN YOU SEE MY DAUGHTER AGAIN, REMIND HER THAT I LOVE HER.

THAT I LOVED HER ENOUGH TO FORGET SHE EVER EXISTED.

CAN YOU IMAGINE SUCH A THING?

LOOK WHO I'M TALKING TO.

OF *COURSE* YOU CAN.

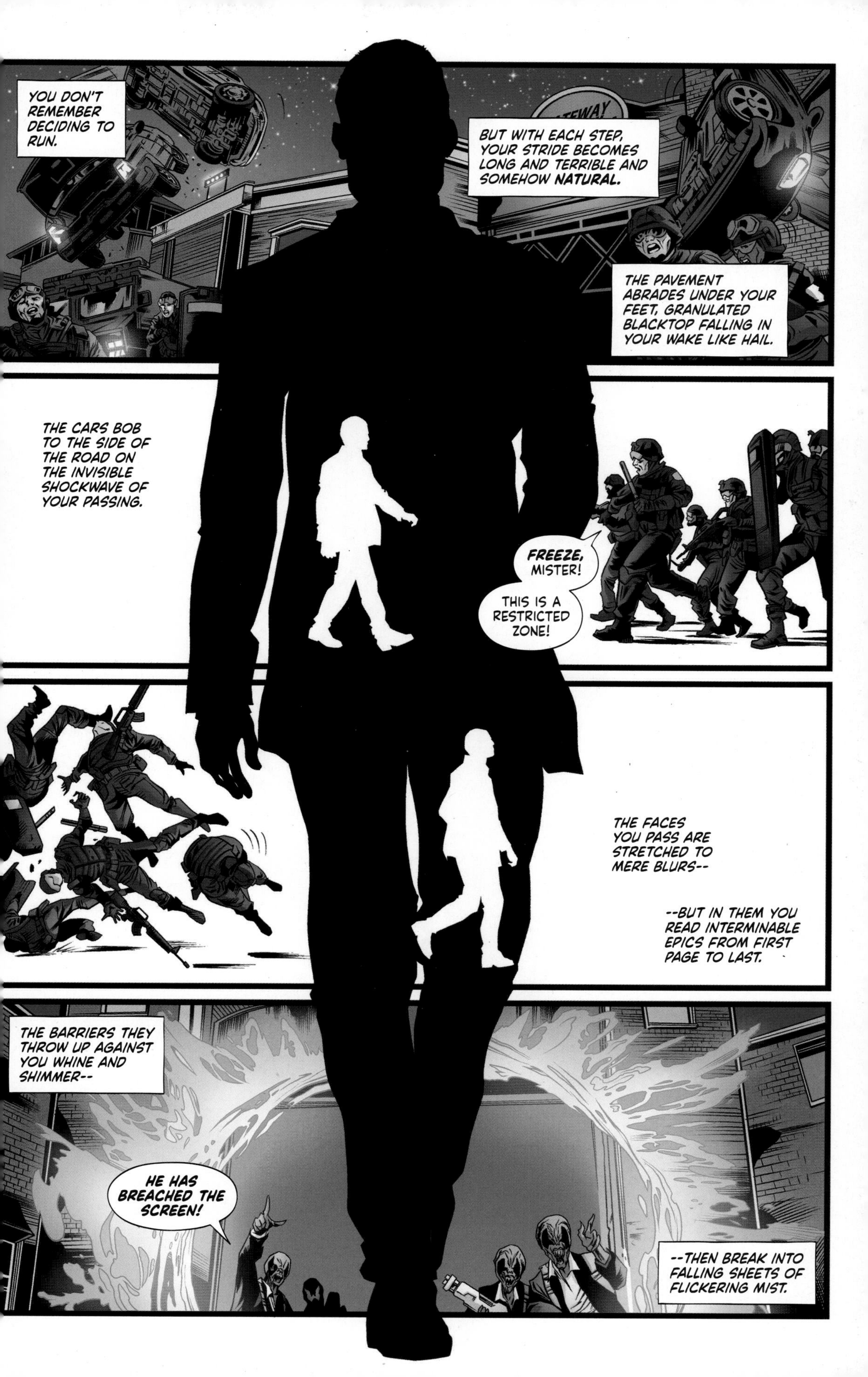
YOU DON'T REMEMBER DECIDING TO RUN.
BUT WITH EACH STEP, YOUR STRIDE BECOMES LONG AND TERRIBLE AND SOMEHOW NATURAL.
THE PAVEMENT ABRADES UNDER YOUR FEET, GRANULATED BLACKTOP FALLING IN YOUR WAKE LIKE HAIL.
THE CARS BOB TO THE SIDE OF THE ROAD ON THE INVISIBLE SHOCKWAVE OF YOUR PASSING.
FREEZE, MISTER!
THIS IS A RESTRICTED ZONE!
THE FACES YOU PASS ARE STRETCHED TO MERE BLURS--
--BUT IN THEM YOU READ INTERMINABLE EPICS FROM FIRST PAGE TO LAST.
THE BARRIERS THEY THROW UP AGAINST YOU WHINE AND SHIMMER--
HE HAS BREACHED THE SCREEN!
--THEN BREAK INTO FALLING SHEETS OF FLICKERING MIST.

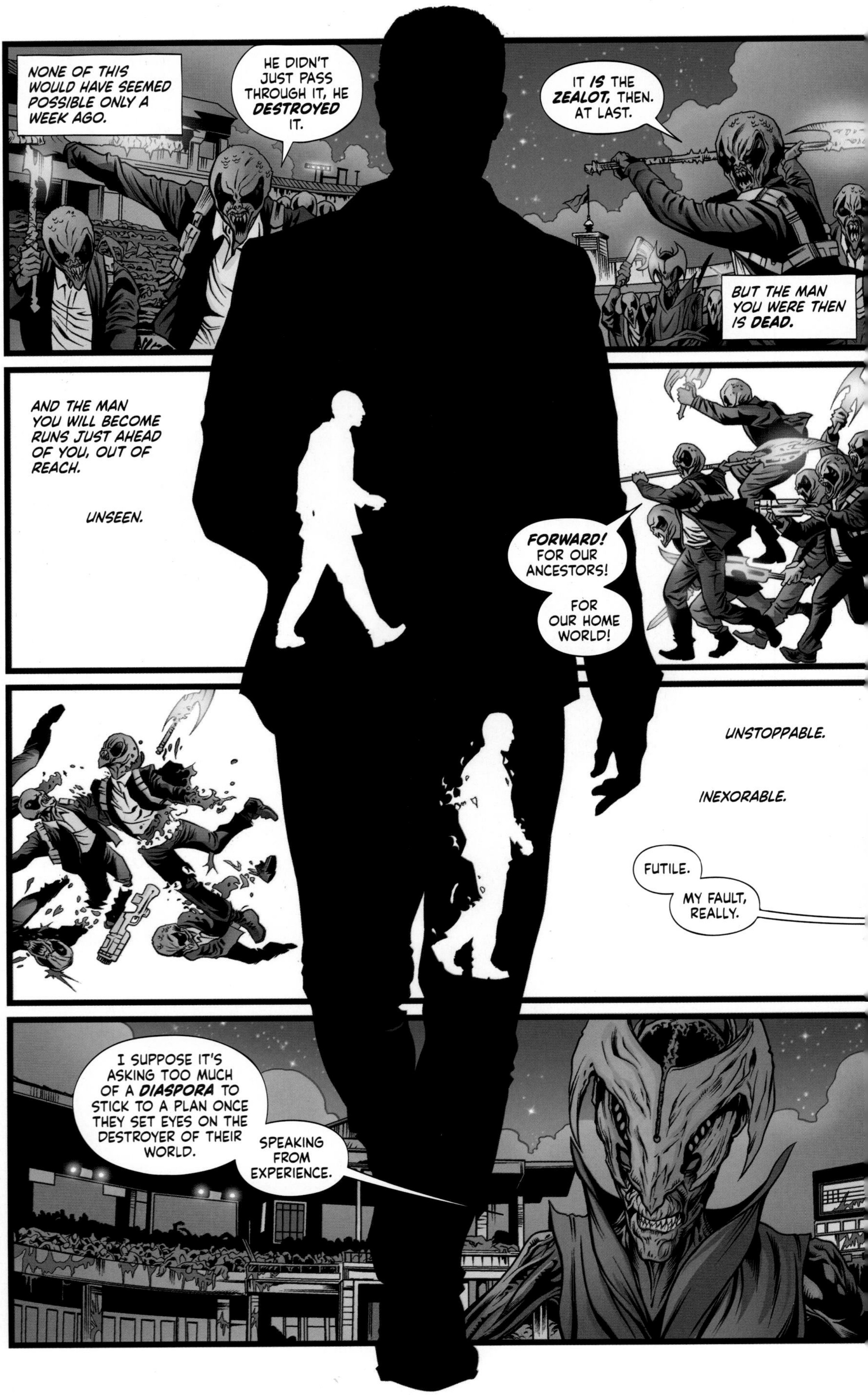
NONE OF THIS WOULD HAVE SEEMED POSSIBLE ONLY A WEEK AGO.
HE DIDN'T JUST PASS THROUGH IT, HE DESTROYED IT.
IT IS THE ZEALOT, THEN. AT LAST.
BUT THE MAN YOU WERE THEN IS DEAD.
AND THE MAN YOU WILL BECOME RUNS JUST AHEAD OF YOU, OUT OF REACH.
UNSEEN.
FORWARD! FOR OUR ANCESTORS!
FOR OUR HOME WORLD!
UNSTOPPABLE.
INEXORABLE.
FUTILE.
MY FAULT, REALLY.
I SUPPOSE IT'S ASKING TOO MUCH OF A DIASPORA TO STICK TO A PLAN ONCE THEY SET EYES ON THE DESTROYER OF THEIR WORLD.
SPEAKING FROM EXPERIENCE.

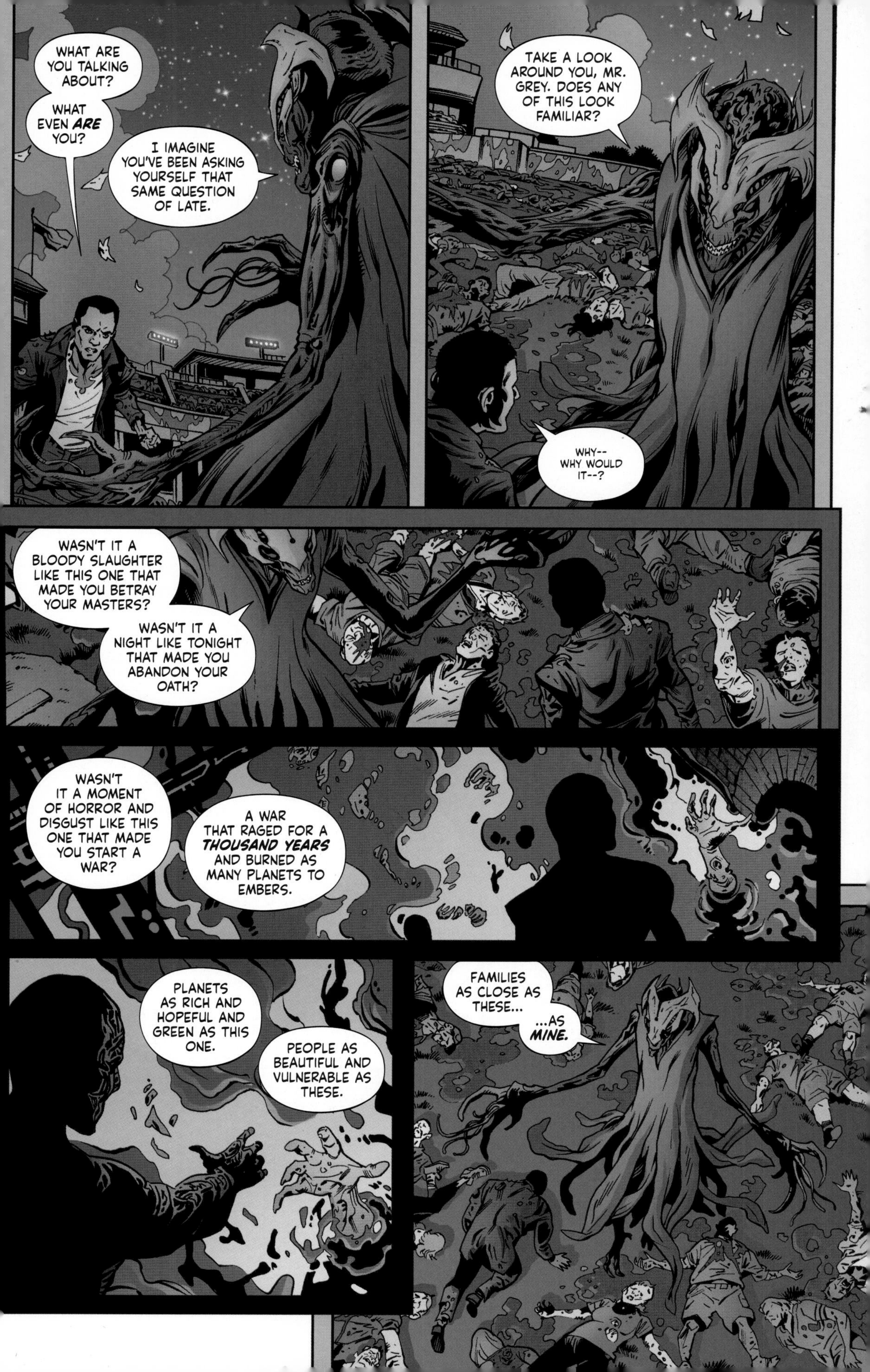
WHAT ARE YOU TALKING ABOUT?
WHAT EVEN ARE YOU?
I IMAGINE YOU'VE BEEN ASKING YOURSELF THAT SAME QUESTION OF LATE.
TAKE A LOOK AROUND YOU, MR. GREY. DOES ANY OF THIS LOOK FAMILIAR?
WHY-- WHY WOULD IT--?
WASN'T IT A BLOODY SLAUGHTER LIKE THIS ONE THAT MADE YOU BETRAY YOUR MASTERS?
WASN'T IT A NIGHT LIKE TONIGHT THAT MADE YOU ABANDON YOUR OATH?
WASN'T IT A MOMENT OF HORROR AND DISGUST LIKE THIS ONE THAT MADE YOU START A WAR?
A WAR THAT RAGED FOR A THOUSAND YEARS AND BURNED AS MANY PLANETS TO EMBERS.
PLANETS AS RICH AND HOPEFUL AND GREEN AS THIS ONE.
PEOPLE AS BEAUTIFUL AND VULNERABLE AS THESE.
FAMILIES AS CLOSE AS THESE...
...AS MINE.

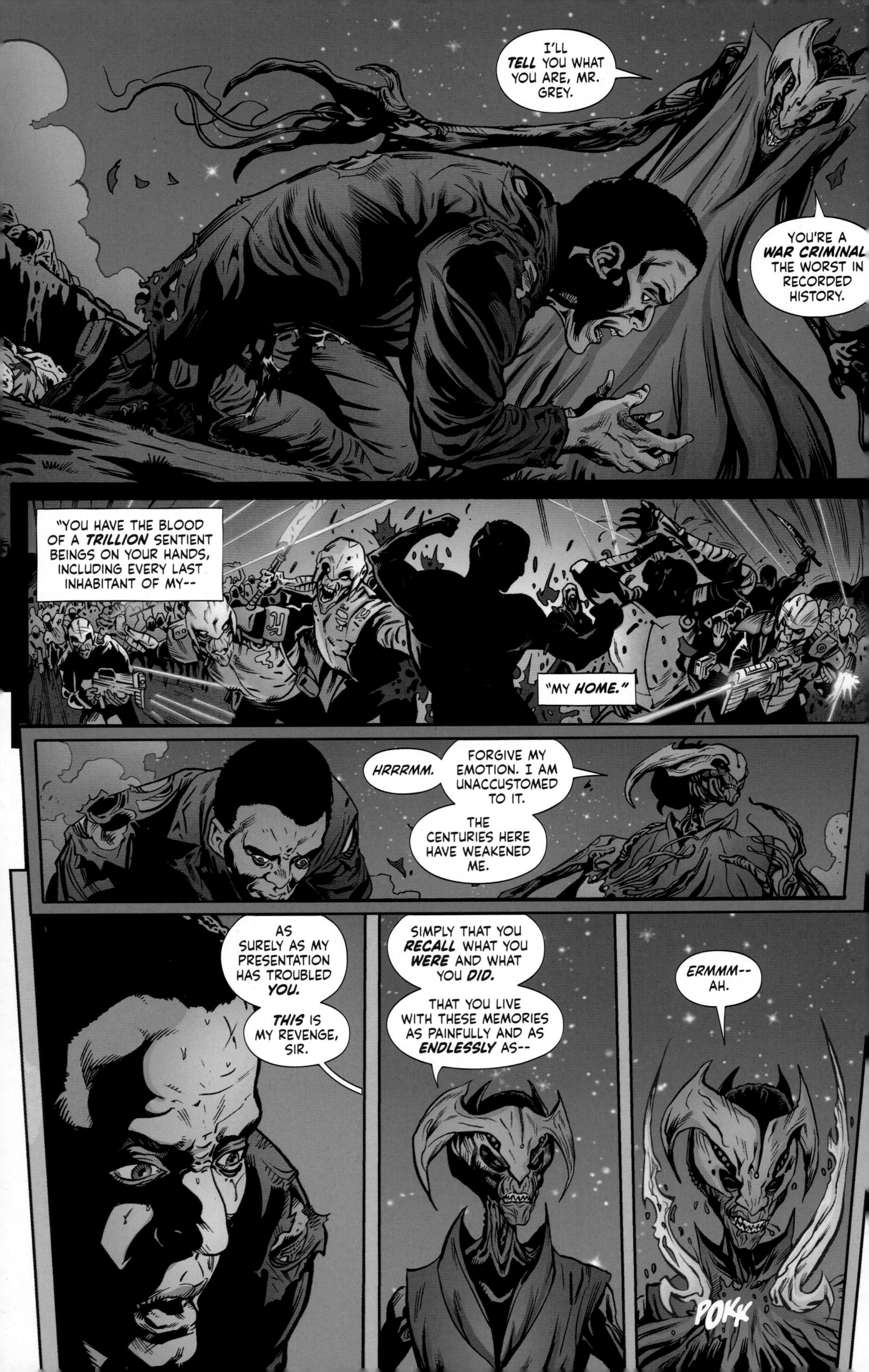

I'LL TELL YOU WHAT YOU ARE, MR. GREY.
YOU'RE A WAR CRIMINAL THE WORST IN RECORDED HISTORY.
"YOU HAVE THE BLOOD OF A TRILLION SENTIENT BEINGS ON YOUR HANDS, INCLUDING EVERY LAST INHABITANT OF MY--
"MY HOME."
HRRRMM.
FORGIVE MY EMOTION. I AM UNACCUSTOMED TO IT.
THE CENTURIES HERE HAVE WEAKENED ME.
AS SURELY AS MY PRESENTATION HAS TROUBLED YOU.
THIS IS MY REVENGE, SIR.
SIMPLY THAT YOU RECALL WHAT YOU WERE AND WHAT YOU DID.
THAT YOU LIVE WITH THESE MEMORIES AS PAINFULLY AND AS ENDLESSLY AS--
ERMMM-- AH.
POKK

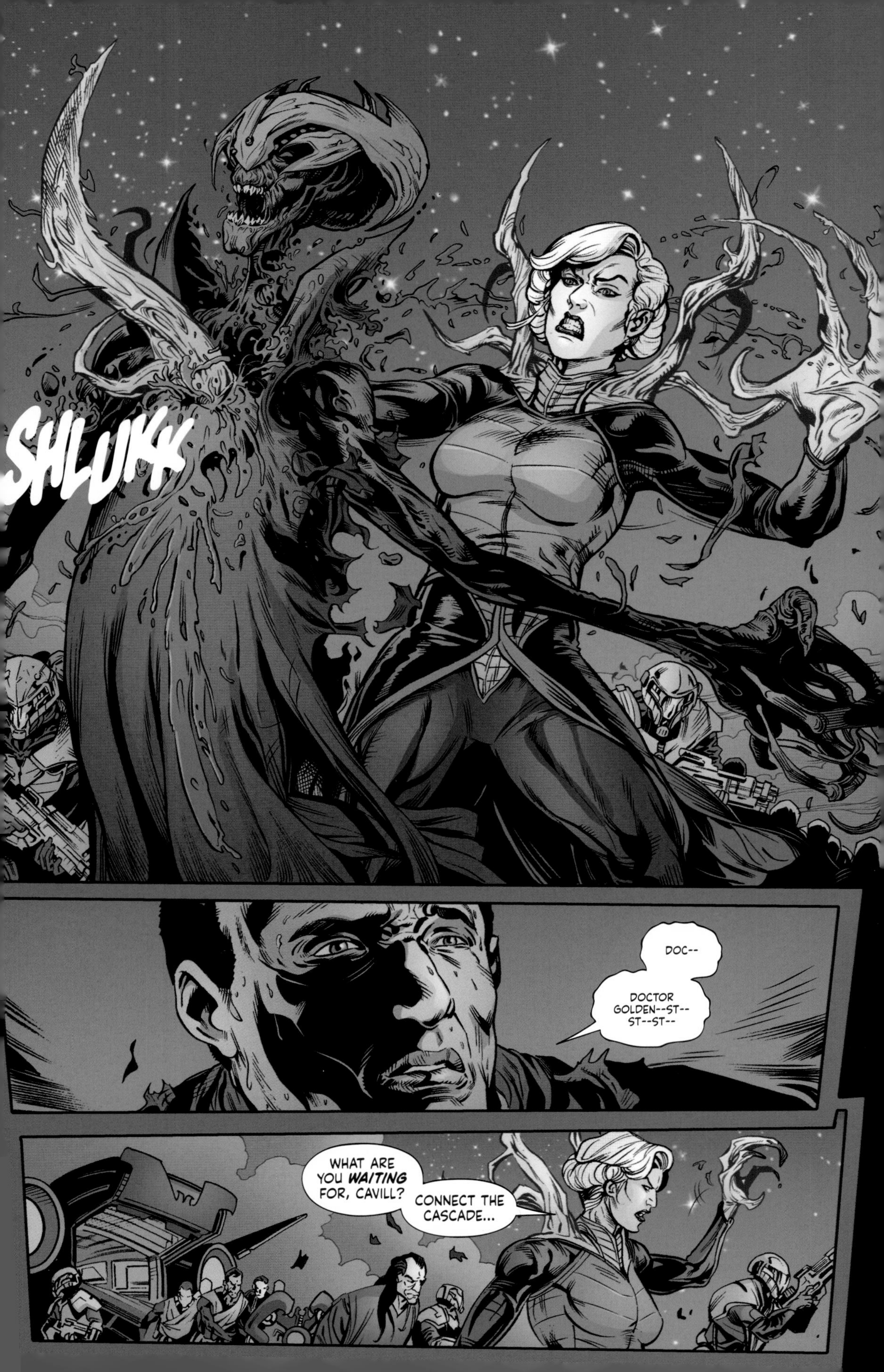
SHLUKK
DOC--
DOCTOR GOLDEN--ST--ST--ST--
WHAT ARE YOU *WAITING* FOR, CAVILL?
CONNECT THE CASCADE...

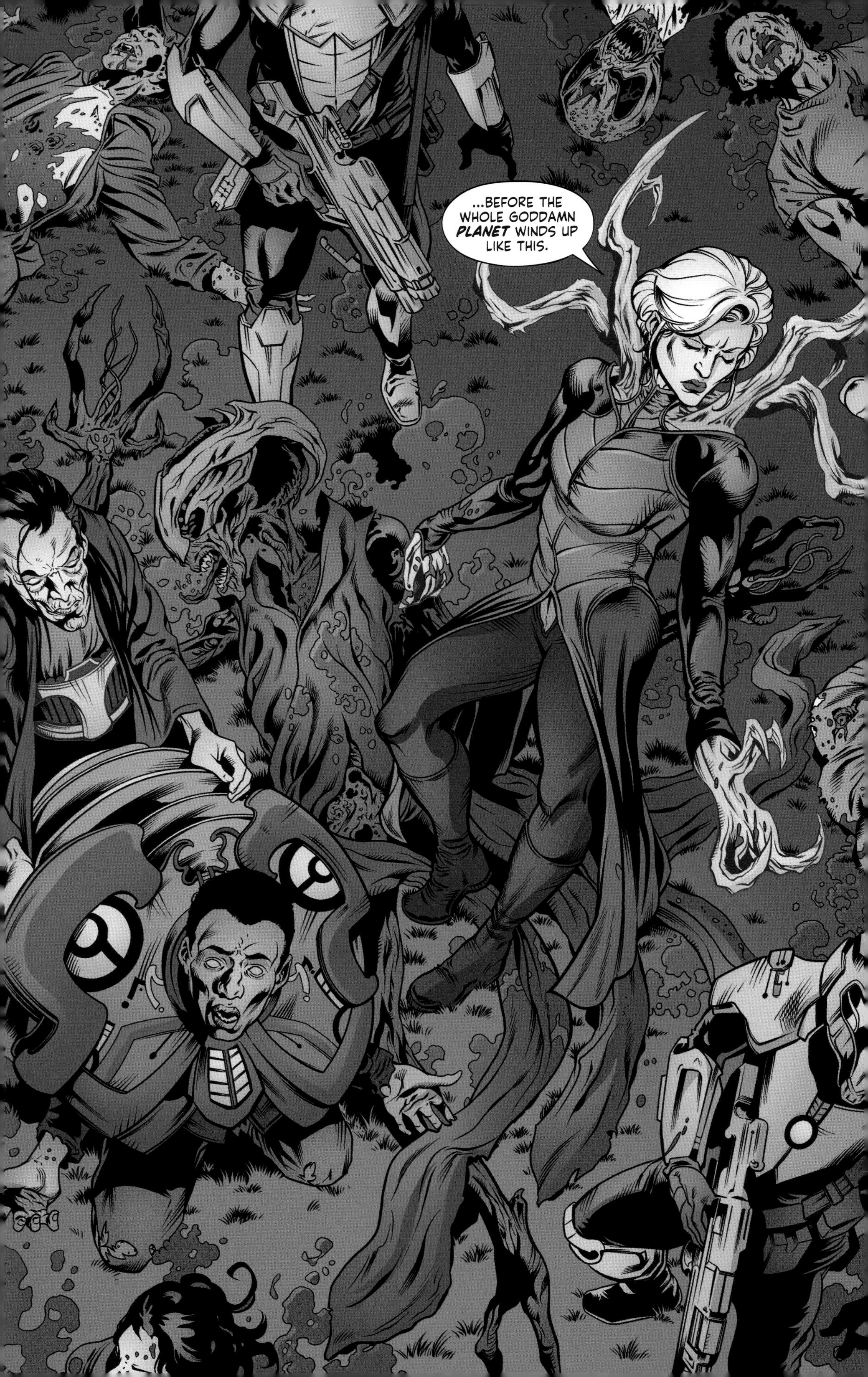
...BEFORE THE WHOLE GODDAMN *PLANET* WINDS UP LIKE THIS.

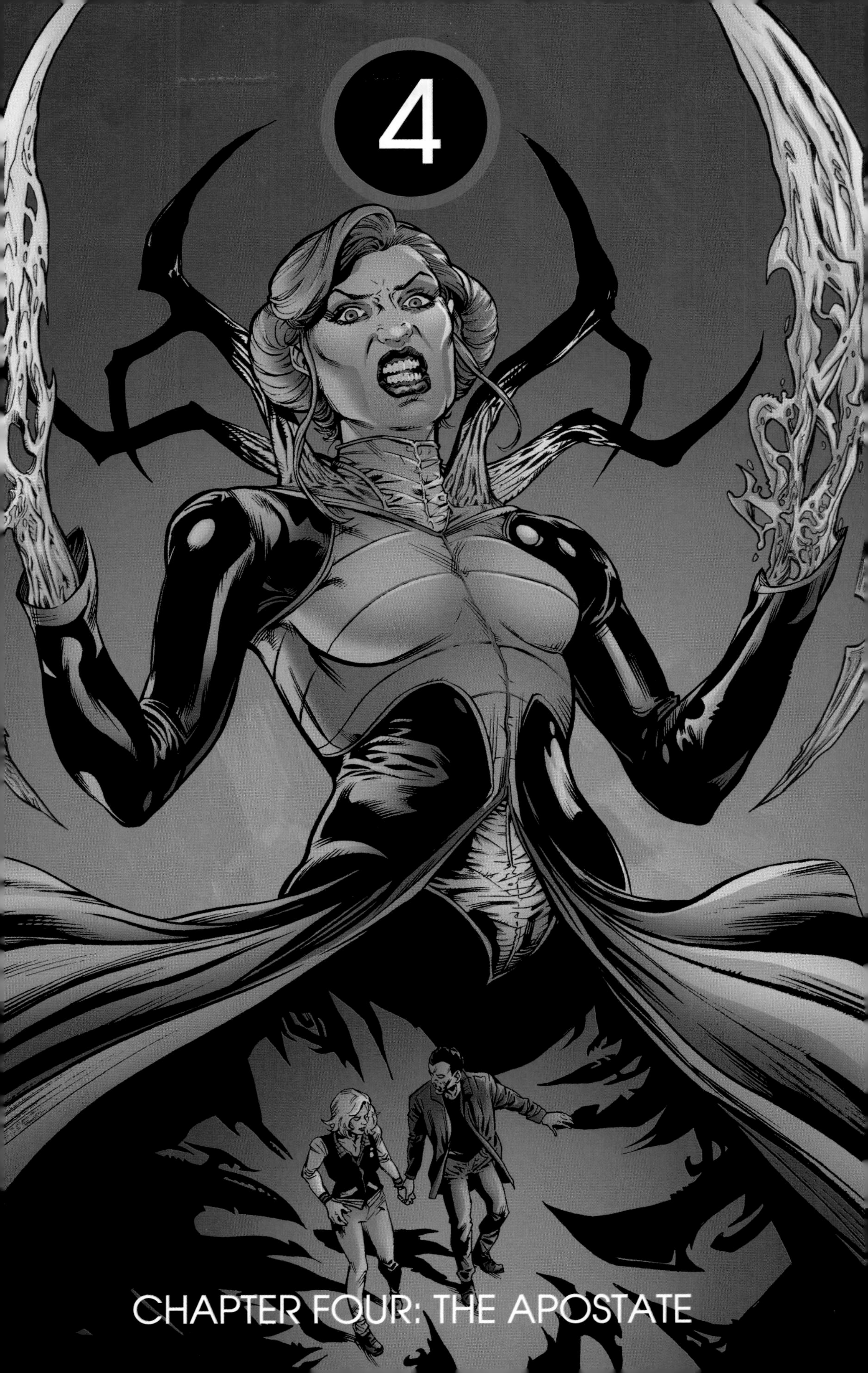
4
CHAPTER FOUR: THE APOSTATE

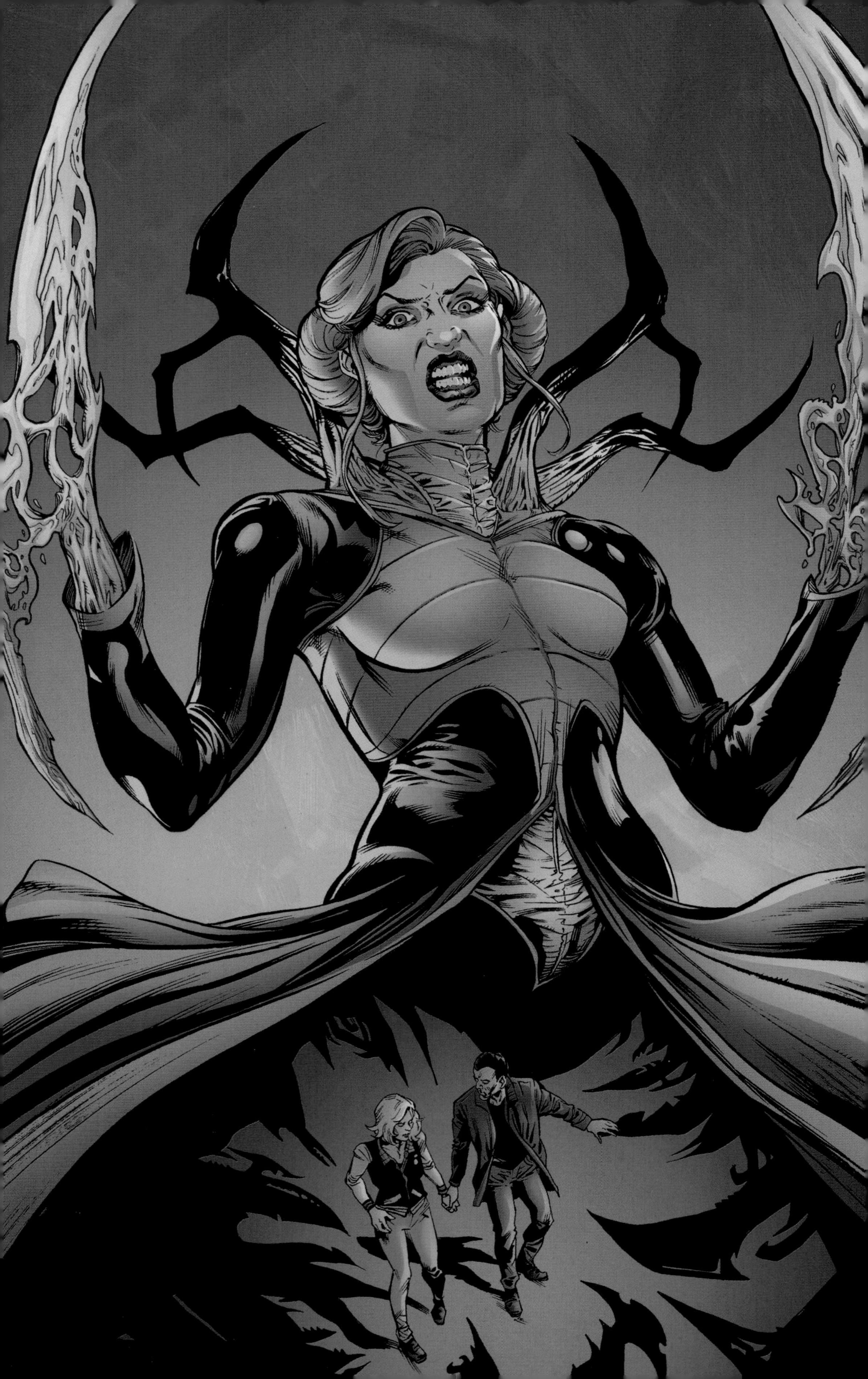

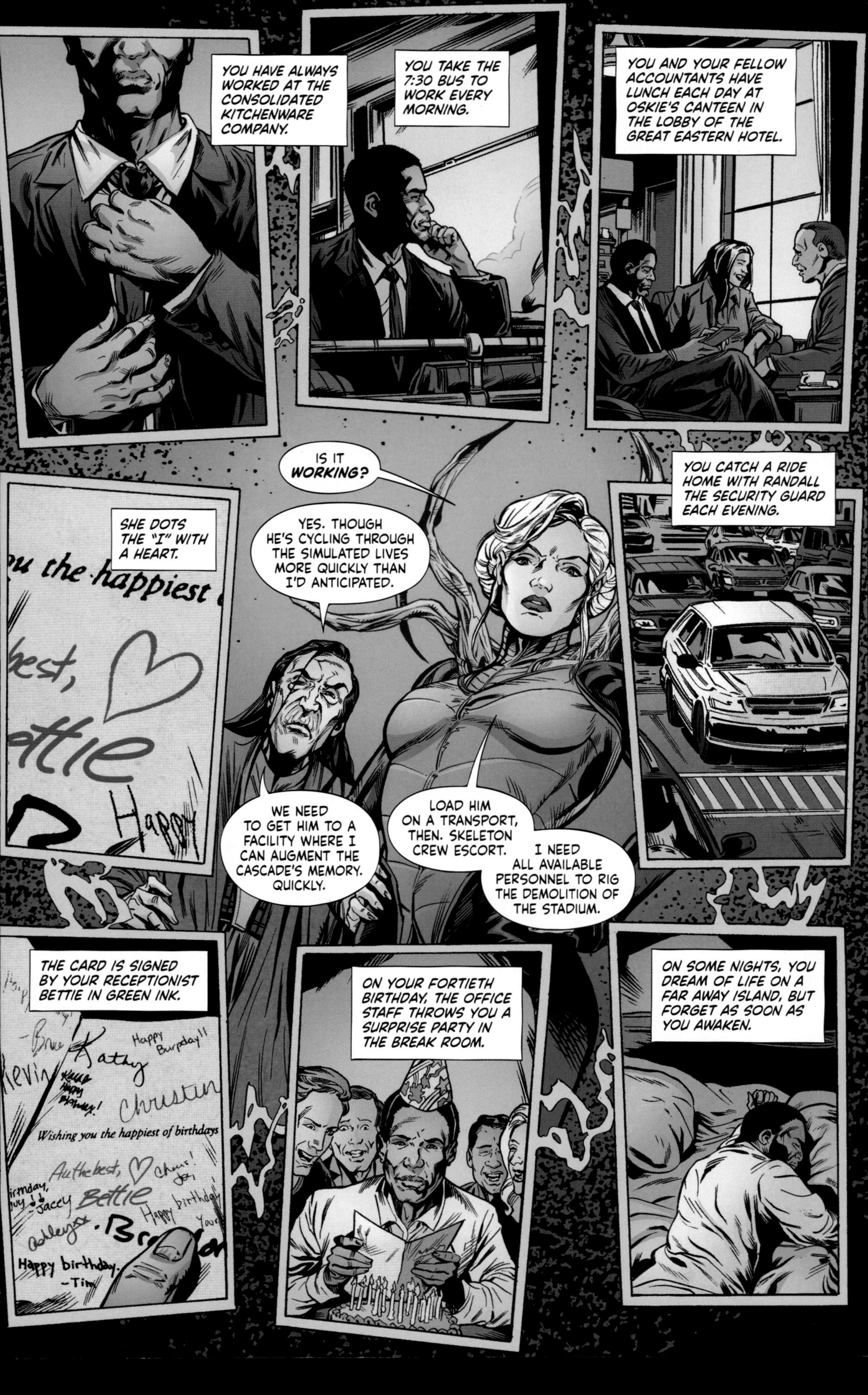

YOU HAVE ALWAYS WORKED AT THE CONSOLIDATED KITCHENWARE COMPANY.
YOU TAKE THE 7:30 BUS TO WORK EVERY MORNING.
YOU AND YOUR FELLOW ACCOUNTANTS HAVE LUNCH EACH DAY AT OSKIE'S CANTEEN IN THE LOBBY OF THE GREAT EASTERN HOTEL.
SHE DOTS THE "I" WITH A HEART.
IS IT *WORKING?*
YES. THOUGH HE'S CYCLING THROUGH THE SIMULATED LIVES MORE QUICKLY THAN I'D ANTICIPATED.
YOU CATCH A RIDE HOME WITH RANDALL THE SECURITY GUARD EACH EVENING.
WE NEED TO GET HIM TO A FACILITY WHERE I CAN AUGMENT THE CASCADE'S MEMORY. QUICKLY.
LOAD HIM ON A TRANSPORT, THEN. SKELETON CREW ESCORT.
I NEED ALL AVAILABLE PERSONNEL TO RIG THE DEMOLITION OF THE STADIUM.
THE CARD IS SIGNED BY YOUR RECEPTIONIST BETTIE IN GREEN INK.
Happy Burpday!!
Kathy
Christin
Wishing you the happiest of birthdays
Bettie
Happy birthday. -Tim
ON YOUR FORTIETH BIRTHDAY, THE OFFICE STAFF THROWS YOU A SURPRISE PARTY IN THE BREAK ROOM.
ON SOME NIGHTS, YOU DREAM OF LIFE ON A FAR AWAY ISLAND, BUT FORGET AS SOON AS YOU AWAKEN.

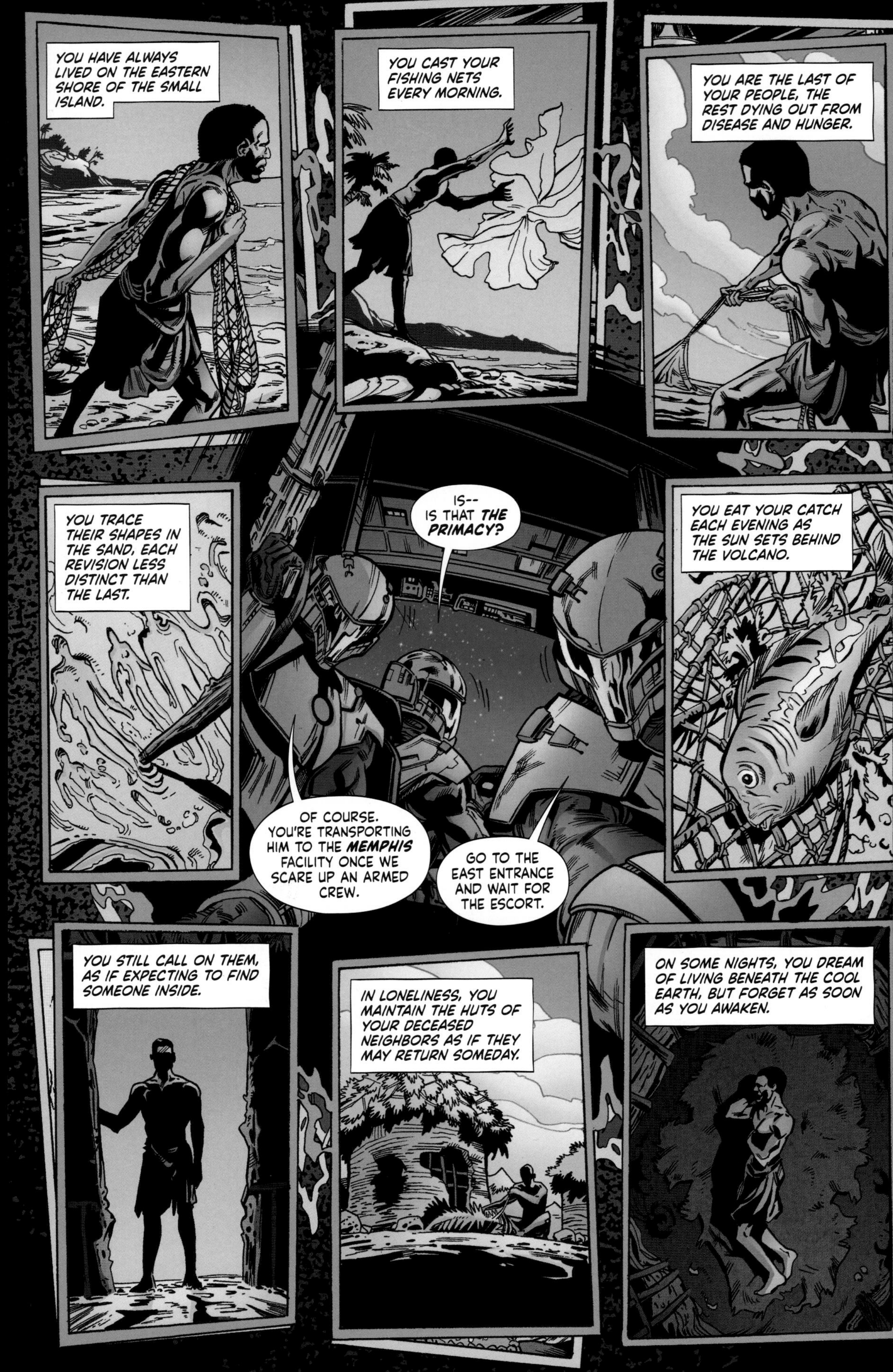
YOU HAVE ALWAYS LIVED ON THE EASTERN SHORE OF THE SMALL ISLAND.
YOU CAST YOUR FISHING NETS EVERY MORNING.
YOU ARE THE LAST OF YOUR PEOPLE, THE REST DYING OUT FROM DISEASE AND HUNGER.
YOU TRACE THEIR SHAPES IN THE SAND, EACH REVISION LESS DISTINCT THAN THE LAST.
IS-- IS THAT THE PRIMACY?
YOU EAT YOUR CATCH EACH EVENING AS THE SUN SETS BEHIND THE VOLCANO.
OF COURSE. YOU'RE TRANSPORTING HIM TO THE MEMPHIS FACILITY ONCE WE SCARE UP AN ARMED CREW.
GO TO THE EAST ENTRANCE AND WAIT FOR THE ESCORT.
YOU STILL CALL ON THEM, AS IF EXPECTING TO FIND SOMEONE INSIDE.
IN LONELINESS, YOU MAINTAIN THE HUTS OF YOUR DECEASED NEIGHBORS AS IF THEY MAY RETURN SOMEDAY.
ON SOME NIGHTS, YOU DREAM OF LIVING BENEATH THE COOL EARTH, BUT FORGET AS SOON AS YOU AWAKEN.

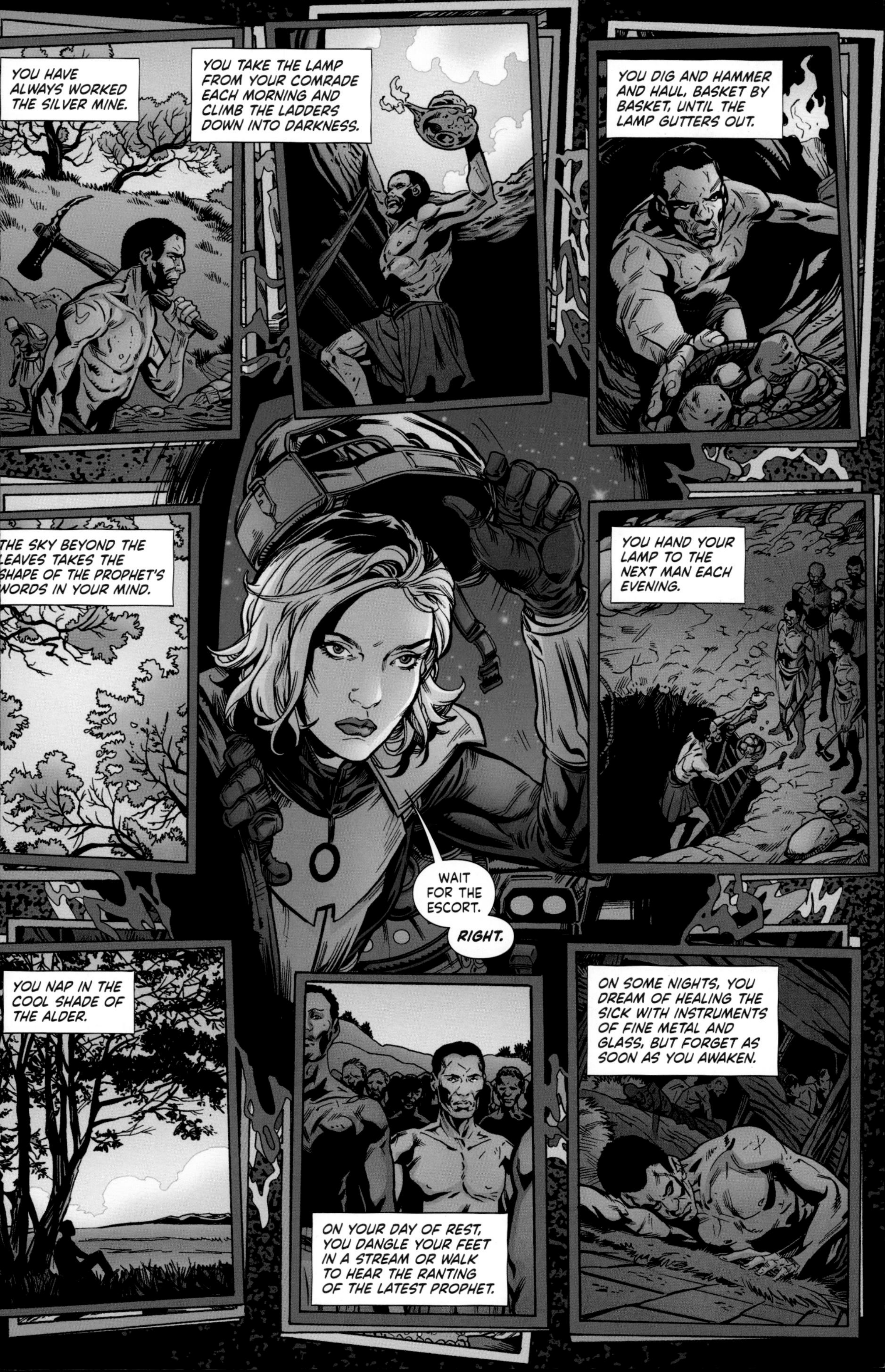
YOU HAVE ALWAYS WORKED THE SILVER MINE.
YOU TAKE THE LAMP FROM YOUR COMRADE EACH MORNING AND CLIMB THE LADDERS DOWN INTO DARKNESS.
YOU DIG AND HAMMER AND HAUL, BASKET BY BASKET, UNTIL THE LAMP GUTTERS OUT.
THE SKY BEYOND THE LEAVES TAKES THE SHAPE OF THE PROPHET'S WORDS IN YOUR MIND.
YOU HAND YOUR LAMP TO THE NEXT MAN EACH EVENING.
WAIT FOR THE ESCORT.
RIGHT.
YOU NAP IN THE COOL SHADE OF THE ALDER.
ON YOUR DAY OF REST, YOU DANGLE YOUR FEET IN A STREAM OR WALK TO HEAR THE RANTING OF THE LATEST PROPHET.
ON SOME NIGHTS, YOU DREAM OF HEALING THE SICK WITH INSTRUMENTS OF FINE METAL AND GLASS, BUT FORGET AS SOON AS YOU AWAKEN.

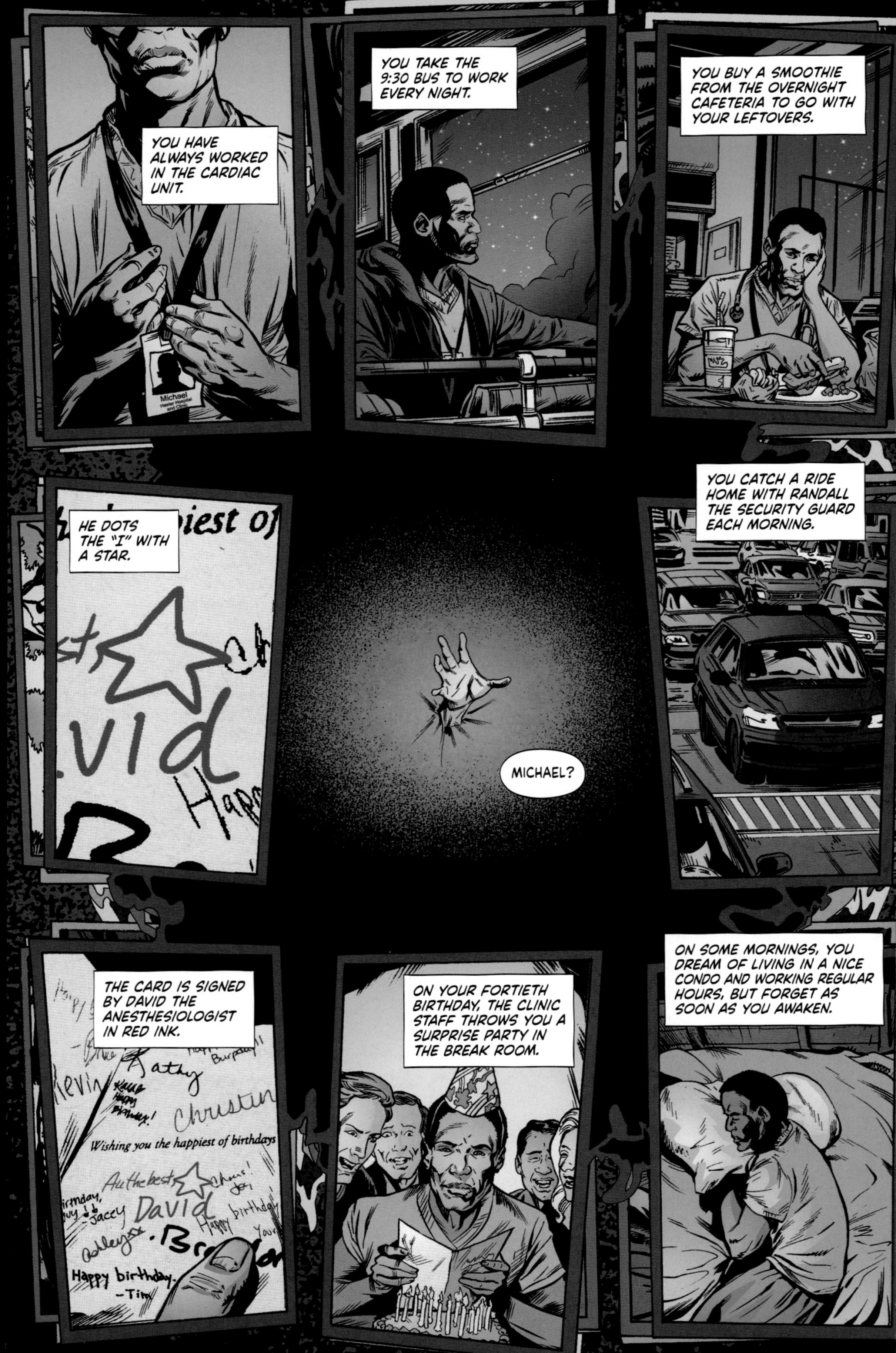
YOU HAVE ALWAYS WORKED IN THE CARDIAC UNIT.
Michael
YOU TAKE THE 9:30 BUS TO WORK EVERY NIGHT.
YOU BUY A SMOOTHIE FROM THE OVERNIGHT CAFETERIA TO GO WITH YOUR LEFTOVERS.
HE DOTS THE "I" WITH A STAR.
MICHAEL?
YOU CATCH A RIDE HOME WITH RANDALL THE SECURITY GUARD EACH MORNING.
THE CARD IS SIGNED BY DAVID THE ANESTHESIOLOGIST IN RED INK.
Kathy
Christin
Wishing you the happiest of birthdays
All the best
David
Happy birthday.
-Tim
ON YOUR FORTIETH BIRTHDAY, THE CLINIC STAFF THROWS YOU A SURPRISE PARTY IN THE BREAK ROOM.
ON SOME MORNINGS, YOU DREAM OF LIVING IN A NICE CONDO AND WORKING REGULAR HOURS, BUT FORGET AS SOON AS YOU AWAKEN.

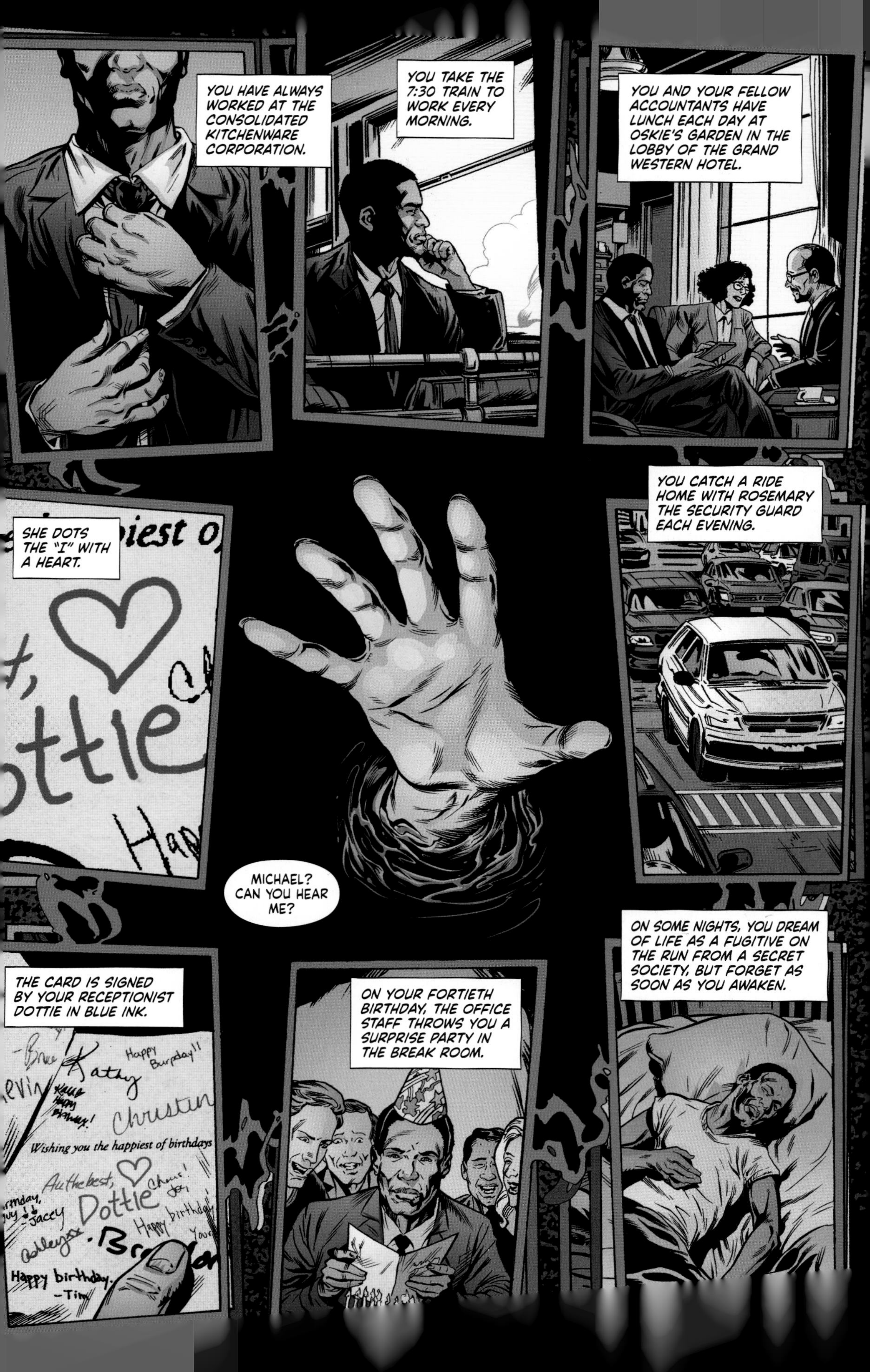
YOU HAVE ALWAYS WORKED AT THE CONSOLIDATED KITCHENWARE CORPORATION.
YOU TAKE THE 7:30 TRAIN TO WORK EVERY MORNING.
YOU AND YOUR FELLOW ACCOUNTANTS HAVE LUNCH EACH DAY AT OSKIE'S GARDEN IN THE LOBBY OF THE GRAND WESTERN HOTEL.
SHE DOTS THE "I" WITH A HEART.
Dottie
YOU CATCH A RIDE HOME WITH ROSEMARY THE SECURITY GUARD EACH EVENING.
MICHAEL? CAN YOU HEAR ME?
THE CARD IS SIGNED BY YOUR RECEPTIONIST DOTTIE IN BLUE INK.
Happy Burpday!!
Wishing you the happiest of birthdays
All the best, Dottie
Happy birthday. -Tim
ON YOUR FORTIETH BIRTHDAY, THE OFFICE STAFF THROWS YOU A SURPRISE PARTY IN THE BREAK ROOM.
ON SOME NIGHTS, YOU DREAM OF LIFE AS A FUGITIVE ON THE RUN FROM A SECRET SOCIETY, BUT FORGET AS SOON AS YOU AWAKEN.

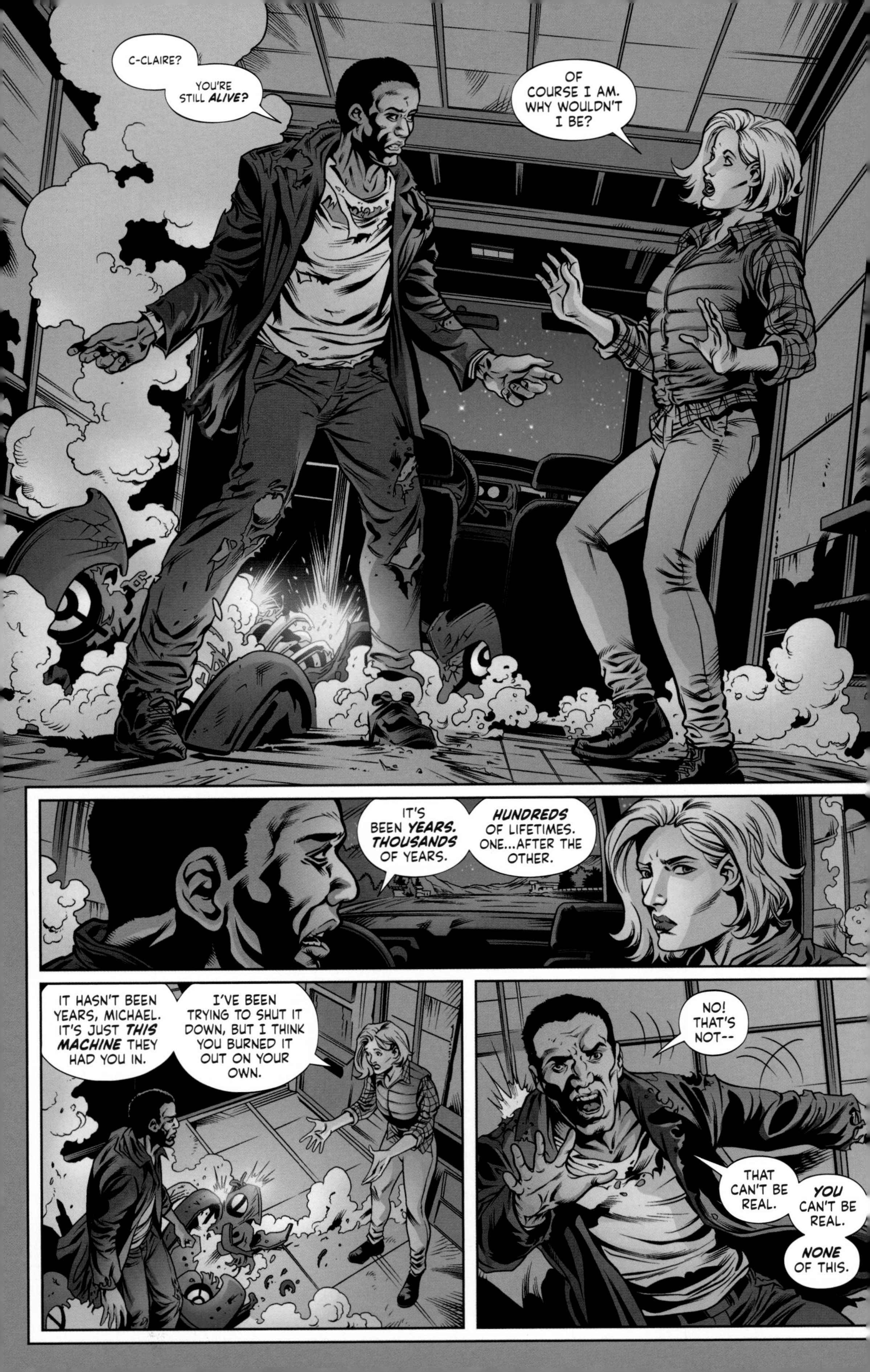
C-CLAIRE?
YOU'RE STILL ALIVE?
OF COURSE I AM. WHY WOULDN'T I BE?
IT'S BEEN YEARS. THOUSANDS OF YEARS.
HUNDREDS OF LIFETIMES. ONE...AFTER THE OTHER.
IT HASN'T BEEN YEARS, MICHAEL. IT'S JUST THIS MACHINE THEY HAD YOU IN.
I'VE BEEN TRYING TO SHUT IT DOWN, BUT I THINK YOU BURNED IT OUT ON YOUR OWN.
NO! THAT'S NOT--
THAT CAN'T BE REAL.
YOU CAN'T BE REAL.
NONE OF THIS.

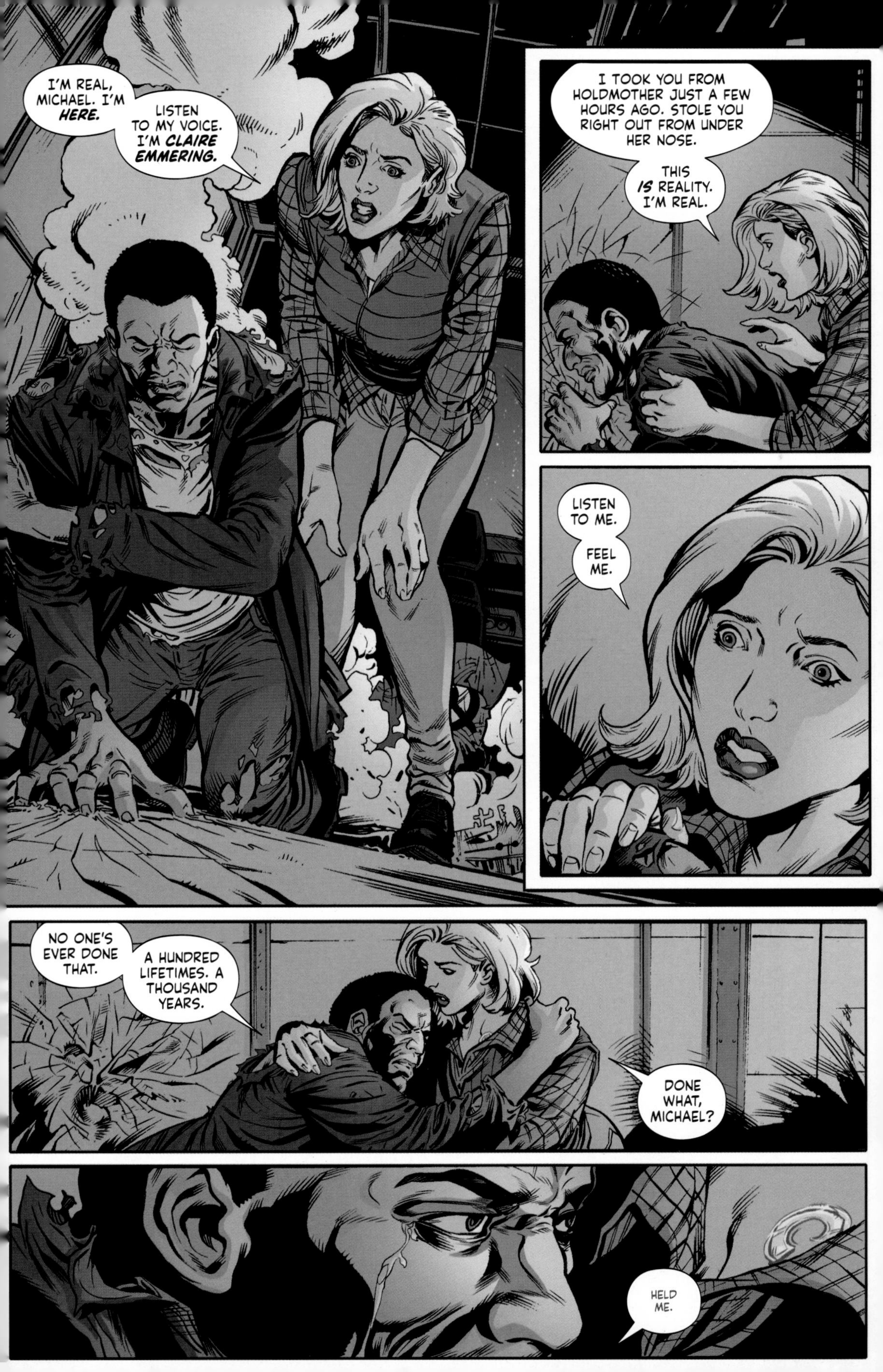
I'M REAL, MICHAEL. I'M **HERE.**
LISTEN TO MY VOICE. I'M ***CLAIRE EMMERING.***
I TOOK YOU FROM HOLDMOTHER JUST A FEW HOURS AGO. STOLE YOU RIGHT OUT FROM UNDER HER NOSE.
THIS ***IS*** REALITY. I'M REAL.
LISTEN TO ME.
FEEL ME.
NO ONE'S EVER DONE THAT.
A HUNDRED LIFETIMES. A THOUSAND YEARS.
DONE WHAT, MICHAEL?
HELD ME.

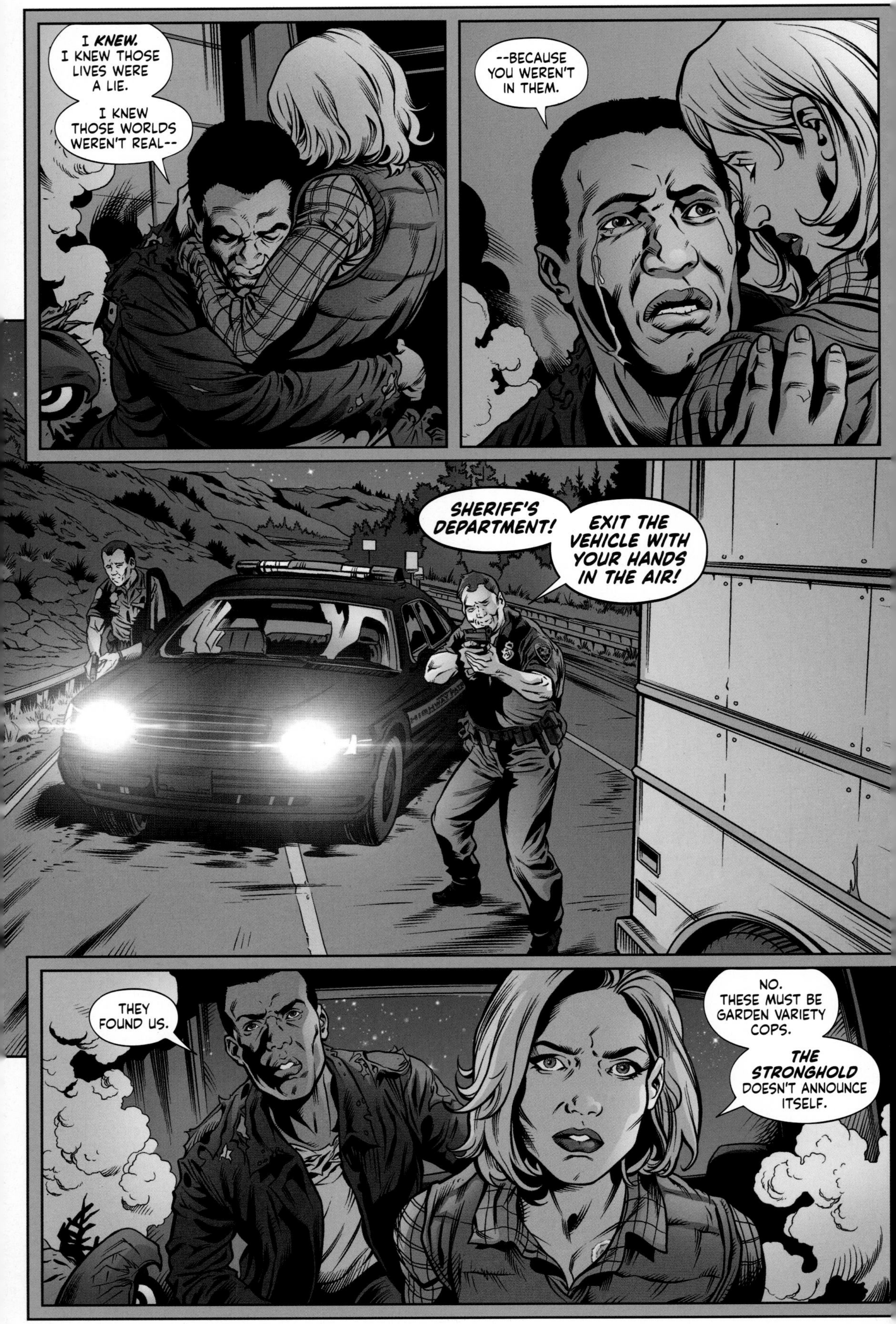
I *KNEW.* I KNEW THOSE LIVES WERE A LIE.
I KNEW THOSE WORLDS WEREN'T REAL--
--BECAUSE YOU WEREN'T IN THEM.
SHERIFF'S DEPARTMENT!
EXIT THE VEHICLE WITH YOUR HANDS IN THE AIR!
THEY FOUND US.
NO. THESE MUST BE GARDEN VARIETY COPS.
THE STRONGHOLD DOESN'T ANNOUNCE ITSELF.

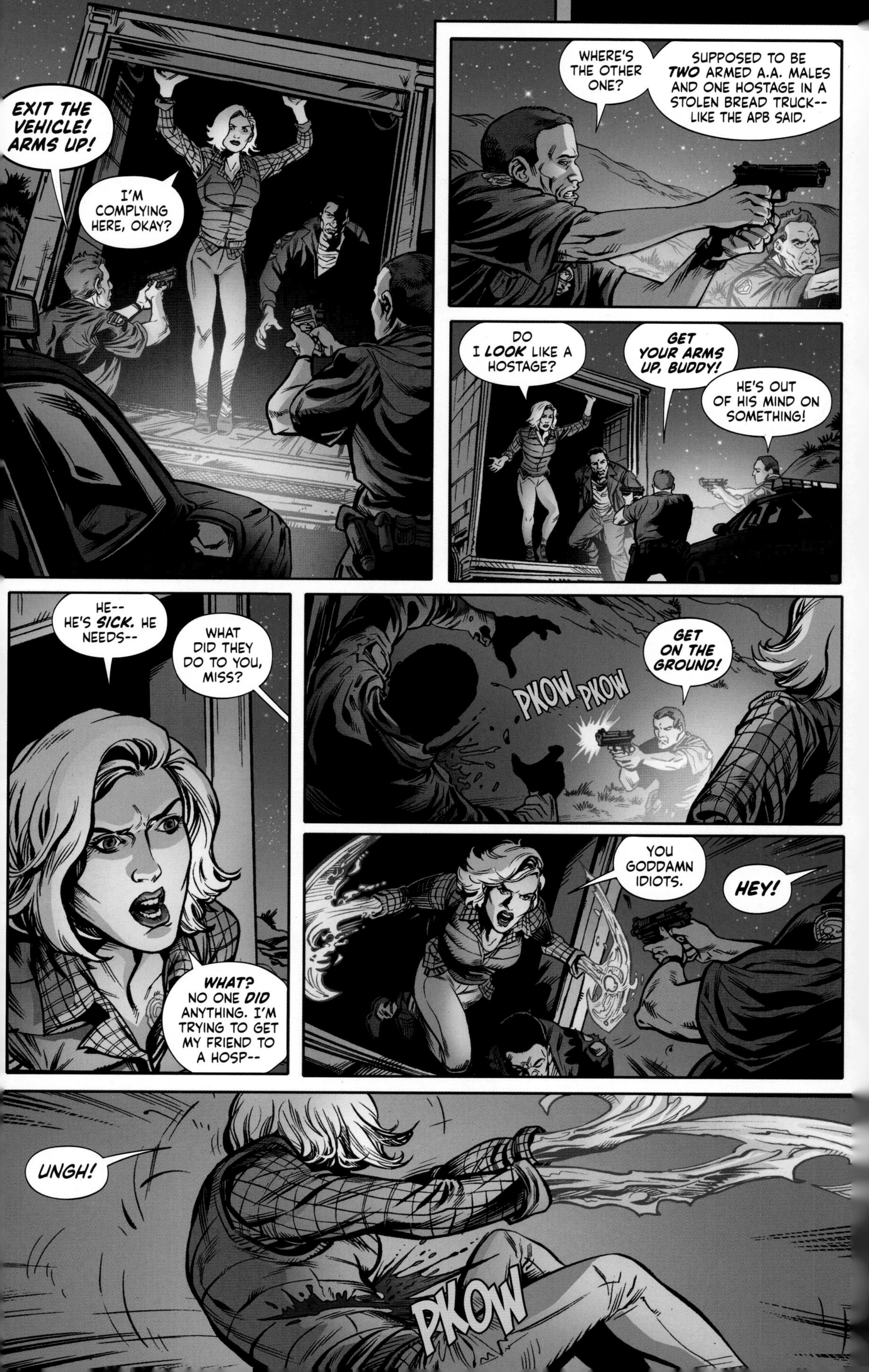
EXIT THE VEHICLE! ARMS UP!
I'M COMPLYING HERE, OKAY?
WHERE'S THE OTHER ONE?
SUPPOSED TO BE TWO ARMED A.A. MALES AND ONE HOSTAGE IN A STOLEN BREAD TRUCK-- LIKE THE APB SAID.
DO I LOOK LIKE A HOSTAGE?
GET YOUR ARMS UP, BUDDY!
HE'S OUT OF HIS MIND ON SOMETHING!
HE-- HE'S SICK. HE NEEDS--
WHAT DID THEY DO TO YOU, MISS?
WHAT? NO ONE DID ANYTHING. I'M TRYING TO GET MY FRIEND TO A HOSP--
GET ON THE GROUND!
PKOW PKOW
YOU GODDAMN IDIOTS.
HEY!
UNGH!
PKOW

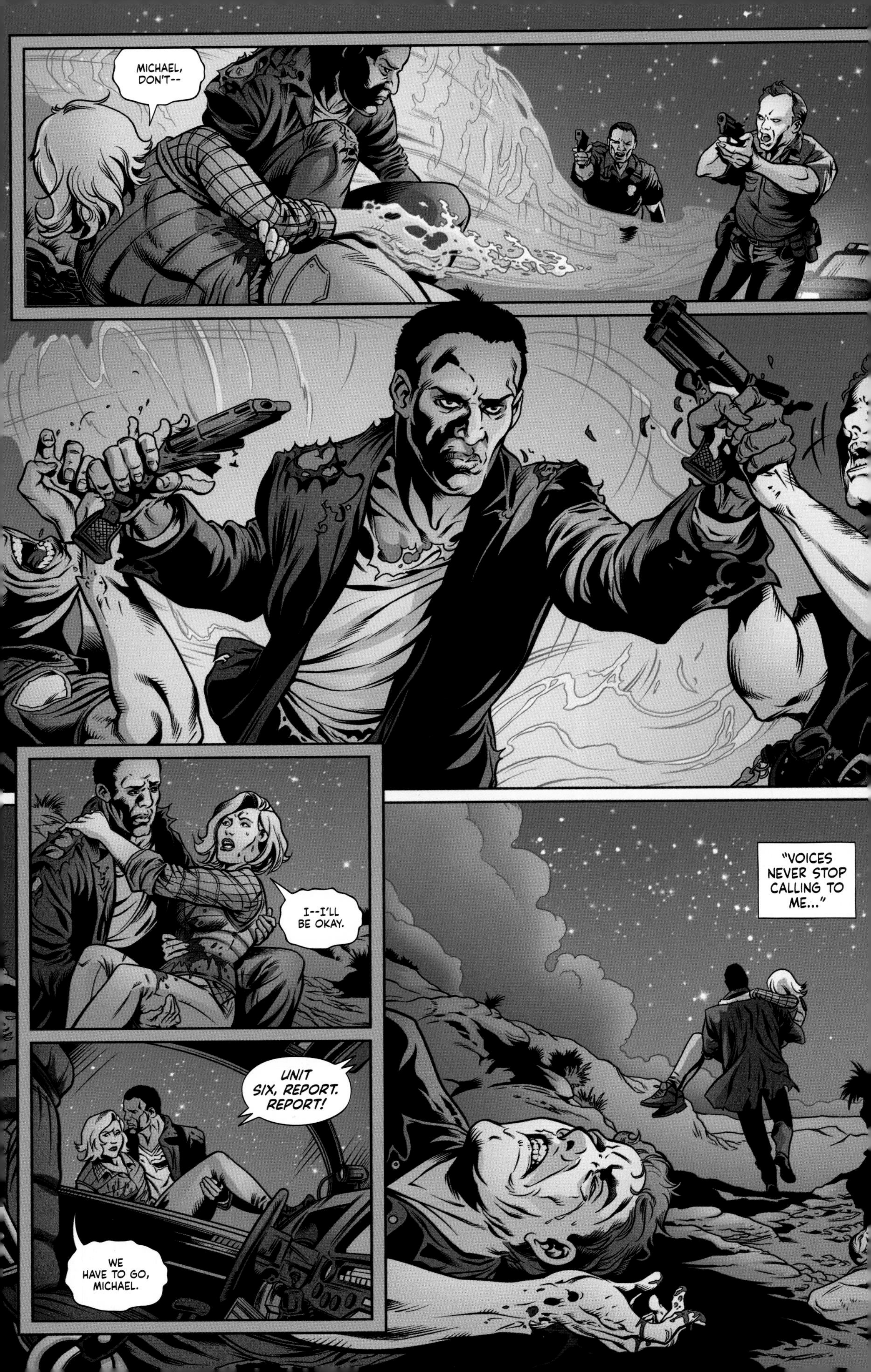
MICHAEL, DON'T--
I--I'LL BE OKAY.
UNIT SIX, REPORT. REPORT!
WE HAVE TO GO, MICHAEL.
"VOICES NEVER STOP CALLING TO ME..."

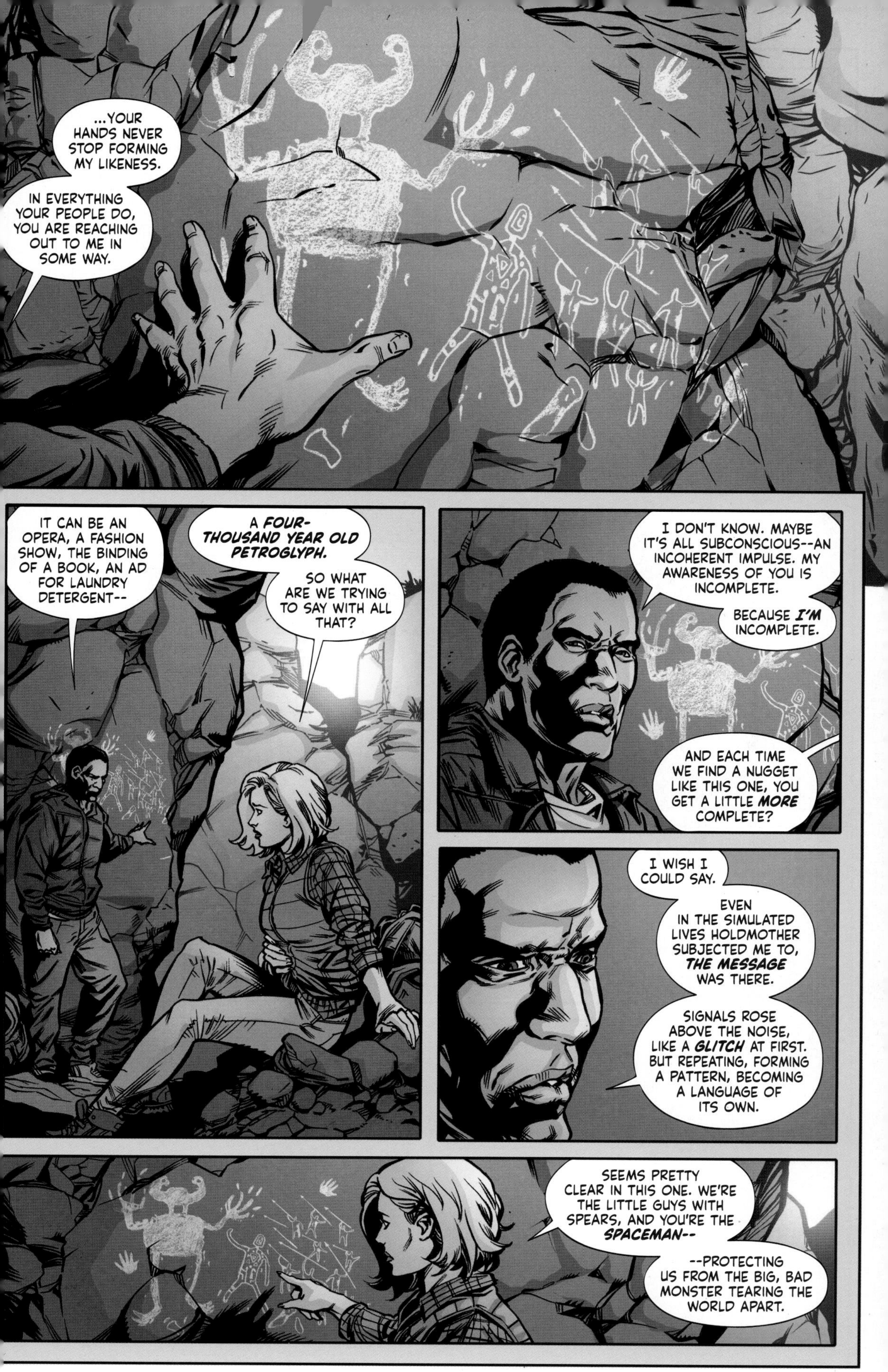

...YOUR HANDS NEVER STOP FORMING MY LIKENESS.
IN EVERYTHING YOUR PEOPLE DO, YOU ARE REACHING OUT TO ME IN SOME WAY.
IT CAN BE AN OPERA, A FASHION SHOW, THE BINDING OF A BOOK, AN AD FOR LAUNDRY DETERGENT--
A *FOUR-THOUSAND YEAR OLD PETROGLYPH.*
SO WHAT ARE WE TRYING TO SAY WITH ALL THAT?
I DON'T KNOW. MAYBE IT'S ALL SUBCONSCIOUS--AN INCOHERENT IMPULSE. MY AWARENESS OF YOU IS INCOMPLETE.
BECAUSE *I'M* INCOMPLETE.
AND EACH TIME WE FIND A NUGGET LIKE THIS ONE, YOU GET A LITTLE *MORE* COMPLETE?
I WISH I COULD SAY.
EVEN IN THE SIMULATED LIVES HOLDMOTHER SUBJECTED ME TO, *THE MESSAGE* WAS THERE.
SIGNALS ROSE ABOVE THE NOISE, LIKE A *GLITCH* AT FIRST. BUT REPEATING, FORMING A PATTERN, BECOMING A LANGUAGE OF ITS OWN.
SEEMS PRETTY CLEAR IN THIS ONE. WE'RE THE LITTLE GUYS WITH SPEARS, AND YOU'RE THE *SPACEMAN--*
--PROTECTING US FROM THE BIG, BAD MONSTER TEARING THE WORLD APART.

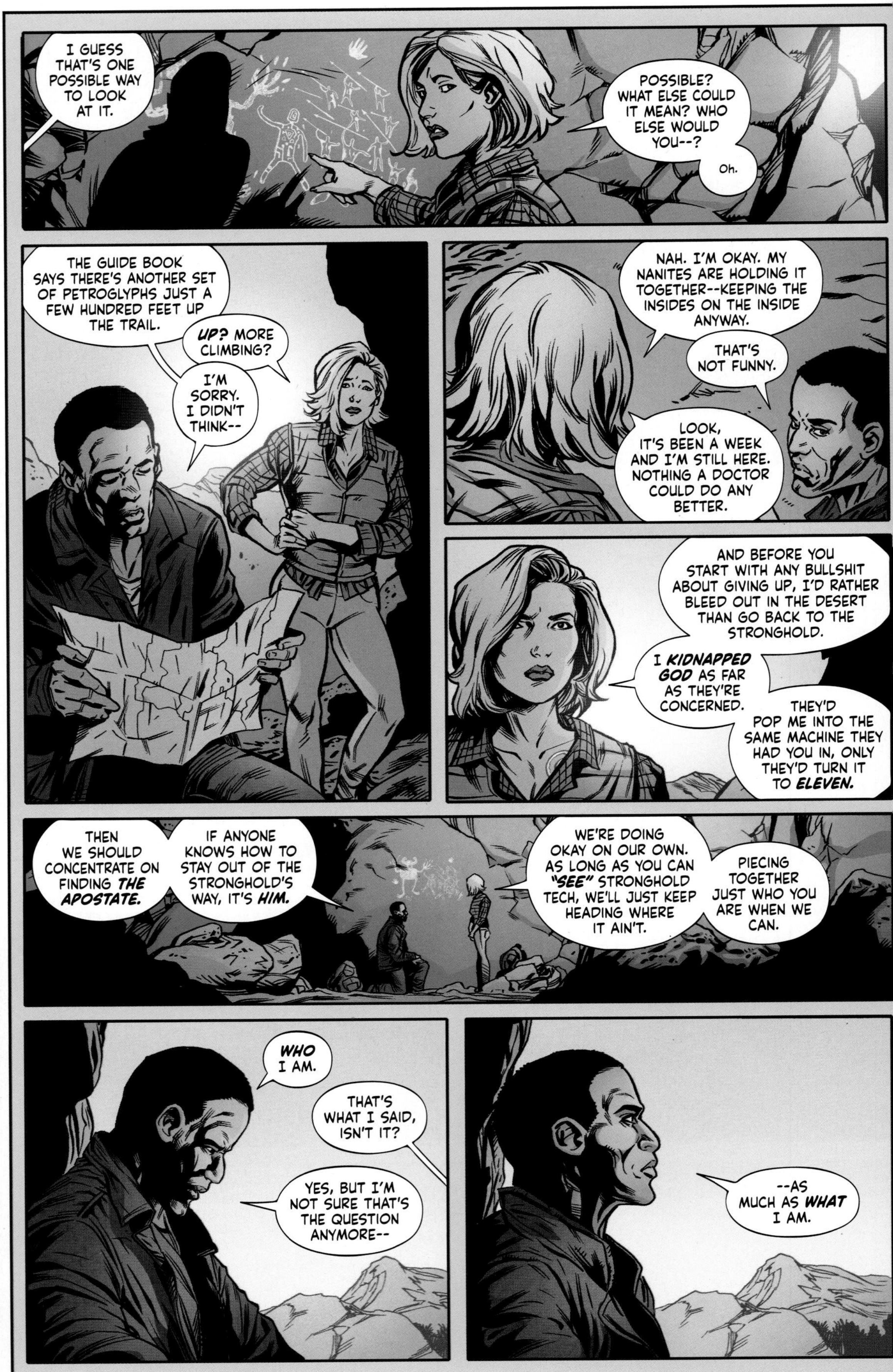
I GUESS THAT'S ONE POSSIBLE WAY TO LOOK AT IT.
POSSIBLE? WHAT ELSE COULD IT MEAN? WHO ELSE WOULD YOU--?
Oh.
THE GUIDE BOOK SAYS THERE'S ANOTHER SET OF PETROGLYPHS JUST A FEW HUNDRED FEET UP THE TRAIL.
UP? MORE CLIMBING?
I'M SORRY. I DIDN'T THINK--
NAH. I'M OKAY. MY NANITES ARE HOLDING IT TOGETHER--KEEPING THE INSIDES ON THE INSIDE ANYWAY.
THAT'S NOT FUNNY.
LOOK, IT'S BEEN A WEEK AND I'M STILL HERE. NOTHING A DOCTOR COULD DO ANY BETTER.
AND BEFORE YOU START WITH ANY BULLSHIT ABOUT GIVING UP, I'D RATHER BLEED OUT IN THE DESERT THAN GO BACK TO THE STRONGHOLD.
I KIDNAPPED GOD AS FAR AS THEY'RE CONCERNED.
THEY'D POP ME INTO THE SAME MACHINE THEY HAD YOU IN, ONLY THEY'D TURN IT TO ELEVEN.
THEN WE SHOULD CONCENTRATE ON FINDING THE APOSTATE.
IF ANYONE KNOWS HOW TO STAY OUT OF THE STRONGHOLD'S WAY, IT'S HIM.
WE'RE DOING OKAY ON OUR OWN. AS LONG AS YOU CAN "SEE" STRONGHOLD TECH, WE'LL JUST KEEP HEADING WHERE IT AIN'T.
PIECING TOGETHER JUST WHO YOU ARE WHEN WE CAN.
WHO I AM.
THAT'S WHAT I SAID, ISN'T IT?
YES, BUT I'M NOT SURE THAT'S THE QUESTION ANYMORE--
--AS MUCH AS WHAT I AM.

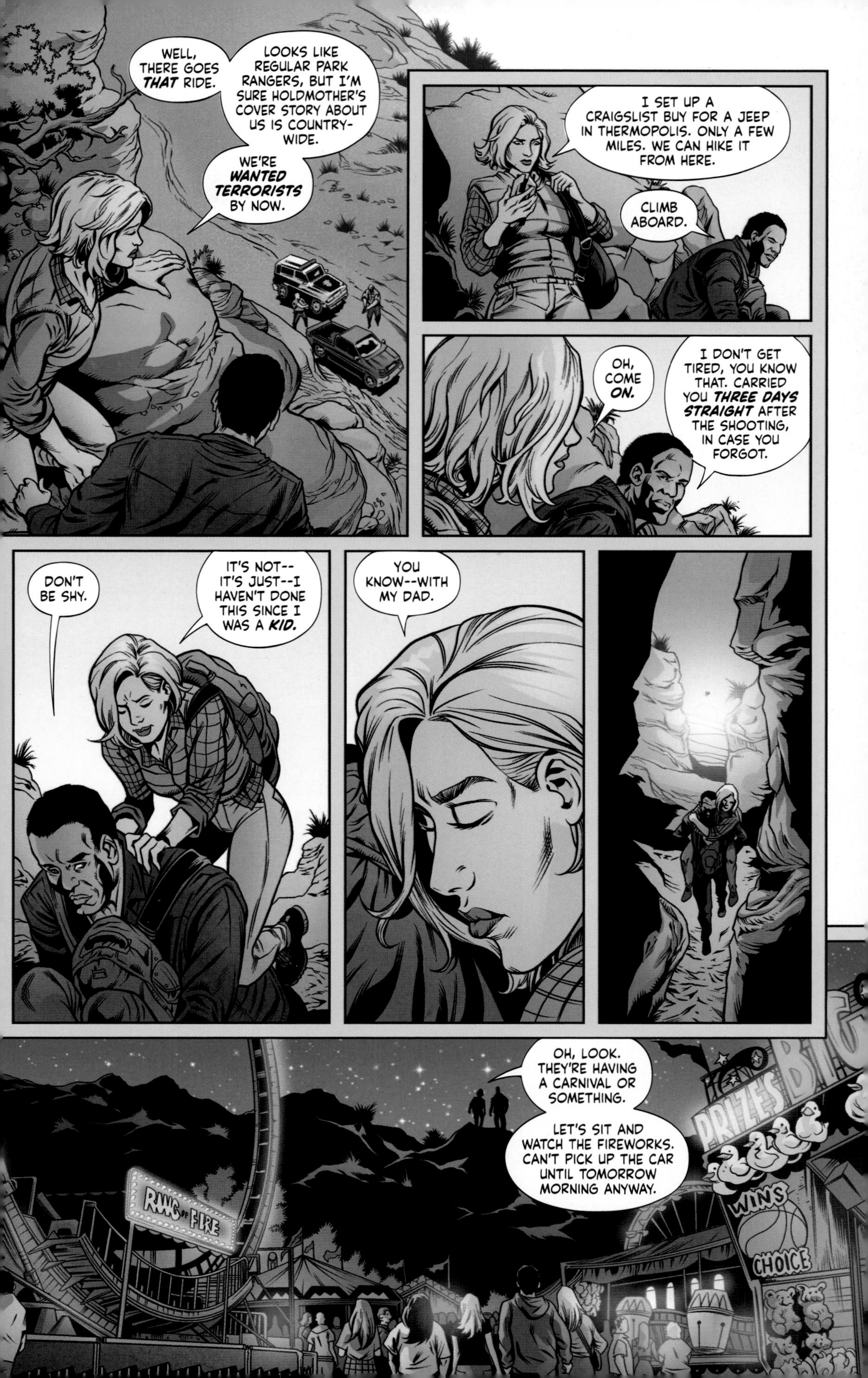
WELL, THERE GOES *THAT* RIDE.
LOOKS LIKE REGULAR PARK RANGERS, BUT I'M SURE HOLDMOTHER'S COVER STORY ABOUT US IS COUNTRY-WIDE.
WE'RE ***WANTED TERRORISTS*** BY NOW.
I SET UP A CRAIGSLIST BUY FOR A JEEP IN THERMOPOLIS. ONLY A FEW MILES. WE CAN HIKE IT FROM HERE.
CLIMB ABOARD.
OH, COME ***ON.***
I DON'T GET TIRED, YOU KNOW THAT. CARRIED YOU ***THREE DAYS STRAIGHT*** AFTER THE SHOOTING, IN CASE YOU FORGOT.
DON'T BE SHY.
IT'S NOT-- IT'S JUST--I HAVEN'T DONE THIS SINCE I WAS A ***KID.***
YOU KNOW--WITH MY DAD.
OH, LOOK. THEY'RE HAVING A CARNIVAL OR SOMETHING.
LET'S SIT AND WATCH THE FIREWORKS. CAN'T PICK UP THE CAR UNTIL TOMORROW MORNING ANYWAY.
RING OF FIRE
PRIZES
WINS
CHOICE

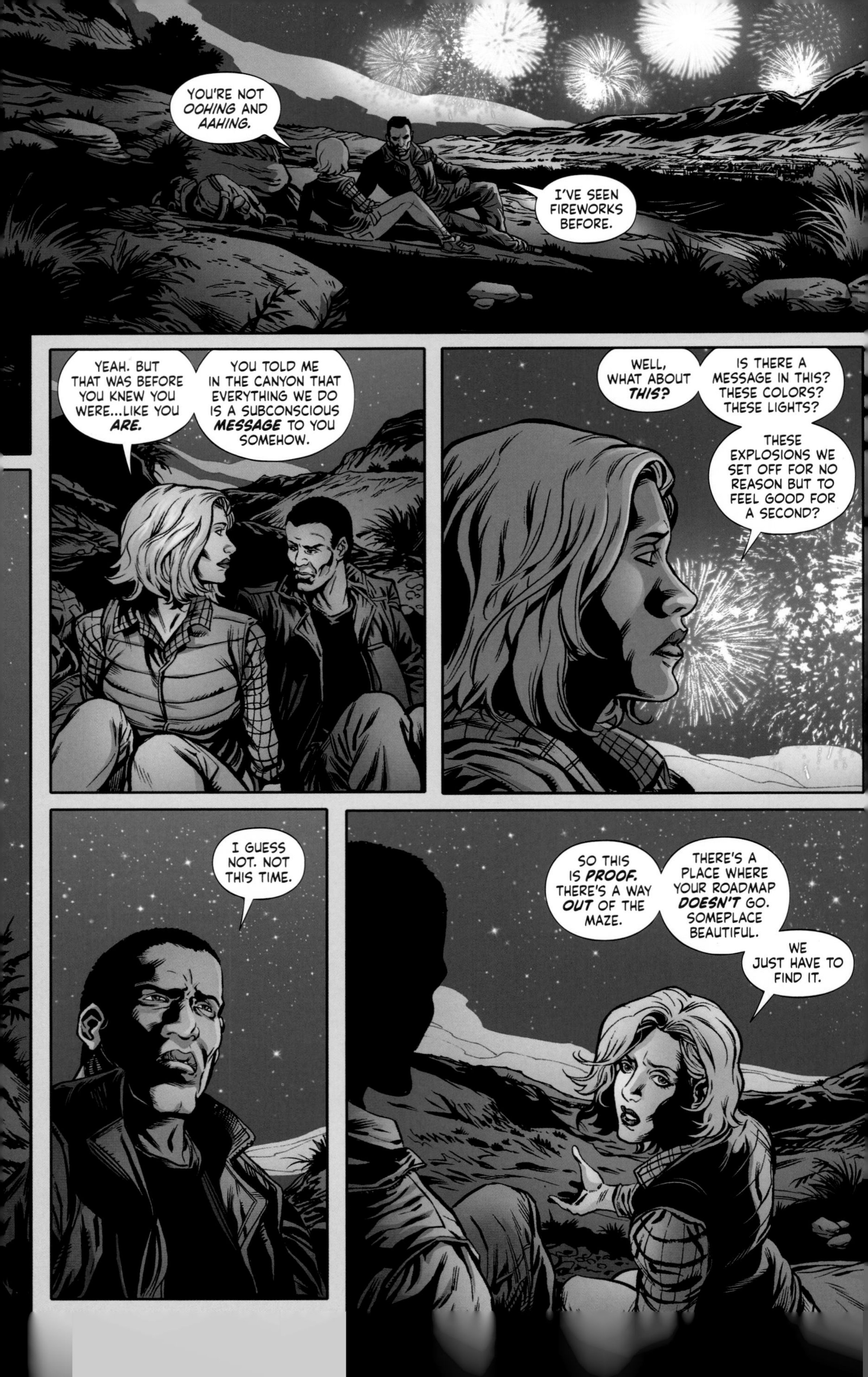
YOU'RE NOT OOHING AND AAHING.
I'VE SEEN FIREWORKS BEFORE.
YEAH. BUT THAT WAS BEFORE YOU KNEW YOU WERE...LIKE YOU ARE.
YOU TOLD ME IN THE CANYON THAT EVERYTHING WE DO IS A SUBCONSCIOUS MESSAGE TO YOU SOMEHOW.
WELL, WHAT ABOUT THIS?
IS THERE A MESSAGE IN THIS? THESE COLORS? THESE LIGHTS?
THESE EXPLOSIONS WE SET OFF FOR NO REASON BUT TO FEEL GOOD FOR A SECOND?
I GUESS NOT. NOT THIS TIME.
SO THIS IS PROOF. THERE'S A WAY OUT OF THE MAZE.
THERE'S A PLACE WHERE YOUR ROADMAP DOESN'T GO. SOMEPLACE BEAUTIFUL.
WE JUST HAVE TO FIND IT.

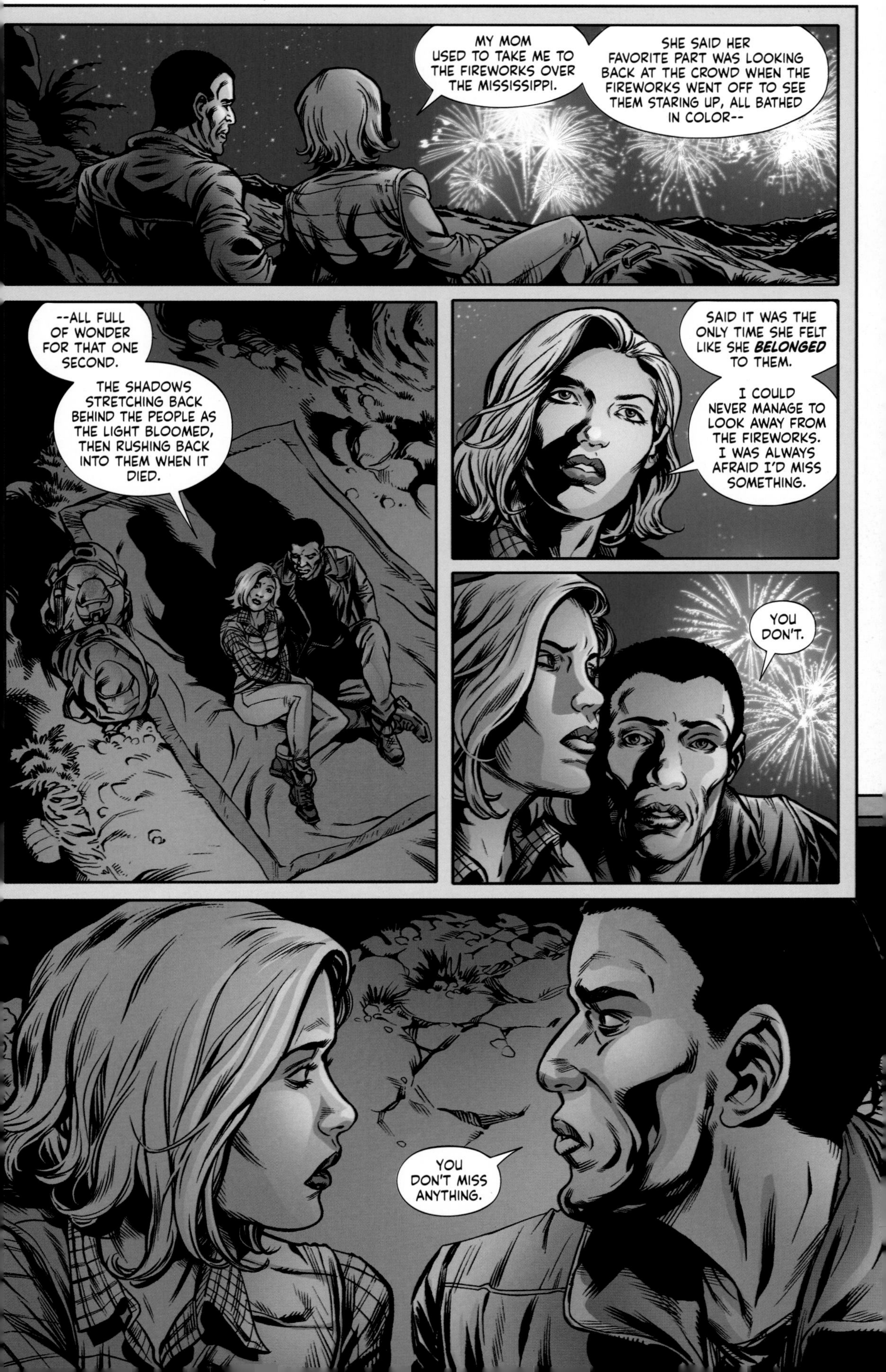
MY MOM USED TO TAKE ME TO THE FIREWORKS OVER THE MISSISSIPPI.
SHE SAID HER FAVORITE PART WAS LOOKING BACK AT THE CROWD WHEN THE FIREWORKS WENT OFF TO SEE THEM STARING UP, ALL BATHED IN COLOR--
--ALL FULL OF WONDER FOR THAT ONE SECOND.
THE SHADOWS STRETCHING BACK BEHIND THE PEOPLE AS THE LIGHT BLOOMED, THEN RUSHING BACK INTO THEM WHEN IT DIED.
SAID IT WAS THE ONLY TIME SHE FELT LIKE SHE ***BELONGED*** TO THEM.
I COULD NEVER MANAGE TO LOOK AWAY FROM THE FIREWORKS. I WAS ALWAYS AFRAID I'D MISS SOMETHING.
YOU DON'T.
YOU DON'T MISS ANYTHING.

MICHAEL, I--

YOU'RE IN PAIN.

WE CAN'T DO THIS ANYMORE, CLAIRE. WE CAN'T KEEP RUNNING.

NO QUITTING. NOT UNTIL YOU KNOW THE TRUTH. NOT UNTIL YOU'RE FREE.

IT'S NOT WORTH ALL THIS.

I CAN JUST GO BACK. I CAN GO BACK TO THE WAY IT WAS *BEFORE*.

YOU REALLY THINK THAT?

LOOK AT ME, MICHAEL. I'M *TWENTY-FOUR* YEARS OLD.

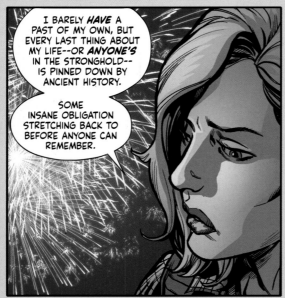

I BARELY *HAVE* A PAST OF MY OWN, BUT EVERY LAST THING ABOUT MY LIFE--OR *ANYONE'S* IN THE STRONGHOLD-- IS PINNED DOWN BY ANCIENT HISTORY.

SOME INSANE OBLIGATION STRETCHING BACK TO BEFORE ANYONE CAN REMEMBER.

IT'S LIKE EVERYTHING THAT COULD EVER REALLY MATTER IN MY LIFE HAS ALREADY HAPPENED AND IT'S ALL JUST PILED UP BEHIND ME--

--*SHOVING* ME INTO THE FUTURE.

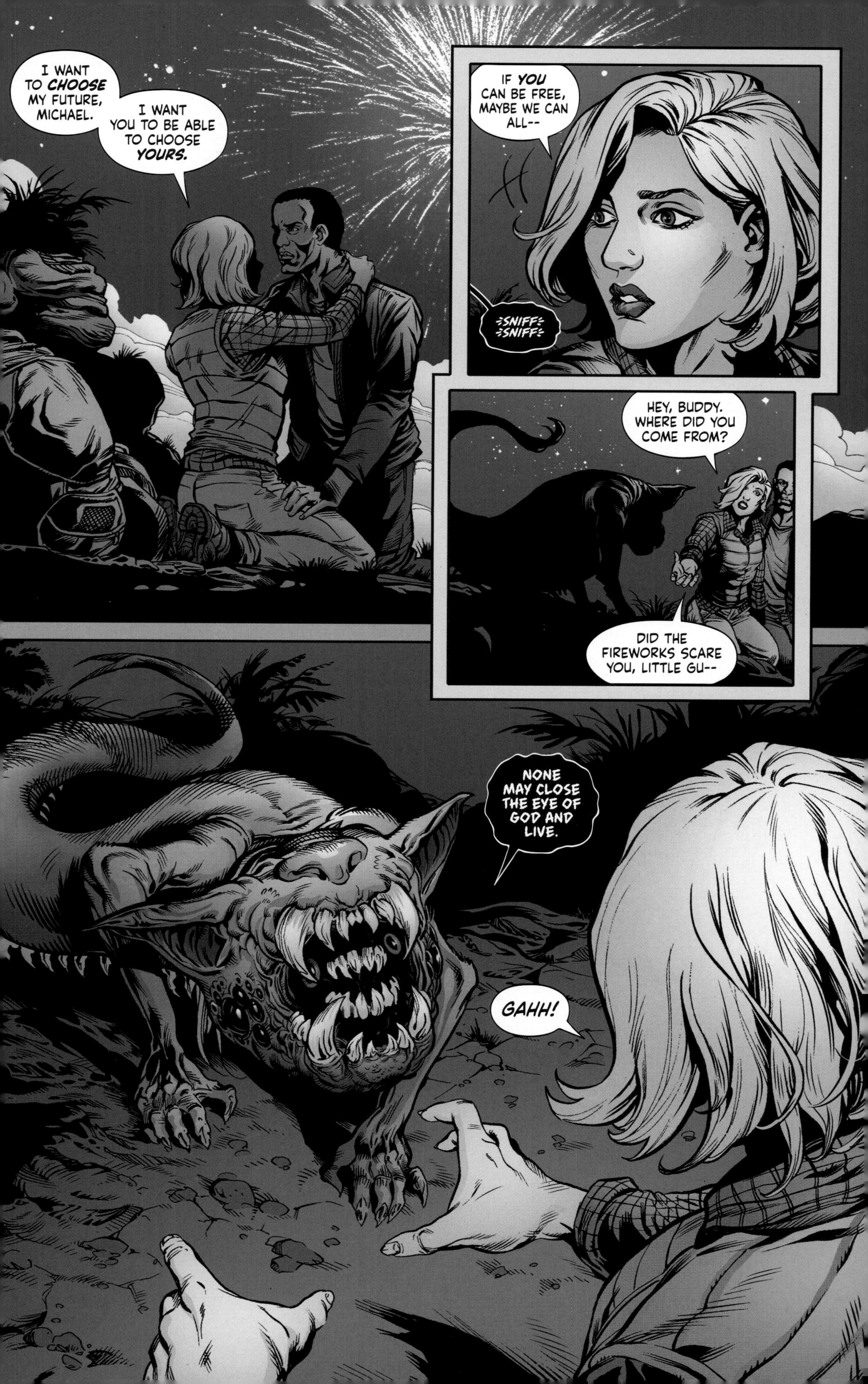

I WANT TO CHOOSE MY FUTURE, MICHAEL.
I WANT YOU TO BE ABLE TO CHOOSE YOURS.
IF YOU CAN BE FREE, MAYBE WE CAN ALL--
SNIFF SNIFF
HEY, BUDDY. WHERE DID YOU COME FROM?
DID THE FIREWORKS SCARE YOU, LITTLE GU--
NONE MAY CLOSE THE EYE OF GOD AND LIVE.
GAHH!

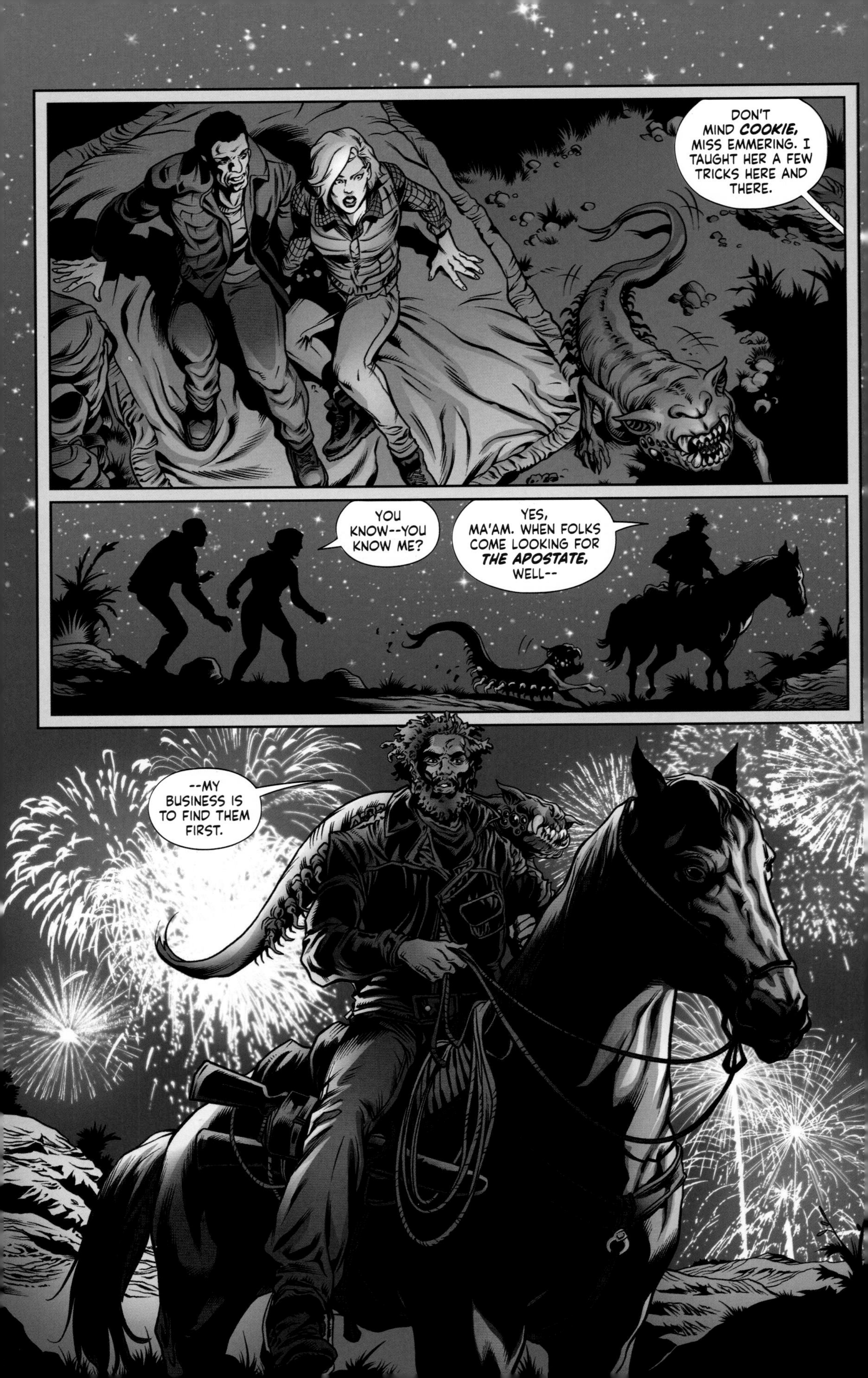
DON'T MIND **COOKIE,** MISS EMMERING. I TAUGHT HER A FEW TRICKS HERE AND THERE.
YOU KNOW--YOU KNOW ME?
YES, MA'AM. WHEN FOLKS COME LOOKING FOR ***THE APOSTATE,*** WELL--
--MY BUSINESS IS TO FIND THEM FIRST.

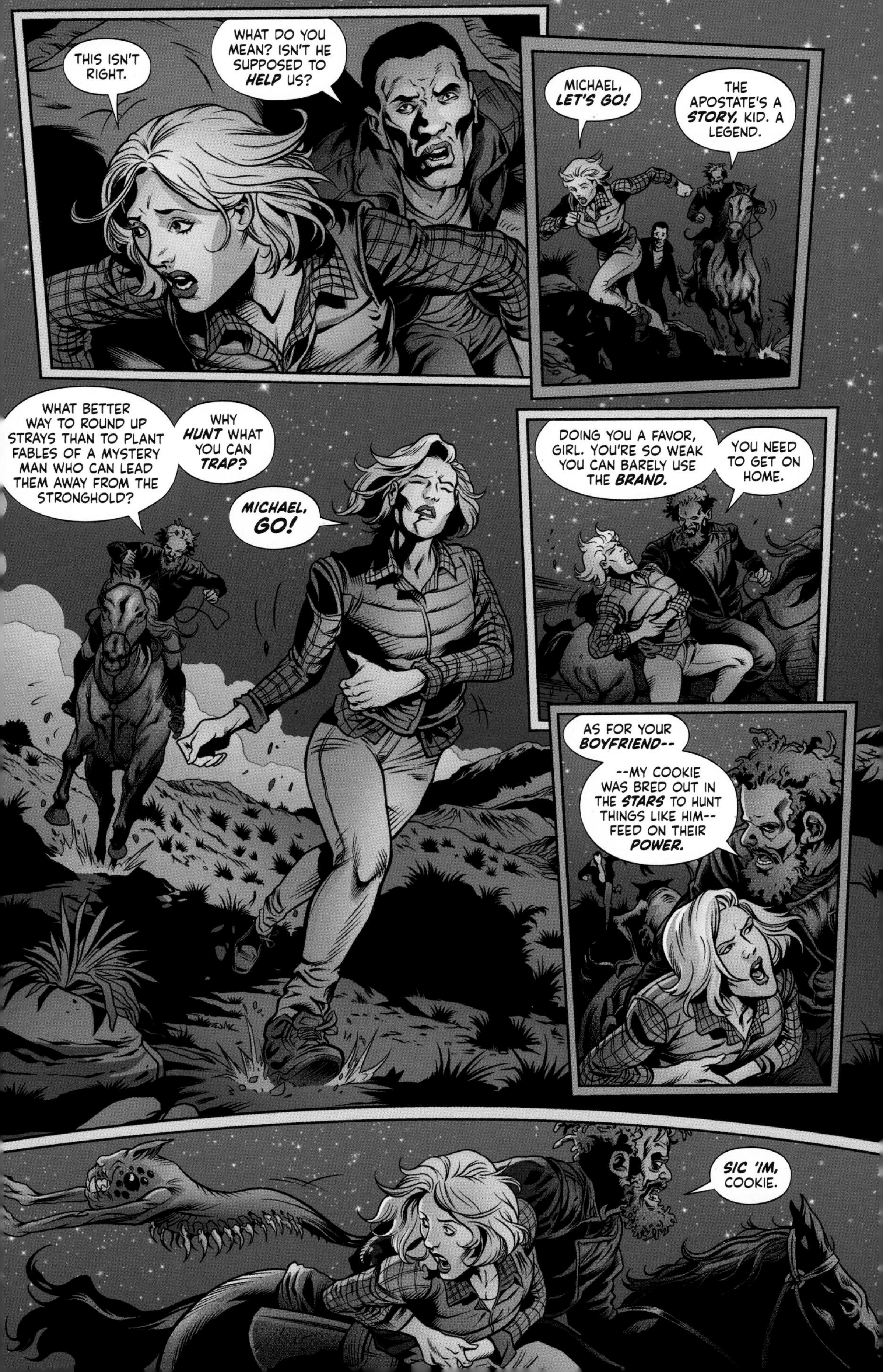
THIS ISN'T RIGHT.
WHAT DO YOU MEAN? ISN'T HE SUPPOSED TO HELP US?
MICHAEL, LET'S GO!
THE APOSTATE'S A STORY, KID. A LEGEND.
WHAT BETTER WAY TO ROUND UP STRAYS THAN TO PLANT FABLES OF A MYSTERY MAN WHO CAN LEAD THEM AWAY FROM THE STRONGHOLD?
WHY HUNT WHAT YOU CAN TRAP?
MICHAEL, GO!
DOING YOU A FAVOR, GIRL. YOU'RE SO WEAK YOU CAN BARELY USE THE BRAND.
YOU NEED TO GET ON HOME.
AS FOR YOUR BOYFRIEND--
--MY COOKIE WAS BRED OUT IN THE STARS TO HUNT THINGS LIKE HIM--FEED ON THEIR POWER.
SIC 'IM, COOKIE.

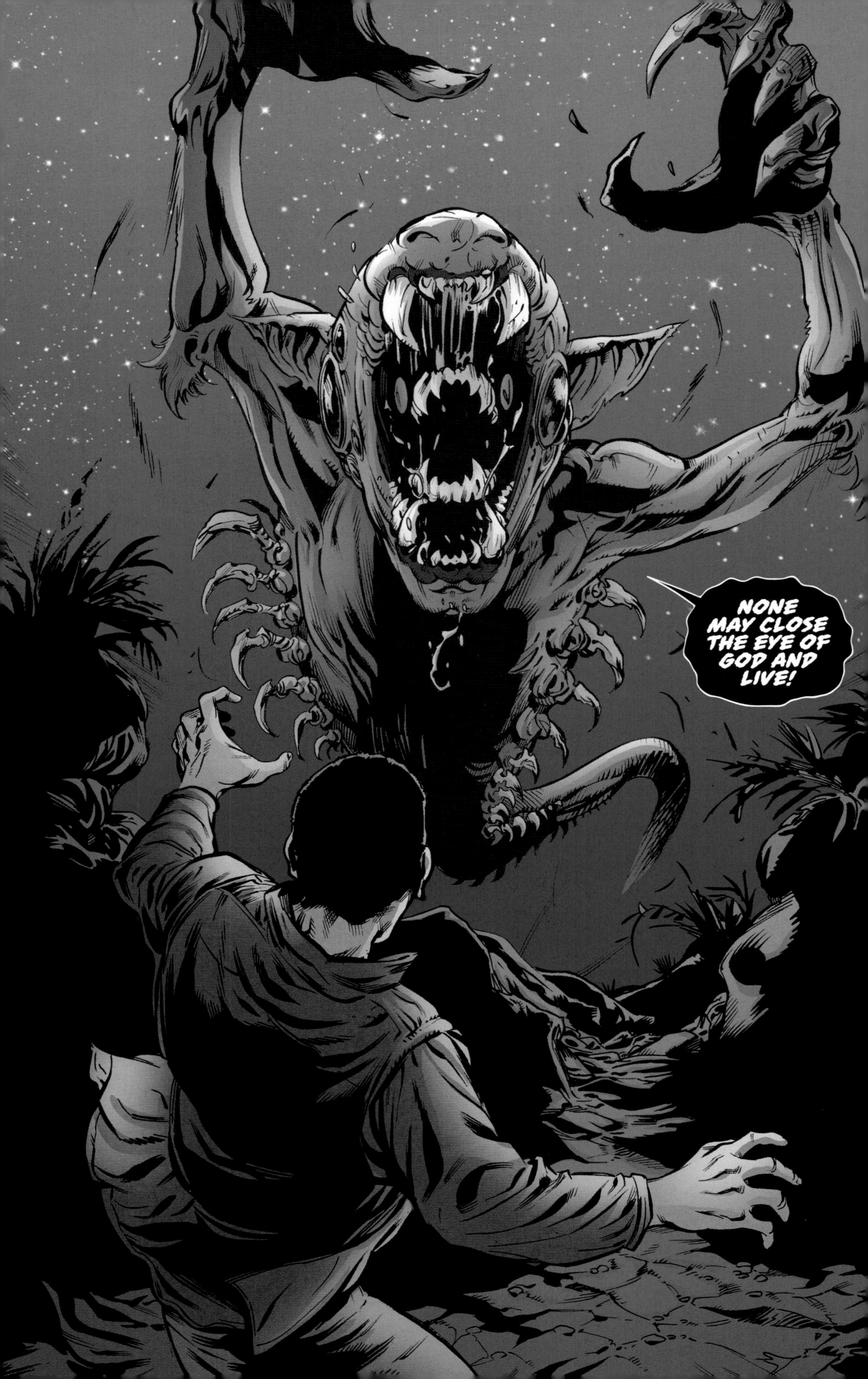
NONE MAY CLOSE THE EYE OF GOD AND LIVE!

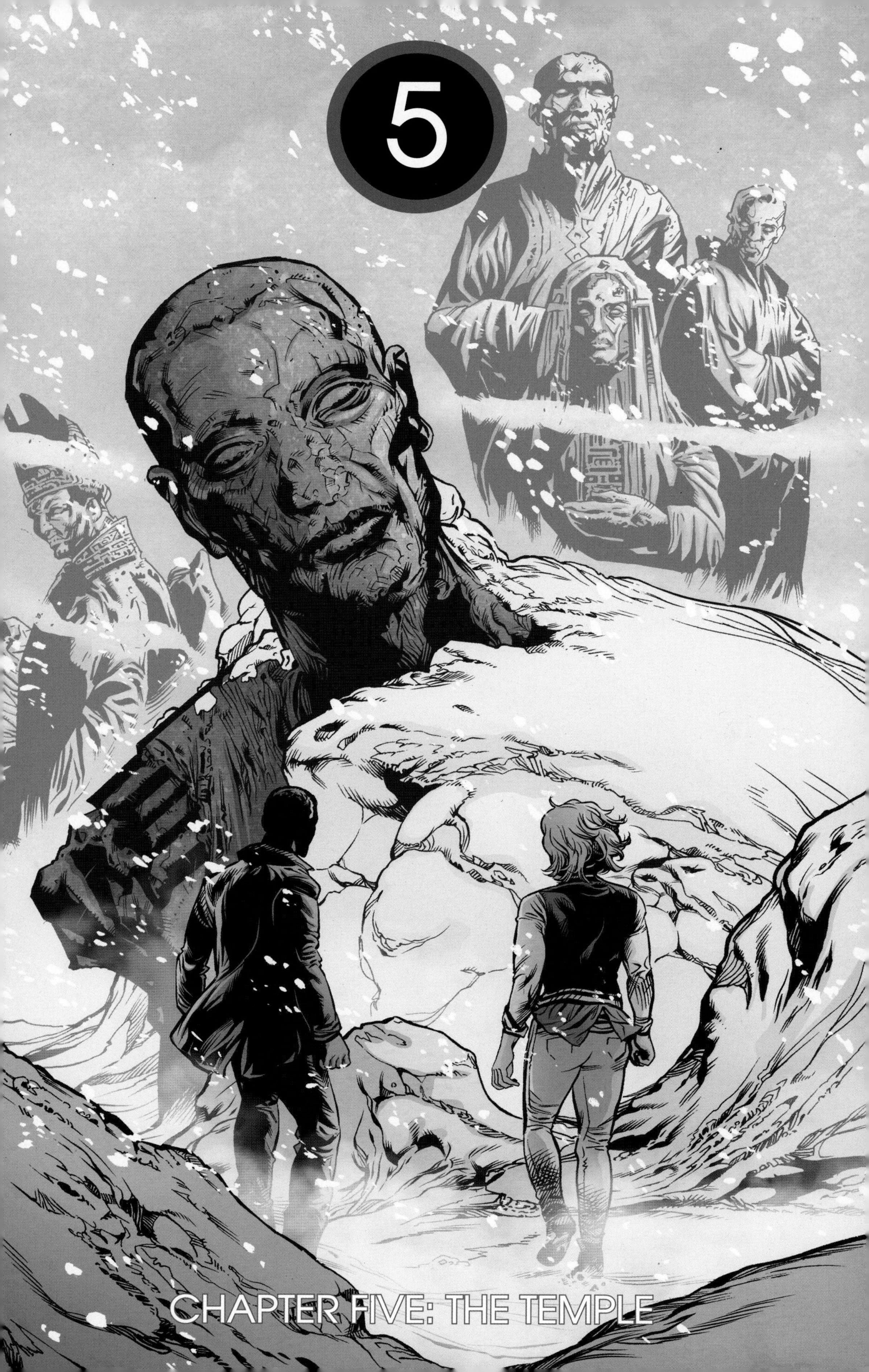
5
CHAPTER FIVE: THE TEMPLE

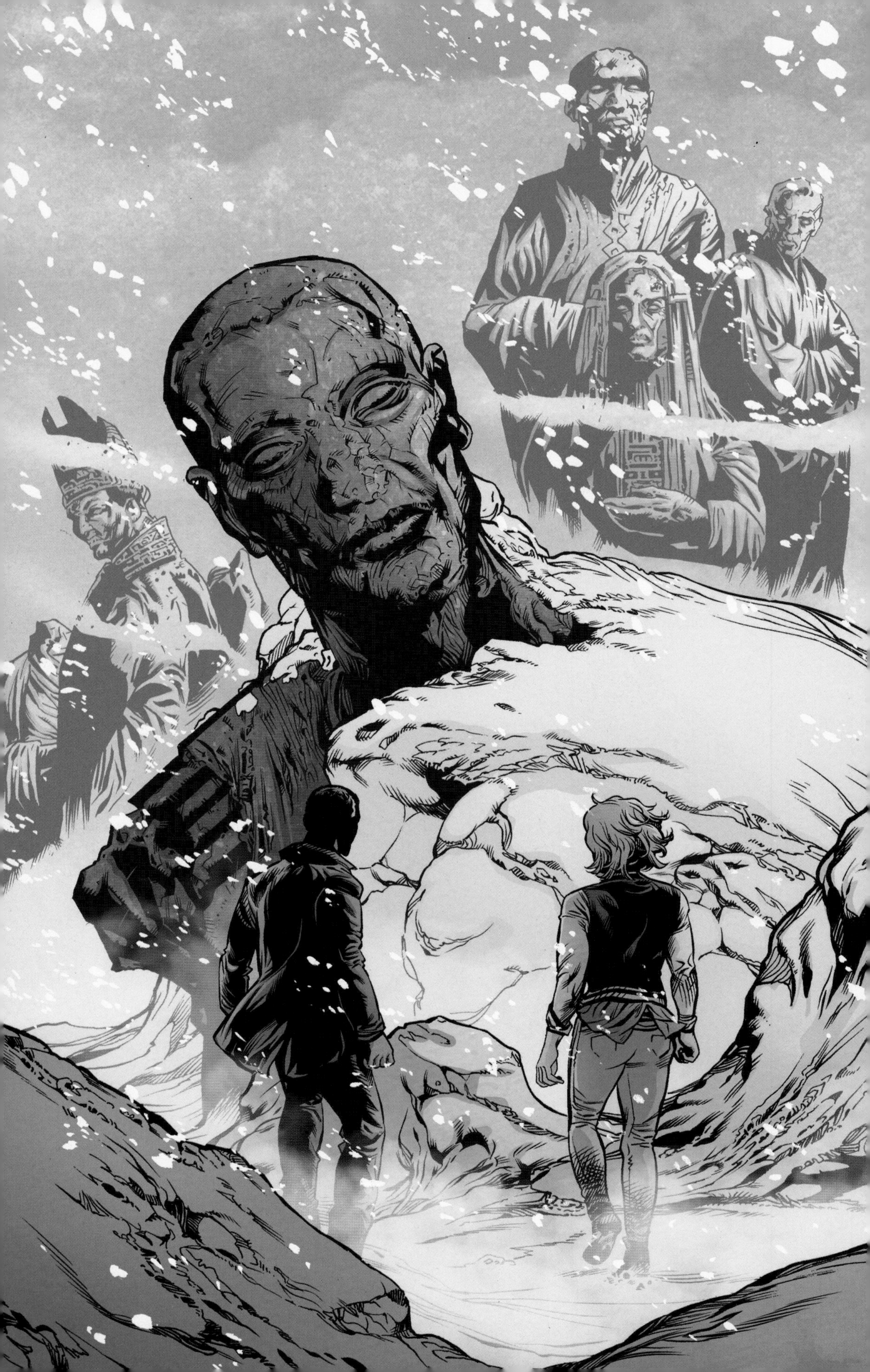

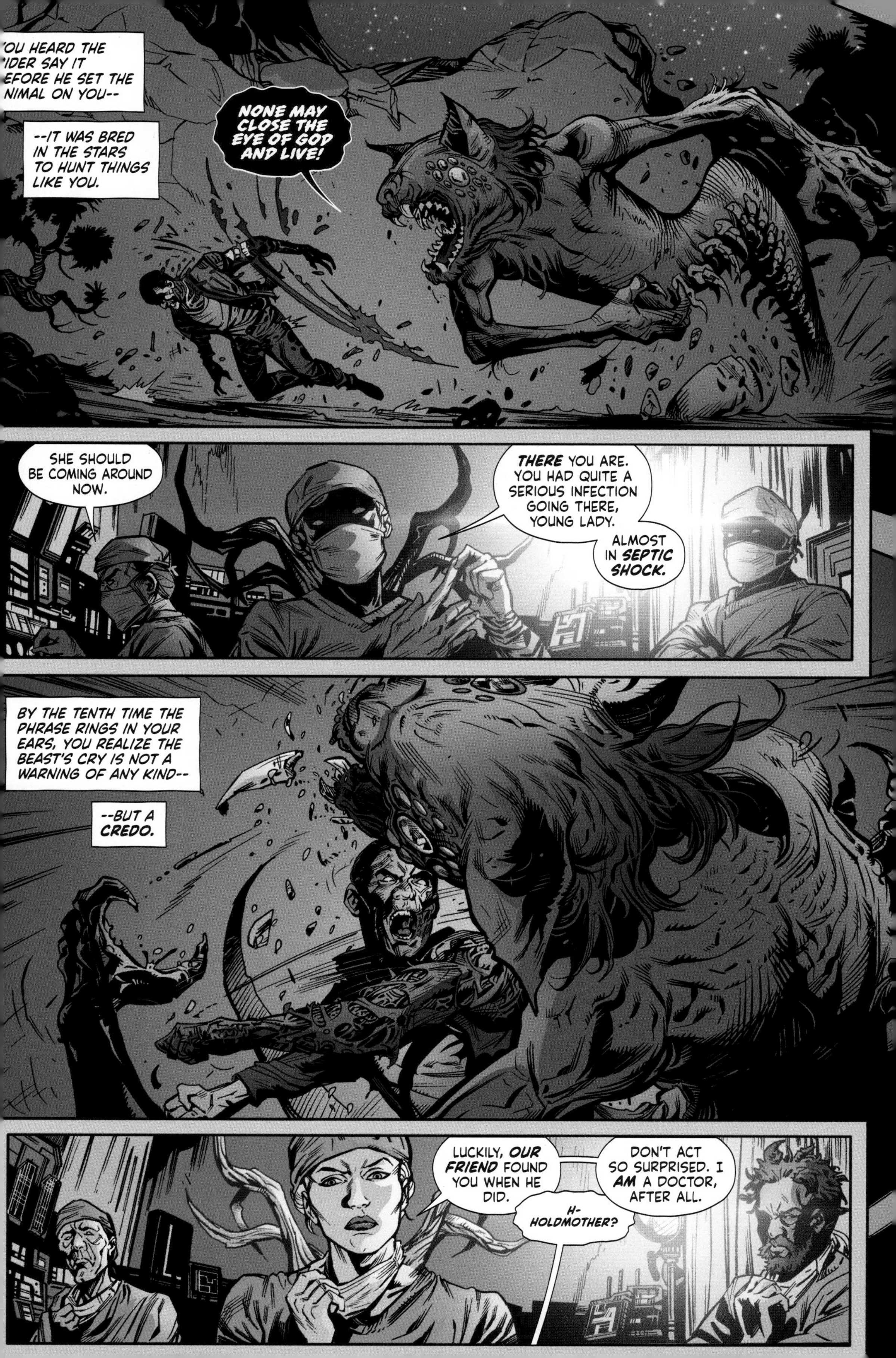

YOU HEARD THE RIDER SAY IT BEFORE HE SET THE ANIMAL ON YOU--
--IT WAS BRED IN THE STARS TO HUNT THINGS LIKE YOU.
NONE MAY CLOSE THE EYE OF GOD AND LIVE!
SHE SHOULD BE COMING AROUND NOW.
THERE YOU ARE. YOU HAD QUITE A SERIOUS INFECTION GOING THERE, YOUNG LADY.
ALMOST IN SEPTIC SHOCK.
BY THE TENTH TIME THE PHRASE RINGS IN YOUR EARS, YOU REALIZE THE BEAST'S CRY IS NOT A WARNING OF ANY KIND--
--BUT A CREDO.
LUCKILY, OUR FRIEND FOUND YOU WHEN HE DID.
DON'T ACT SO SURPRISED. I AM A DOCTOR, AFTER ALL.
H-HOLDMOTHER?

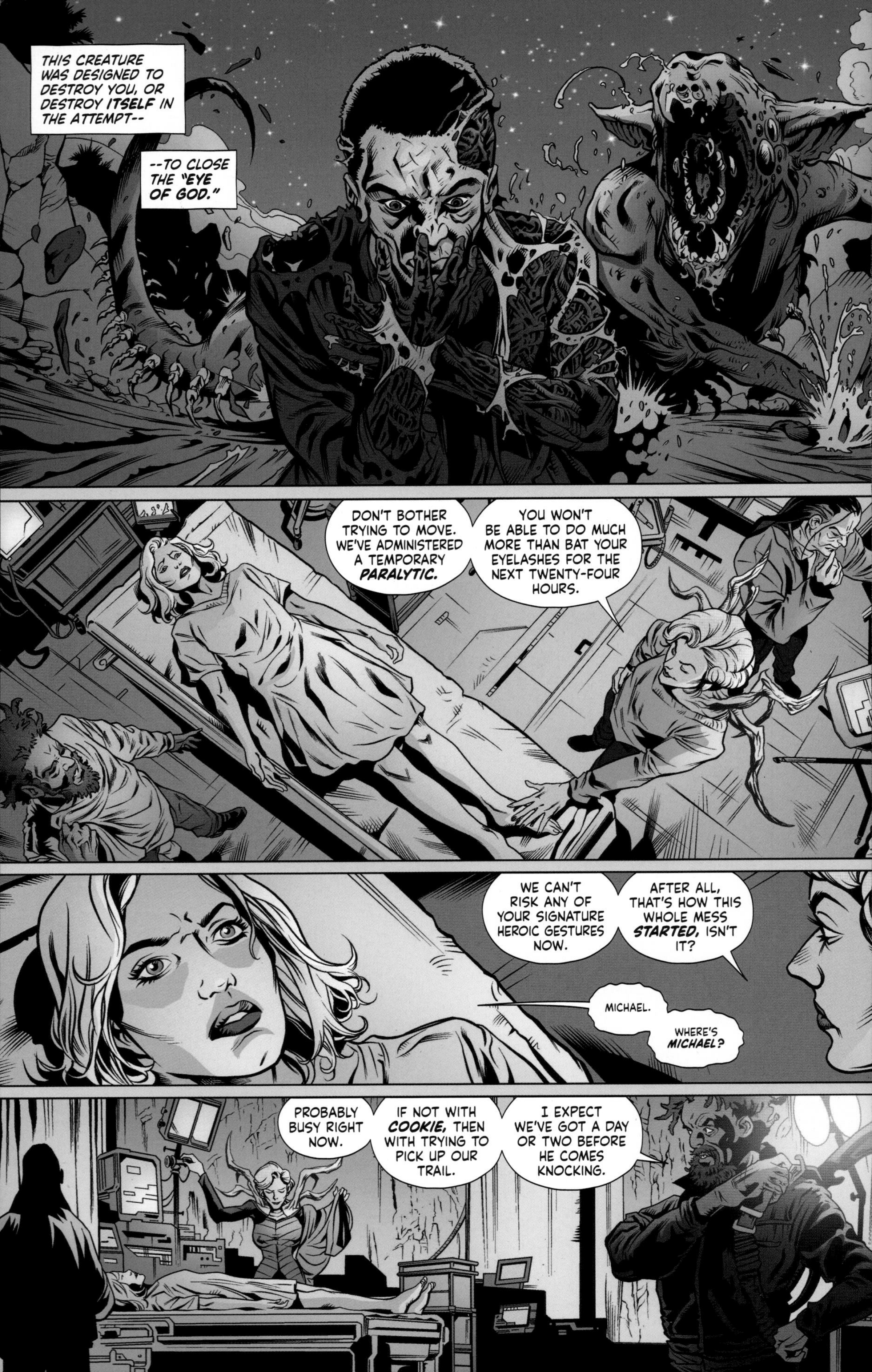
THIS CREATURE WAS DESIGNED TO DESTROY YOU, OR DESTROY ITSELF IN THE ATTEMPT--
--TO CLOSE THE "EYE OF GOD."
DON'T BOTHER TRYING TO MOVE. WE'VE ADMINISTERED A TEMPORARY PARALYTIC.
YOU WON'T BE ABLE TO DO MUCH MORE THAN BAT YOUR EYELASHES FOR THE NEXT TWENTY-FOUR HOURS.
WE CAN'T RISK ANY OF YOUR SIGNATURE HEROIC GESTURES NOW.
AFTER ALL, THAT'S HOW THIS WHOLE MESS STARTED, ISN'T IT?
MICHAEL.
WHERE'S MICHAEL?
PROBABLY BUSY RIGHT NOW.
IF NOT WITH COOKIE, THEN WITH TRYING TO PICK UP OUR TRAIL.
I EXPECT WE'VE GOT A DAY OR TWO BEFORE HE COMES KNOCKING.

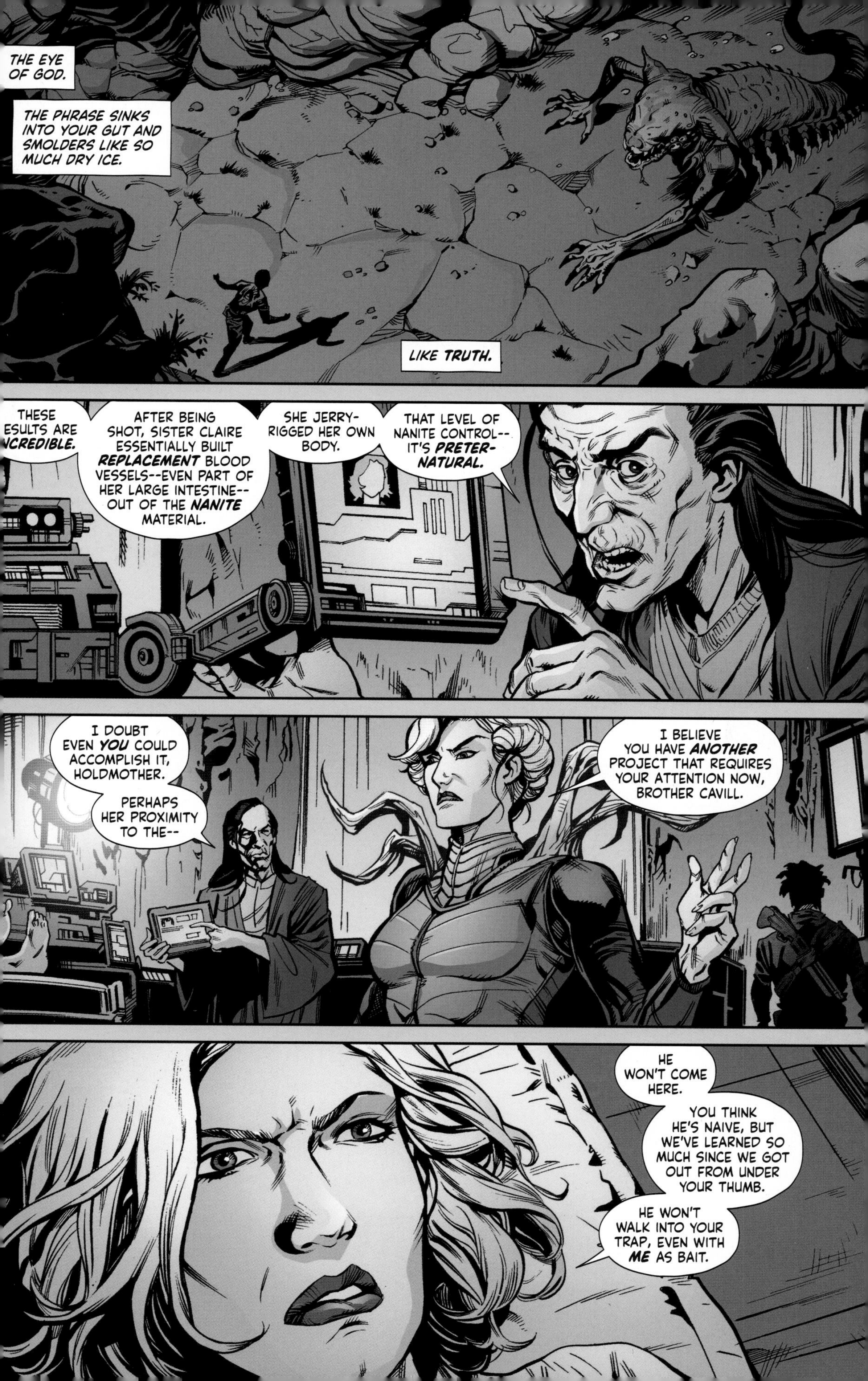
THE EYE OF GOD.
THE PHRASE SINKS INTO YOUR GUT AND SMOLDERS LIKE SO MUCH DRY ICE.
LIKE TRUTH.
THESE ESULTS ARE NCREDIBLE.
AFTER BEING SHOT, SISTER CLAIRE ESSENTIALLY BUILT REPLACEMENT BLOOD VESSELS--EVEN PART OF HER LARGE INTESTINE--OUT OF THE NANITE MATERIAL.
SHE JERRY-RIGGED HER OWN BODY.
THAT LEVEL OF NANITE CONTROL--IT'S PRETER-NATURAL.
I DOUBT EVEN YOU COULD ACCOMPLISH IT, HOLDMOTHER.
PERHAPS HER PROXIMITY TO THE--
I BELIEVE YOU HAVE ANOTHER PROJECT THAT REQUIRES YOUR ATTENTION NOW, BROTHER CAVILL.
HE WON'T COME HERE.
YOU THINK HE'S NAIVE, BUT WE'VE LEARNED SO MUCH SINCE WE GOT OUT FROM UNDER YOUR THUMB.
HE WON'T WALK INTO YOUR TRAP, EVEN WITH ME AS BAIT.

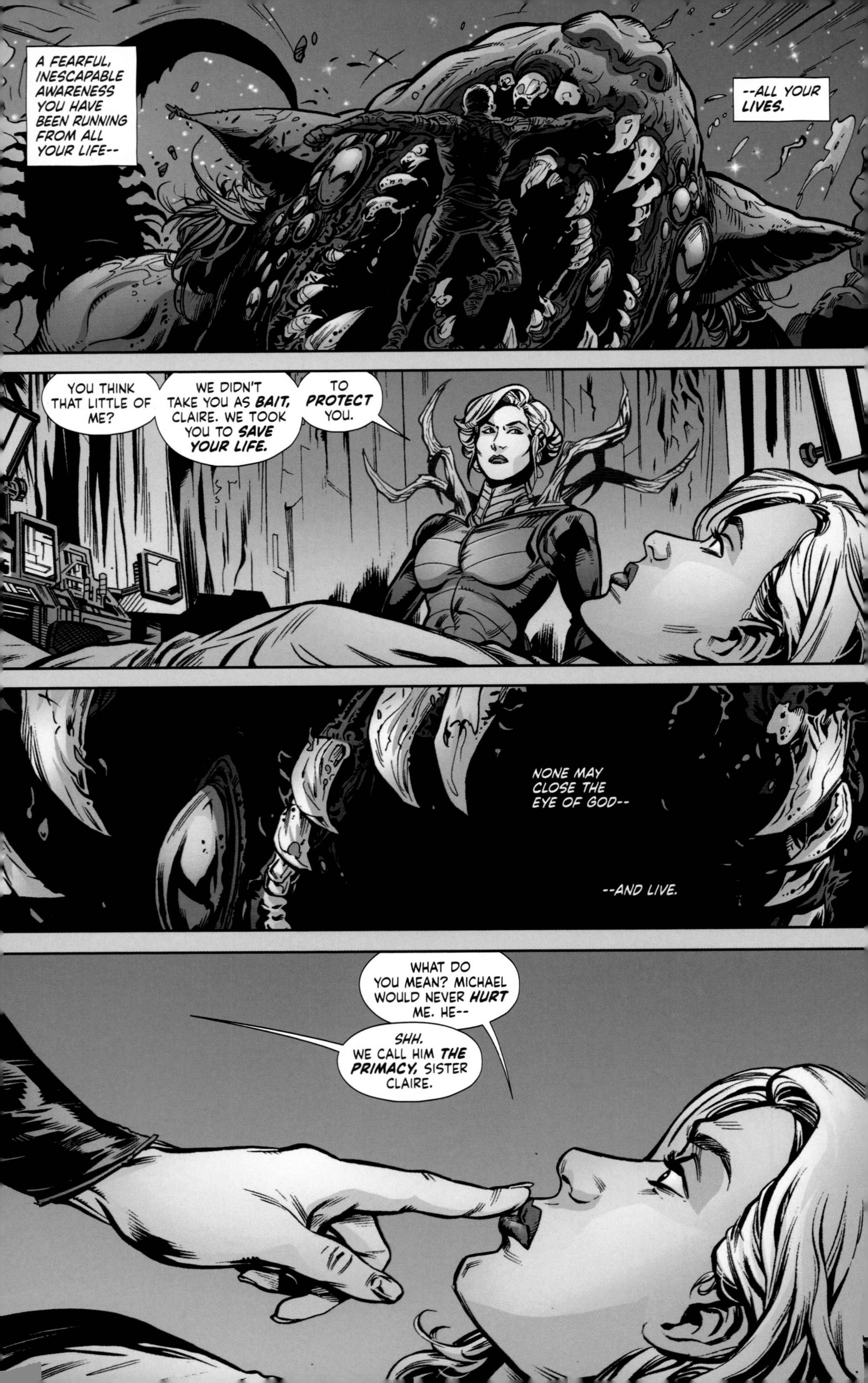
A FEARFUL, INESCAPABLE AWARENESS YOU HAVE BEEN RUNNING FROM ALL YOUR LIFE--
--ALL YOUR LIVES.
YOU THINK THAT LITTLE OF ME?
WE DIDN'T TAKE YOU AS BAIT, CLAIRE. WE TOOK YOU TO SAVE YOUR LIFE.
TO PROTECT YOU.
NONE MAY CLOSE THE EYE OF GOD--
--AND LIVE.
WHAT DO YOU MEAN? MICHAEL WOULD NEVER HURT ME. HE--
SHH. WE CALL HIM THE PRIMACY, SISTER CLAIRE.

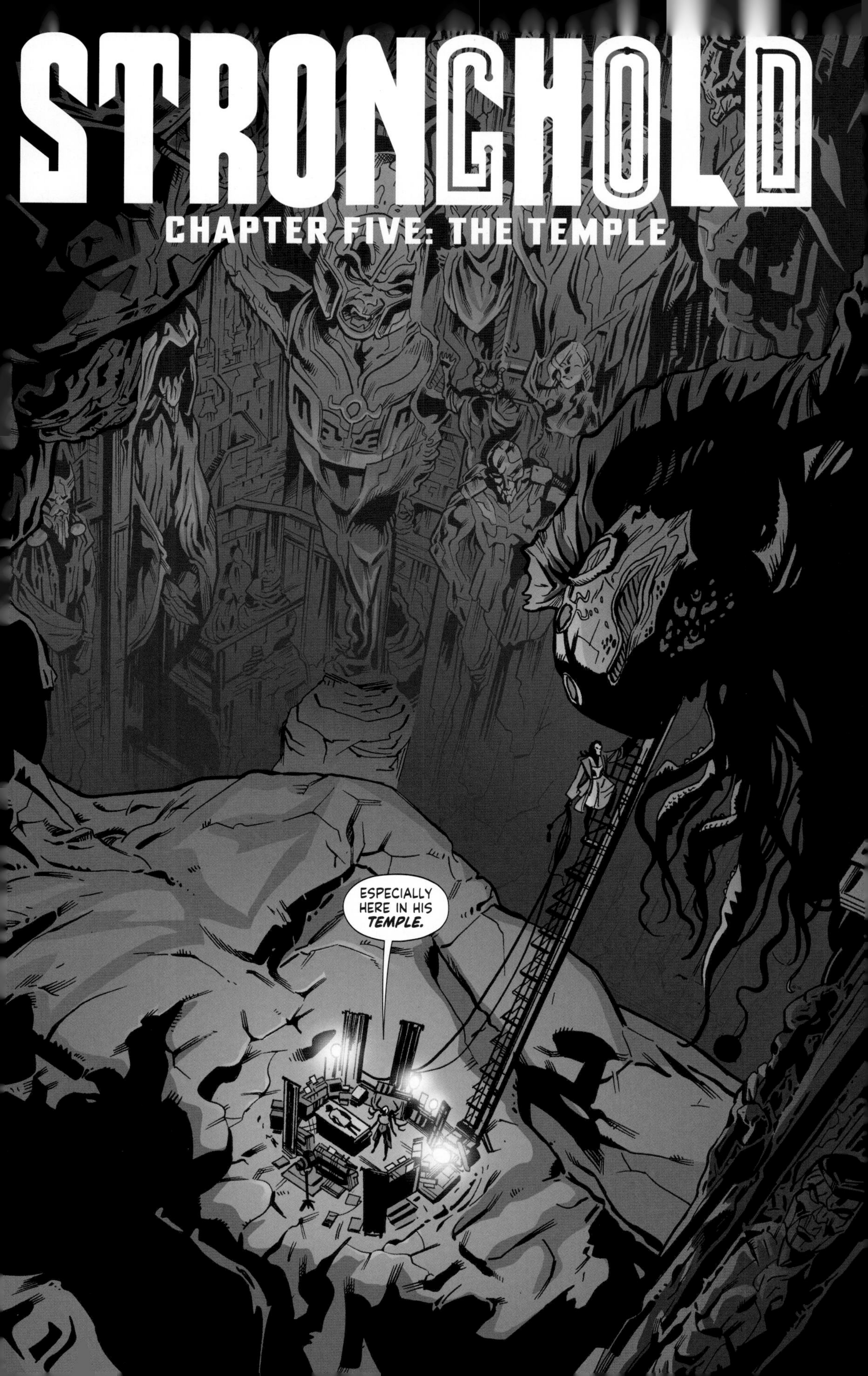
STRONGHOLD
CHAPTER FIVE: THE TEMPLE
ESPECIALLY HERE IN HIS TEMPLE.

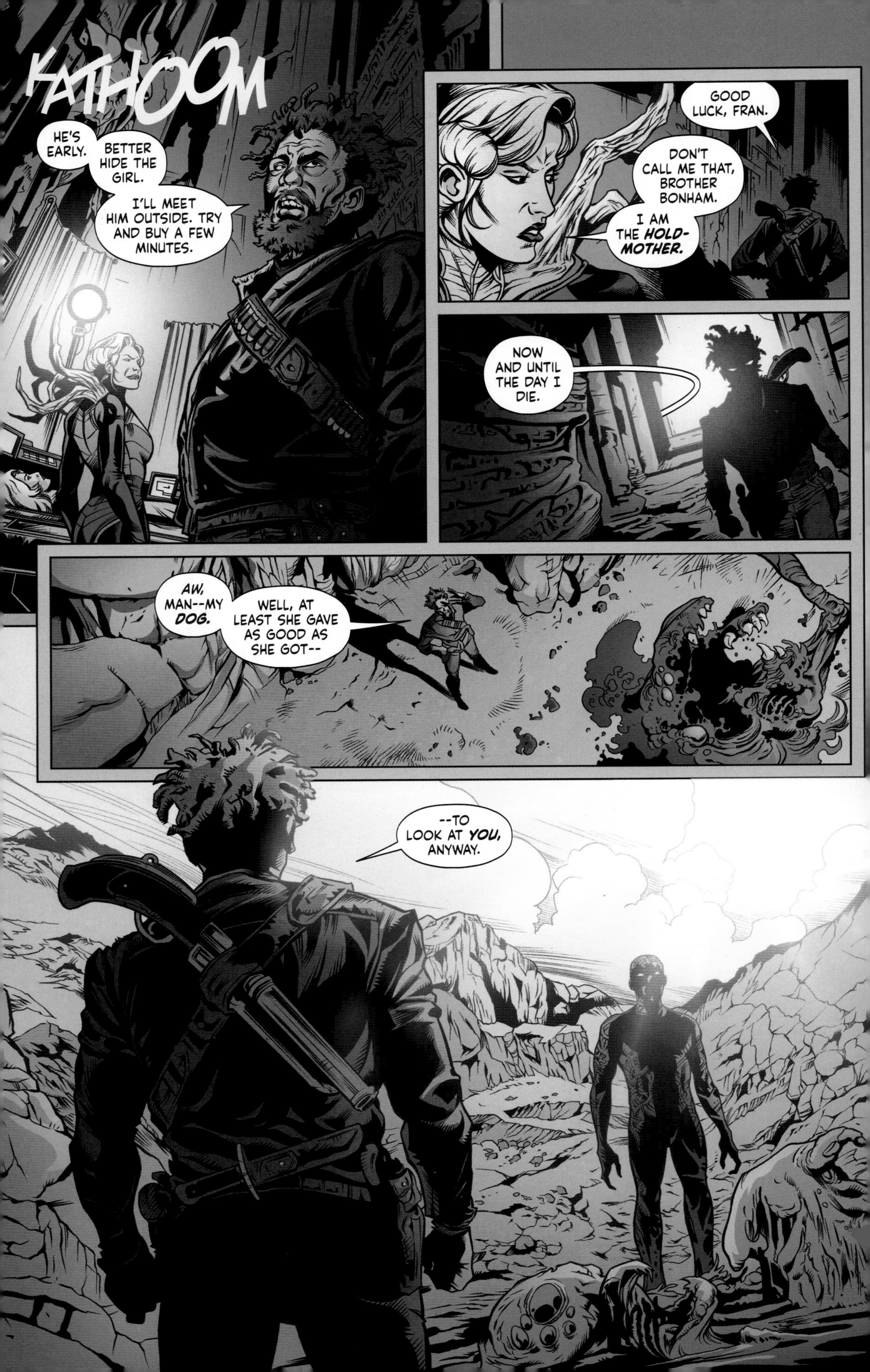
KATHOOM
HE'S EARLY.
BETTER HIDE THE GIRL.
I'LL MEET HIM OUTSIDE. TRY AND BUY A FEW MINUTES.
GOOD LUCK, FRAN.
DON'T CALL ME THAT, BROTHER BONHAM.
I AM THE *HOLD-MOTHER.*
NOW AND UNTIL THE DAY I DIE.
AW, MAN--MY *DOG.*
WELL, AT LEAST SHE GAVE AS GOOD AS SHE GOT--
--TO LOOK AT *YOU,* ANYWAY.

YOUR ANIMAL KEPT TRYING TO EAT ME, SO I *LET* IT.

I ASSUMED ONCE ITS MISSION WAS ACCOMPLISHED IT WOULD RETURN TO ITS MASTER.

THE HUMAN PARTS OF MY FORM WERE...

"DIGESTED" IS THE WORD YOU'RE LOOKING FOR.

I--I AM NOT A MAN. THAT IS CLEAR NOW.

MAYBE I NEVER *WAS.* NEVER EVEN *ALIVE* AT ALL.

WOULDN'T GO THAT FAR. YOU'RE RIGHT BETWEEN *MACHINE AND MAN,* I SUSPECT.

HELL, MACHINE AND *GOD* IS MORE LIKE IT. SOMETHING NO ONE ELSE'S EVER BEEN.

A MACHINE NO ONE IN THE GODDAMNED UNIVERSE KNOWS HOW TO TURN OFF.

TOUGH TO HEAR, I KNOW.

CLAIRE...

CLAIRE IS INSIDE, ISN'T SHE?

ALONG WITH A WHOLE LOT OF OTHER THINGS YOU AREN'T READY TO SEE OR HEAR.

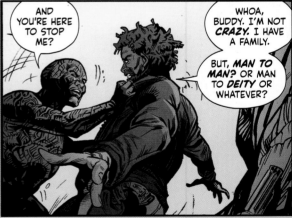

AND YOU'RE HERE TO STOP ME?

WHOA, BUDDY. I'M NOT *CRAZY.* I HAVE A FAMILY.

BUT, *MAN TO MAN?* OR MAN TO *DEITY* OR WHATEVER?

YOU DON'T WANT WHAT'S IN THERE.

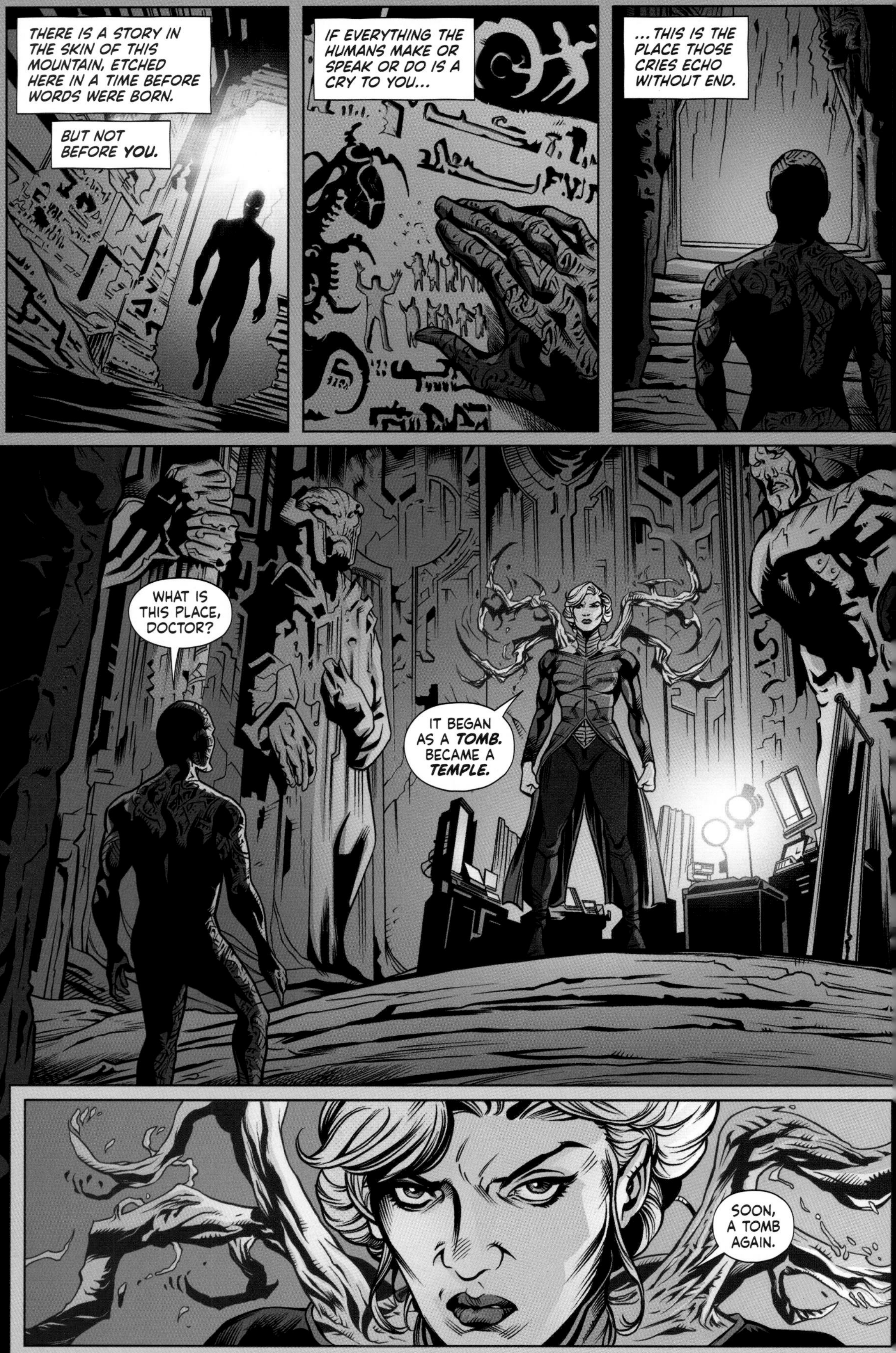
THERE IS A STORY IN THE SKIN OF THIS MOUNTAIN, ETCHED HERE IN A TIME BEFORE WORDS WERE BORN.
BUT NOT BEFORE **YOU.**
IF EVERYTHING THE HUMANS MAKE OR SPEAK OR DO IS A CRY TO YOU...
...THIS IS THE PLACE THOSE CRIES ECHO WITHOUT END.
WHAT IS THIS PLACE, DOCTOR?
IT BEGAN AS A **TOMB.** BECAME A **TEMPLE.**
SOON, A TOMB AGAIN.

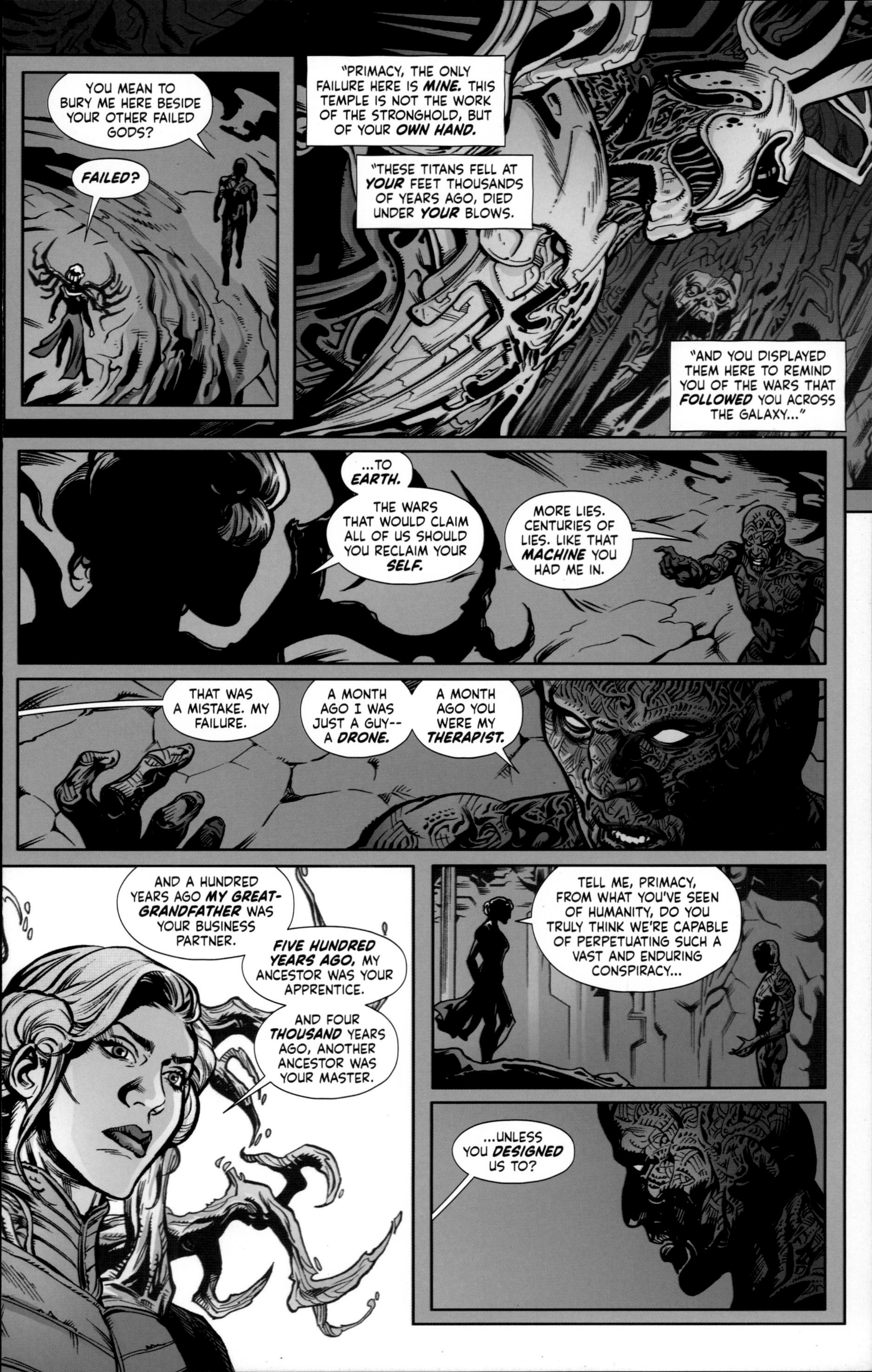
YOU MEAN TO BURY ME HERE BESIDE YOUR OTHER FAILED GODS?
FAILED?
"PRIMACY, THE ONLY FAILURE HERE IS MINE. THIS TEMPLE IS NOT THE WORK OF THE STRONGHOLD, BUT OF YOUR OWN HAND.
"THESE TITANS FELL AT YOUR FEET THOUSANDS OF YEARS AGO, DIED UNDER YOUR BLOWS.
"AND YOU DISPLAYED THEM HERE TO REMIND YOU OF THE WARS THAT FOLLOWED YOU ACROSS THE GALAXY..."
...TO EARTH.
THE WARS THAT WOULD CLAIM ALL OF US SHOULD YOU RECLAIM YOUR SELF.
MORE LIES. CENTURIES OF LIES. LIKE THAT MACHINE YOU HAD ME IN.
THAT WAS A MISTAKE. MY FAILURE.
A MONTH AGO I WAS JUST A GUY-- A DRONE.
A MONTH AGO YOU WERE MY THERAPIST.
AND A HUNDRED YEARS AGO MY GREAT-GRANDFATHER WAS YOUR BUSINESS PARTNER.
FIVE HUNDRED YEARS AGO, MY ANCESTOR WAS YOUR APPRENTICE.
AND FOUR THOUSAND YEARS AGO, ANOTHER ANCESTOR WAS YOUR MASTER.
TELL ME, PRIMACY, FROM WHAT YOU'VE SEEN OF HUMANITY, DO YOU TRULY THINK WE'RE CAPABLE OF PERPETUATING SUCH A VAST AND ENDURING CONSPIRACY...
...UNLESS YOU DESIGNED US TO?

THAT *IDIOT.*
THAT ABSOLUTE
MADWOMAN.

WHAT--WHAT'S
HAPPENING?

SHE'S
ACTUALLY TRYING
TO *REASON*
WITH HIM.

SHE THINKS
TELLING HIM THE
TRUTH WILL SOMEHOW
RETURN US ALL TO
OUR FUTILE STATUS
QUO--

--WHEN WE
HAVE THE MEANS
TO *END* THIS CYCLE
IN OUR VERY
HANDS.

END
IT?

WITH THIS
VERY ALIEN
CONSTRUCT,
GIRL.

TRUE, THE
PRIMACY DEFEATED
IT ONCE, LONG AGO,
LEFT IT FOR A
TROPHY.

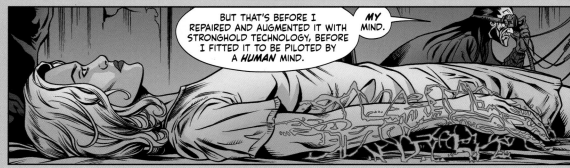

BUT THAT'S BEFORE I
REPAIRED AND AUGMENTED IT WITH
STRONGHOLD TECHNOLOGY, BEFORE
I FITTED IT TO BE PILOTED BY
A *HUMAN* MIND.

MY
MIND.

I CAN *SEE*
THROUGH ITS
EYES.

I KNOW
WHAT *IT*
KNEW.

MY
GOD--WHAT IT
REMEMBERS!

THE
PRIMACY
DESERVES *DEATH!*

DEATH!

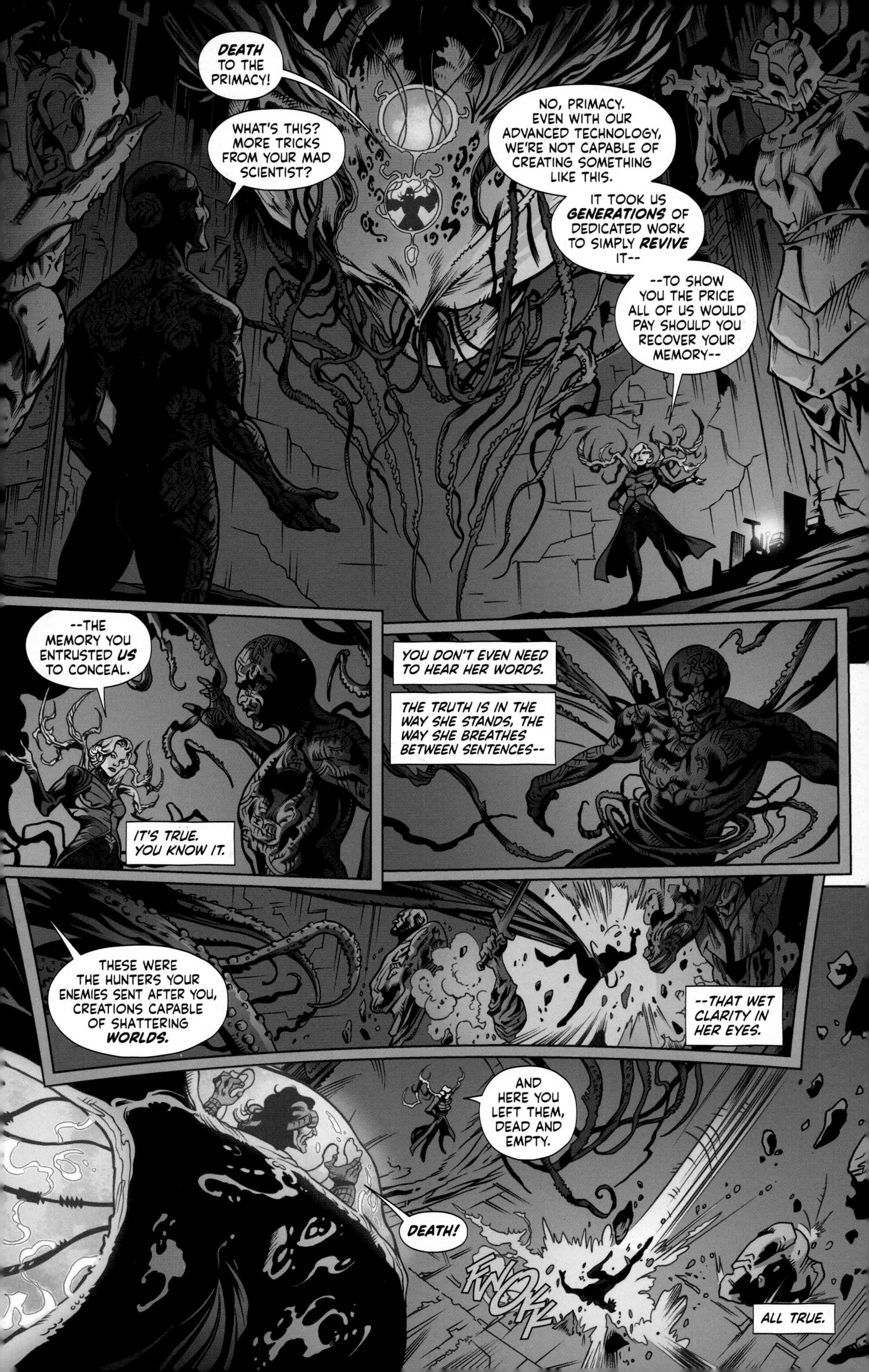

DEATH TO THE PRIMACY!
WHAT'S THIS? MORE TRICKS FROM YOUR MAD SCIENTIST?
NO, PRIMACY. EVEN WITH OUR ADVANCED TECHNOLOGY, WE'RE NOT CAPABLE OF CREATING SOMETHING LIKE THIS.
IT TOOK US GENERATIONS OF DEDICATED WORK TO SIMPLY REVIVE IT--
--TO SHOW YOU THE PRICE ALL OF US WOULD PAY SHOULD YOU RECOVER YOUR MEMORY--
--THE MEMORY YOU ENTRUSTED US TO CONCEAL.
IT'S TRUE. YOU KNOW IT.
YOU DON'T EVEN NEED TO HEAR HER WORDS.
THE TRUTH IS IN THE WAY SHE STANDS, THE WAY SHE BREATHES BETWEEN SENTENCES--
THESE WERE THE HUNTERS YOUR ENEMIES SENT AFTER YOU, CREATIONS CAPABLE OF SHATTERING WORLDS.
--THAT WET CLARITY IN HER EYES.
AND HERE YOU LEFT THEM, DEAD AND EMPTY.
DEATH!
FWOK
ALL TRUE.

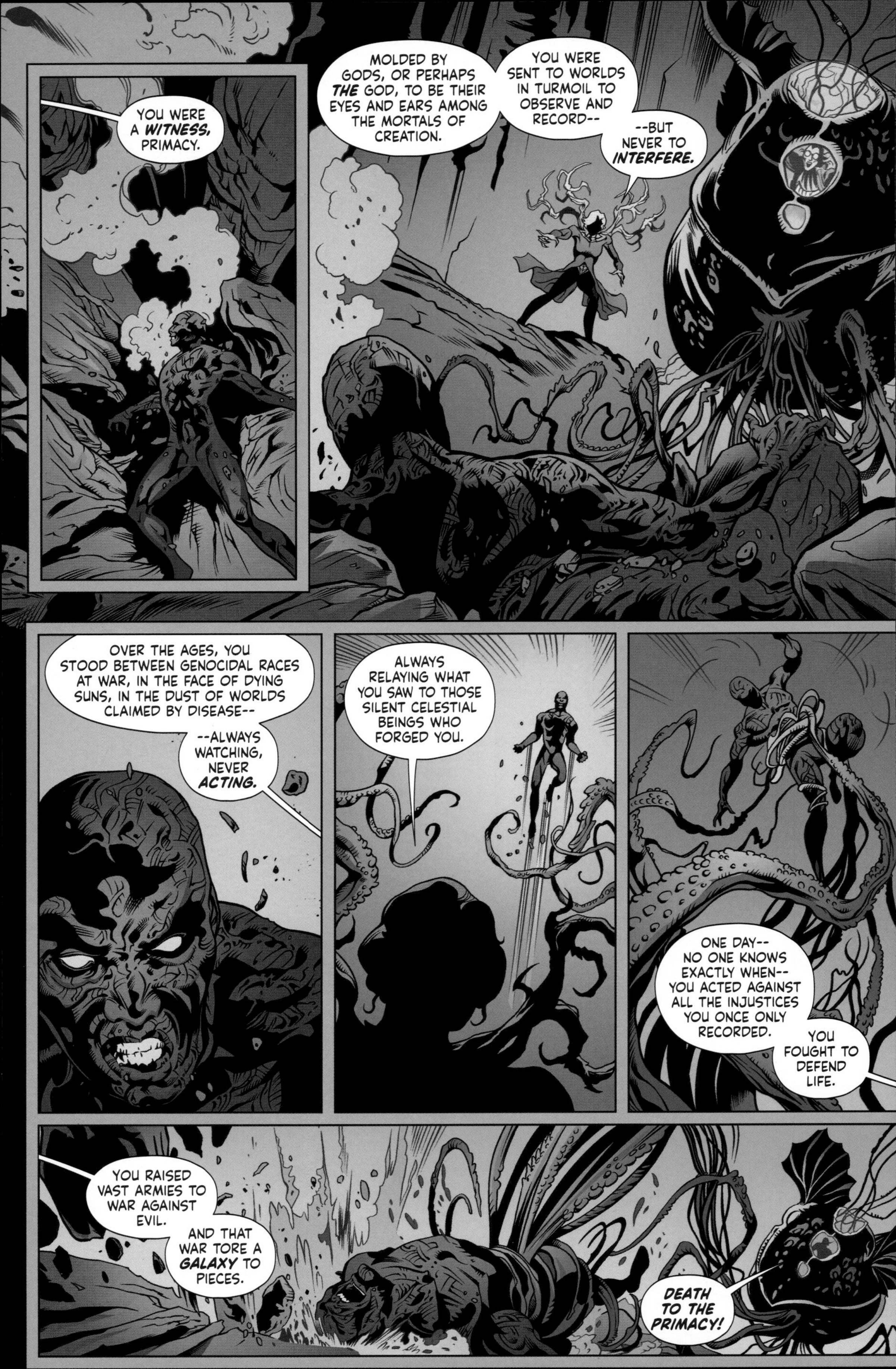
YOU WERE A *WITNESS,* PRIMACY.
MOLDED BY GODS, OR PERHAPS *THE* GOD, TO BE THEIR EYES AND EARS AMONG THE MORTALS OF CREATION.
YOU WERE SENT TO WORLDS IN TURMOIL TO OBSERVE AND RECORD--
--BUT NEVER TO *INTERFERE.*
OVER THE AGES, YOU STOOD BETWEEN GENOCIDAL RACES AT WAR, IN THE FACE OF DYING SUNS, IN THE DUST OF WORLDS CLAIMED BY DISEASE--
--ALWAYS WATCHING, NEVER *ACTING.*
ALWAYS RELAYING WHAT YOU SAW TO THOSE SILENT CELESTIAL BEINGS WHO FORGED YOU.
ONE DAY-- NO ONE KNOWS EXACTLY WHEN-- YOU ACTED AGAINST ALL THE INJUSTICES YOU ONCE ONLY RECORDED.
YOU FOUGHT TO DEFEND LIFE.
YOU RAISED VAST ARMIES TO WAR AGAINST EVIL.
AND THAT WAR TORE A *GALAXY* TO PIECES.
DEATH TO THE PRIMACY!

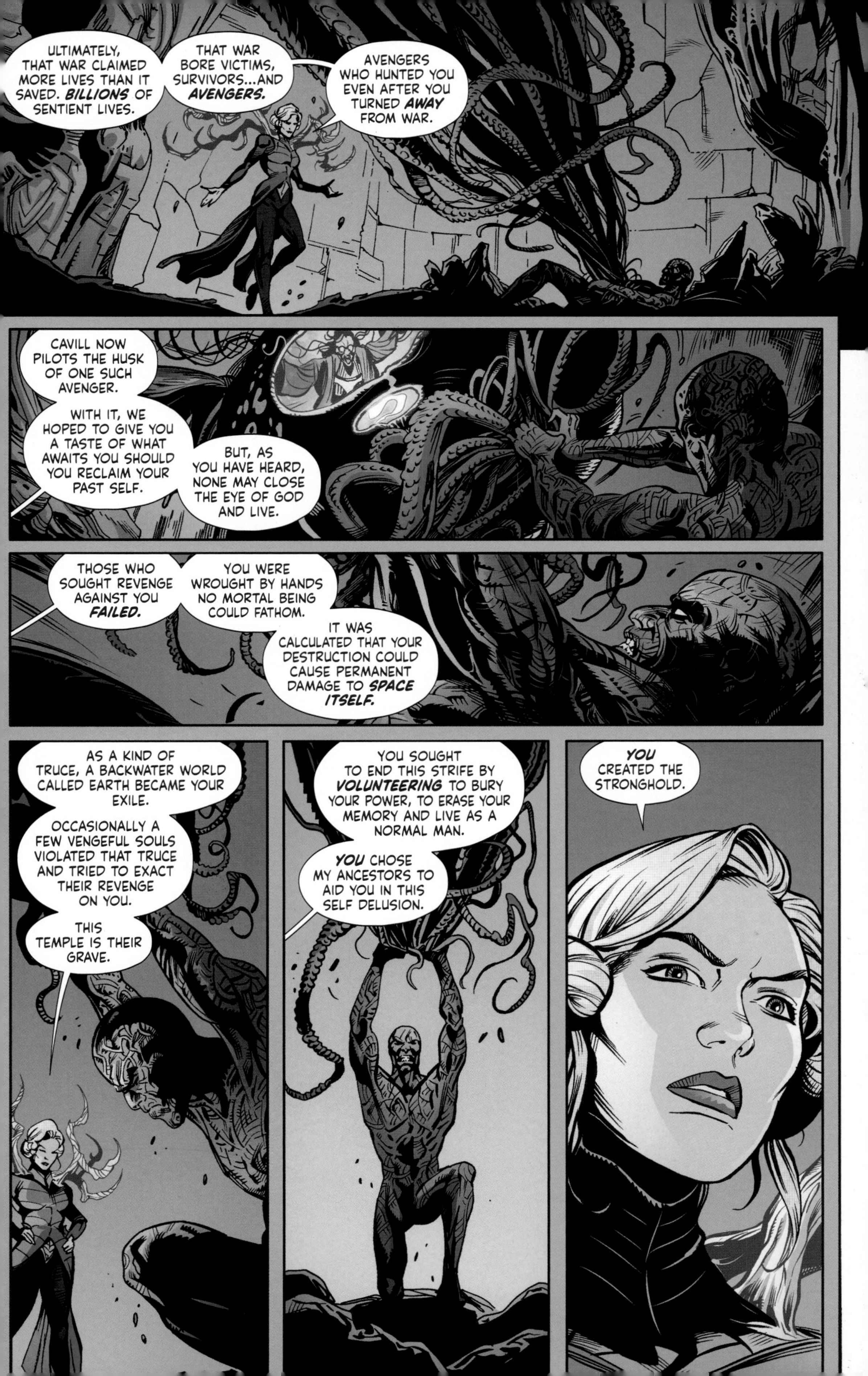
ULTIMATELY, THAT WAR CLAIMED MORE LIVES THAN IT SAVED. ***BILLIONS*** OF SENTIENT LIVES.
THAT WAR BORE VICTIMS, SURVIVORS...AND ***AVENGERS.***
AVENGERS WHO HUNTED YOU EVEN AFTER YOU TURNED ***AWAY*** FROM WAR.
CAVILL NOW PILOTS THE HUSK OF ONE SUCH AVENGER.
WITH IT, WE HOPED TO GIVE YOU A TASTE OF WHAT AWAITS YOU SHOULD YOU RECLAIM YOUR PAST SELF.
BUT, AS YOU HAVE HEARD, NONE MAY CLOSE THE EYE OF GOD AND LIVE.
THOSE WHO SOUGHT REVENGE AGAINST YOU ***FAILED.***
YOU WERE WROUGHT BY HANDS NO MORTAL BEING COULD FATHOM.
IT WAS CALCULATED THAT YOUR DESTRUCTION COULD CAUSE PERMANENT DAMAGE TO ***SPACE ITSELF.***
AS A KIND OF TRUCE, A BACKWATER WORLD CALLED EARTH BECAME YOUR EXILE.
OCCASIONALLY A FEW VENGEFUL SOULS VIOLATED THAT TRUCE AND TRIED TO EXACT THEIR REVENGE ON YOU.
THIS TEMPLE IS THEIR GRAVE.
YOU SOUGHT TO END THIS STRIFE BY ***VOLUNTEERING*** TO BURY YOUR POWER, TO ERASE YOUR MEMORY AND LIVE AS A NORMAL MAN.
YOU CHOSE MY ANCESTORS TO AID YOU IN THIS SELF DELUSION.
YOU CREATED THE STRONGHOLD.

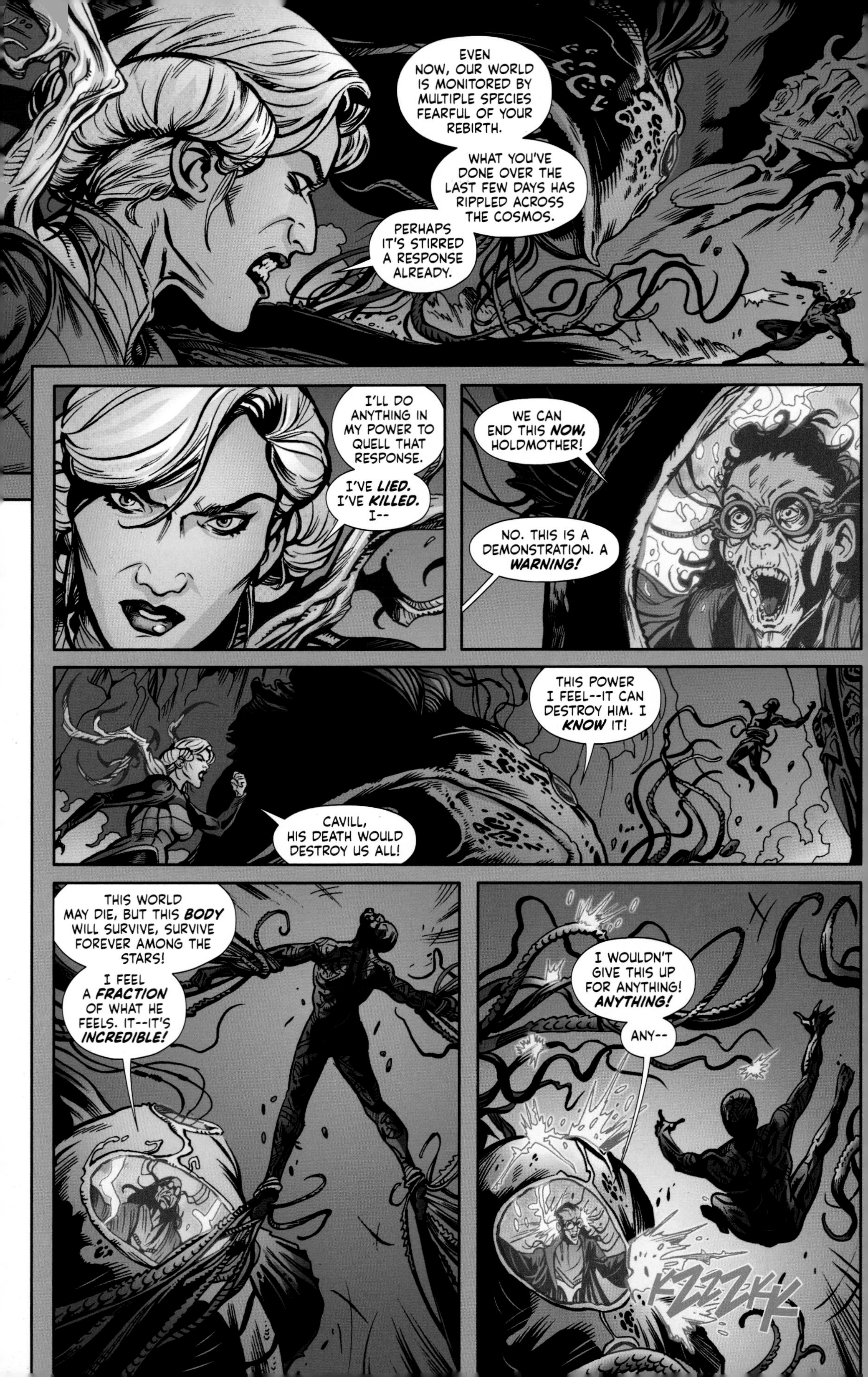
EVEN NOW, OUR WORLD IS MONITORED BY MULTIPLE SPECIES FEARFUL OF YOUR REBIRTH.
WHAT YOU'VE DONE OVER THE LAST FEW DAYS HAS RIPPLED ACROSS THE COSMOS.
PERHAPS IT'S STIRRED A RESPONSE ALREADY.
I'LL DO ANYTHING IN MY POWER TO QUELL THAT RESPONSE.
I'VE *LIED.* I'VE *KILLED.* I--
WE CAN END THIS *NOW,* HOLDMOTHER!
NO. THIS IS A DEMONSTRATION. A ***WARNING!***
THIS POWER I FEEL--IT CAN DESTROY HIM. I ***KNOW*** IT!
CAVILL, HIS DEATH WOULD DESTROY US ALL!
THIS WORLD MAY DIE, BUT THIS ***BODY*** WILL SURVIVE, SURVIVE FOREVER AMONG THE STARS!
I FEEL A ***FRACTION*** OF WHAT HE FEELS. IT--IT'S ***INCREDIBLE!***
I WOULDN'T GIVE THIS UP FOR ANYTHING! ***ANYTHING!***
ANY--
KZZZKK

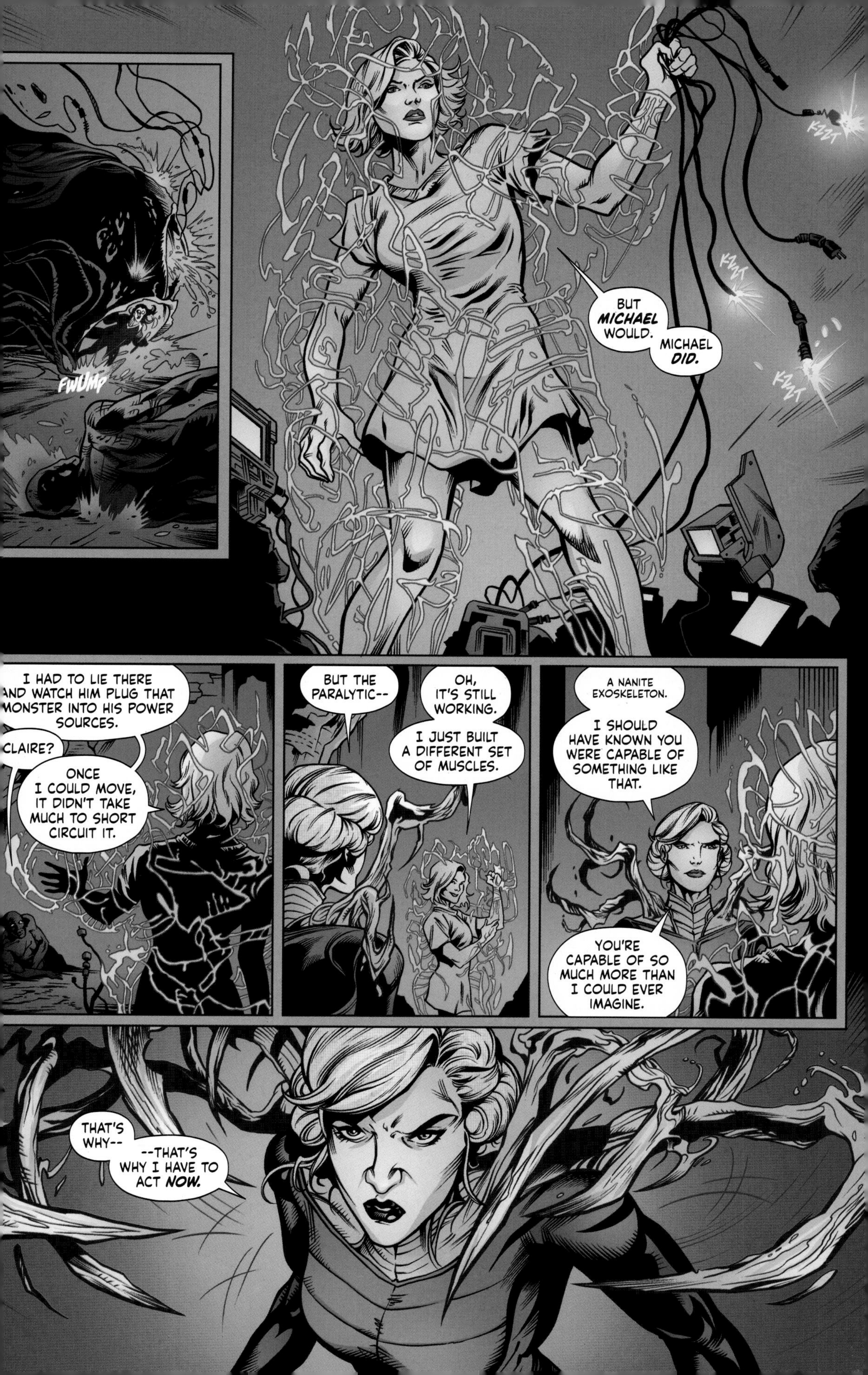
FWUMP
KZZT
BUT MICHAEL WOULD.
MICHAEL DID.
KZZT
KZZT
I HAD TO LIE THERE AND WATCH HIM PLUG THAT MONSTER INTO HIS POWER SOURCES.
CLAIRE?
ONCE I COULD MOVE, IT DIDN'T TAKE MUCH TO SHORT CIRCUIT IT.
BUT THE PARALYTIC--
OH, IT'S STILL WORKING.
I JUST BUILT A DIFFERENT SET OF MUSCLES.
A NANITE EXOSKELETON.
I SHOULD HAVE KNOWN YOU WERE CAPABLE OF SOMETHING LIKE THAT.
YOU'RE CAPABLE OF SO MUCH MORE THAN I COULD EVER IMAGINE.
THAT'S WHY--
--THAT'S WHY I HAVE TO ACT NOW.

WHAT ARE YOU DOING?

THERE'S ONLY ONE WAY TO PROVE MYSELF. I HAVE TO *SHOW* HIM.

IT'S THE ONLY WAY, PRIMACY. IF I DON'T--IF I DON'T, SOMEDAY *CLAIRE* WILL.

STOP THIS MADNESS!

I SEE IT IN HER. SHE COULDN'T LIVE WITH LETTING YOU SUFFER IN IGNORANCE.

EVENTUALLY SHE'D *LEARN* THE TRUTH.

SHE WOULD BE BRAVE ENOUGH TO--

--TO MAKE THE *SACRIFICE* I'VE BEEN AFRAID TO.

SACRIFICE?

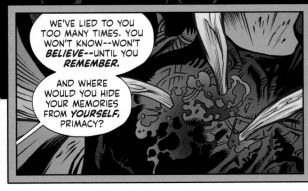

WE'VE LIED TO YOU TOO MANY TIMES. YOU WON'T KNOW--WON'T *BELIEVE*--UNTIL YOU *REMEMBER*.

AND WHERE WOULD YOU HIDE YOUR MEMORIES FROM *YOURSELF*, PRIMACY?

WHERE WOULD YOU CONCEAL YOUR IDENTITY THAT YOU DARE NOT TAKE IT BACK--

--BUT *WITHIN* THOSE YOU LOVE?

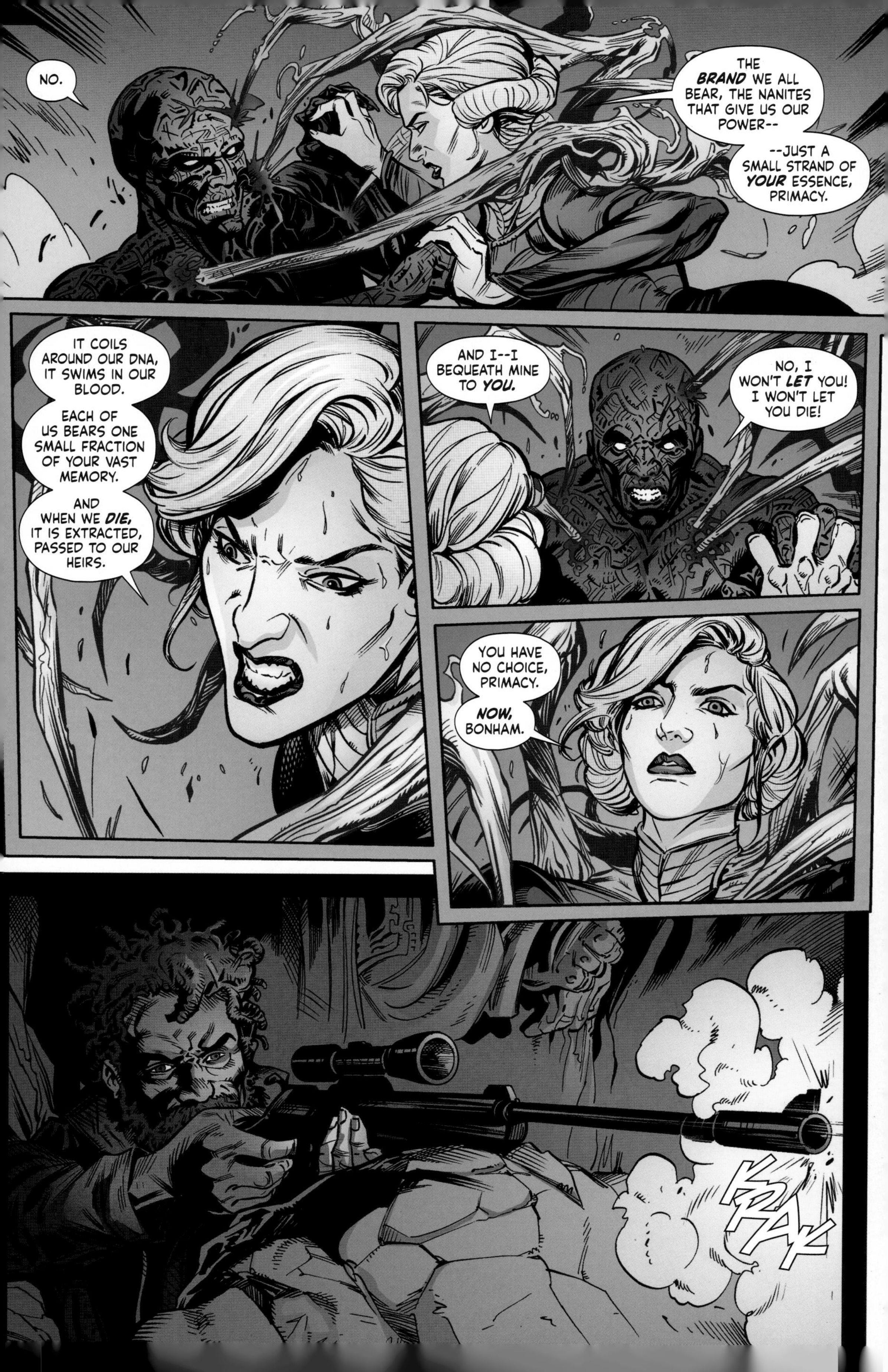

NO.
THE BRAND WE ALL BEAR, THE NANITES THAT GIVE US OUR POWER--
--JUST A SMALL STRAND OF YOUR ESSENCE, PRIMACY.
IT COILS AROUND OUR DNA, IT SWIMS IN OUR BLOOD.
EACH OF US BEARS ONE SMALL FRACTION OF YOUR VAST MEMORY.
AND WHEN WE DIE, IT IS EXTRACTED, PASSED TO OUR HEIRS.
AND I--I BEQUEATH MINE TO YOU.
NO, I WON'T LET YOU! I WON'T LET YOU DIE!
YOU HAVE NO CHOICE, PRIMACY.
NOW, BONHAM.
KRAK

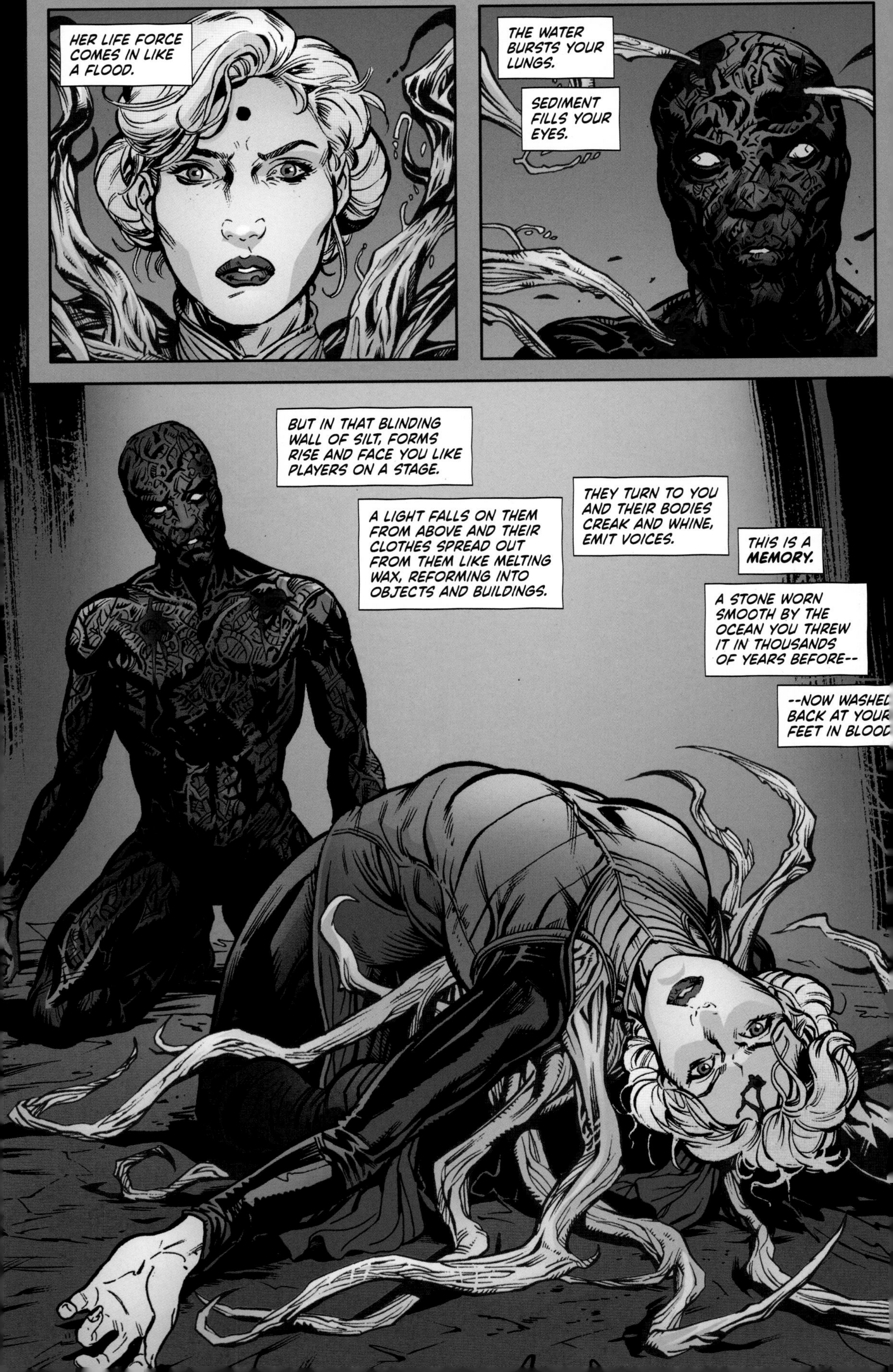
HER LIFE FORCE COMES IN LIKE A FLOOD.
THE WATER BURSTS YOUR LUNGS.
SEDIMENT FILLS YOUR EYES.
BUT IN THAT BLINDING WALL OF SILT, FORMS RISE AND FACE YOU LIKE PLAYERS ON A STAGE.
A LIGHT FALLS ON THEM FROM ABOVE AND THEIR CLOTHES SPREAD OUT FROM THEM LIKE MELTING WAX, REFORMING INTO OBJECTS AND BUILDINGS.
THEY TURN TO YOU AND THEIR BODIES CREAK AND WHINE, EMIT VOICES.
THIS IS A MEMORY.
A STONE WORN SMOOTH BY THE OCEAN YOU THREW IT IN THOUSANDS OF YEARS BEFORE--
--NOW WASHEL BACK AT YOUR FEET IN BLOOD

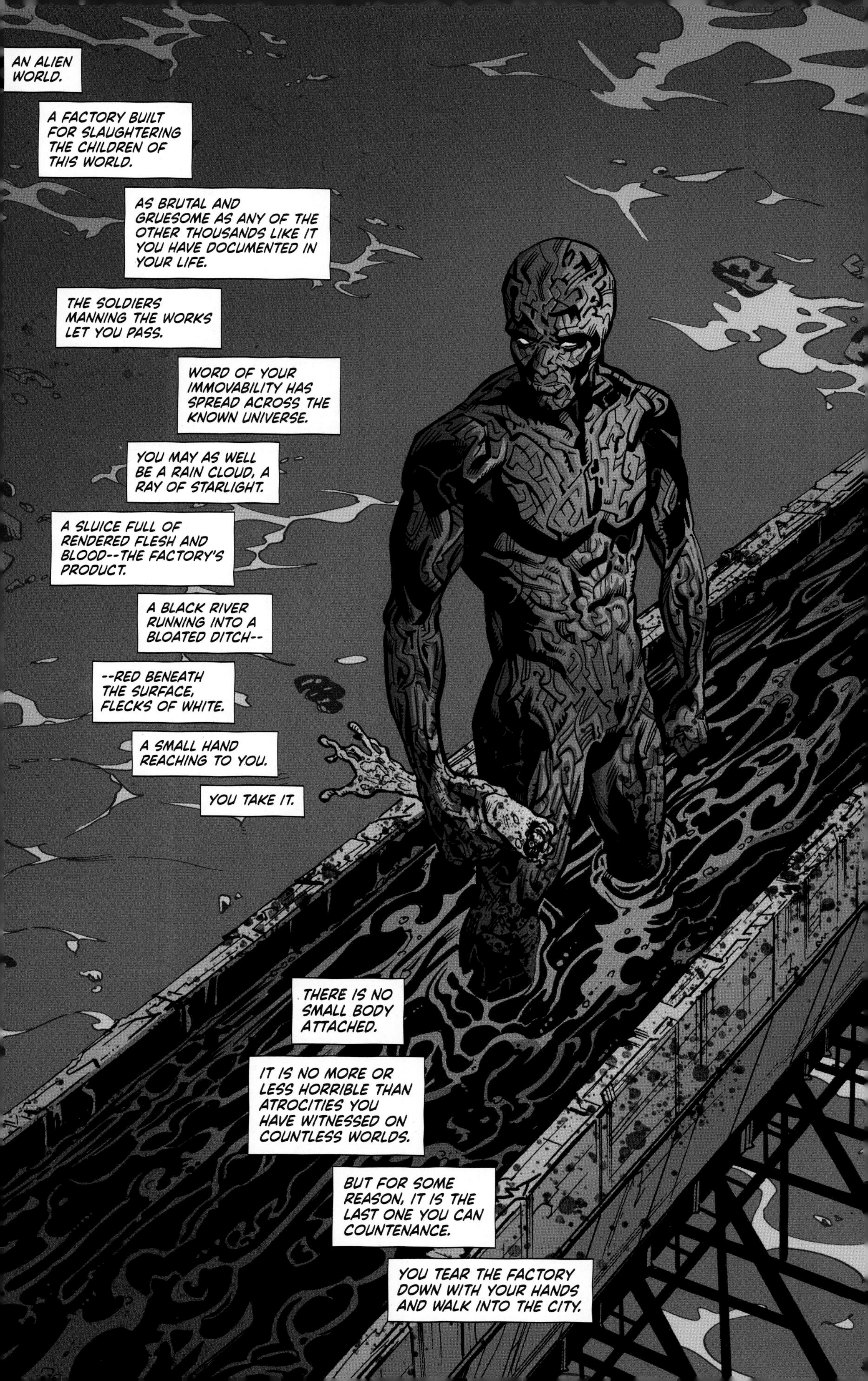
AN ALIEN WORLD.
A FACTORY BUILT FOR SLAUGHTERING THE CHILDREN OF THIS WORLD.
AS BRUTAL AND GRUESOME AS ANY OF THE OTHER THOUSANDS LIKE IT YOU HAVE DOCUMENTED IN YOUR LIFE.
THE SOLDIERS MANNING THE WORKS LET YOU PASS.
WORD OF YOUR IMMOVABILITY HAS SPREAD ACROSS THE KNOWN UNIVERSE.
YOU MAY AS WELL BE A RAIN CLOUD, A RAY OF STARLIGHT.
A SLUICE FULL OF RENDERED FLESH AND BLOOD--THE FACTORY'S PRODUCT.
A BLACK RIVER RUNNING INTO A BLOATED DITCH--
--RED BENEATH THE SURFACE, FLECKS OF WHITE.
A SMALL HAND REACHING TO YOU.
YOU TAKE IT.
THERE IS NO SMALL BODY ATTACHED.
IT IS NO MORE OR LESS HORRIBLE THAN ATROCITIES YOU HAVE WITNESSED ON COUNTLESS WORLDS.
BUT FOR SOME REASON, IT IS THE LAST ONE YOU CAN COUNTENANCE.
YOU TEAR THE FACTORY DOWN WITH YOUR HANDS AND WALK INTO THE CITY.

WITH YOUR HANDS.

BONHAM! **NOW!**

FRAN, I SHOT YOU IN THE HEAD THREE DAYS AGO.

DIDN'T TAKE.

YOUR PLAN WORKED, HOLDMOTHER. YOU TRANSFERRED YOUR MEMORY TO MICHAEL.

YOU **DID** DIE.

FOR A TIME.

YOU-- YOU HEALED ME? AFTER ALL I DID TO YOU?

A SMALL THING. YOU DID ONLY WHAT I ASKED.

THE MEMORY YOU HELD--AND ITS **POWER**--REMAIN WITH ME.

THEN THIS-- THIS DOESN'T END. ALL THIS **BULLSHIT,** IT JUST KEEPS GOING AND--

IT ENDS TODAY. HAVING SEEN THE SHADOW OF MY LEGACY, I AM CONTENT TO LET IT LIE.

I AM CONTENT TO BE NOTHING MORE THAN MICHAEL GREY.

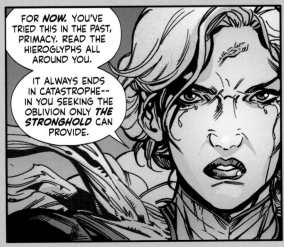

FOR **NOW.** YOU'VE TRIED THIS IN THE PAST, PRIMACY. READ THE HIEROGLYPHS ALL AROUND YOU.

IT ALWAYS ENDS IN CATASTROPHE-- IN YOU SEEKING THE OBLIVION ONLY **THE STRONGHOLD** CAN PROVIDE.

MAYBE.

BUT THIS TIME HE'S NOT DOING IT ALONE.

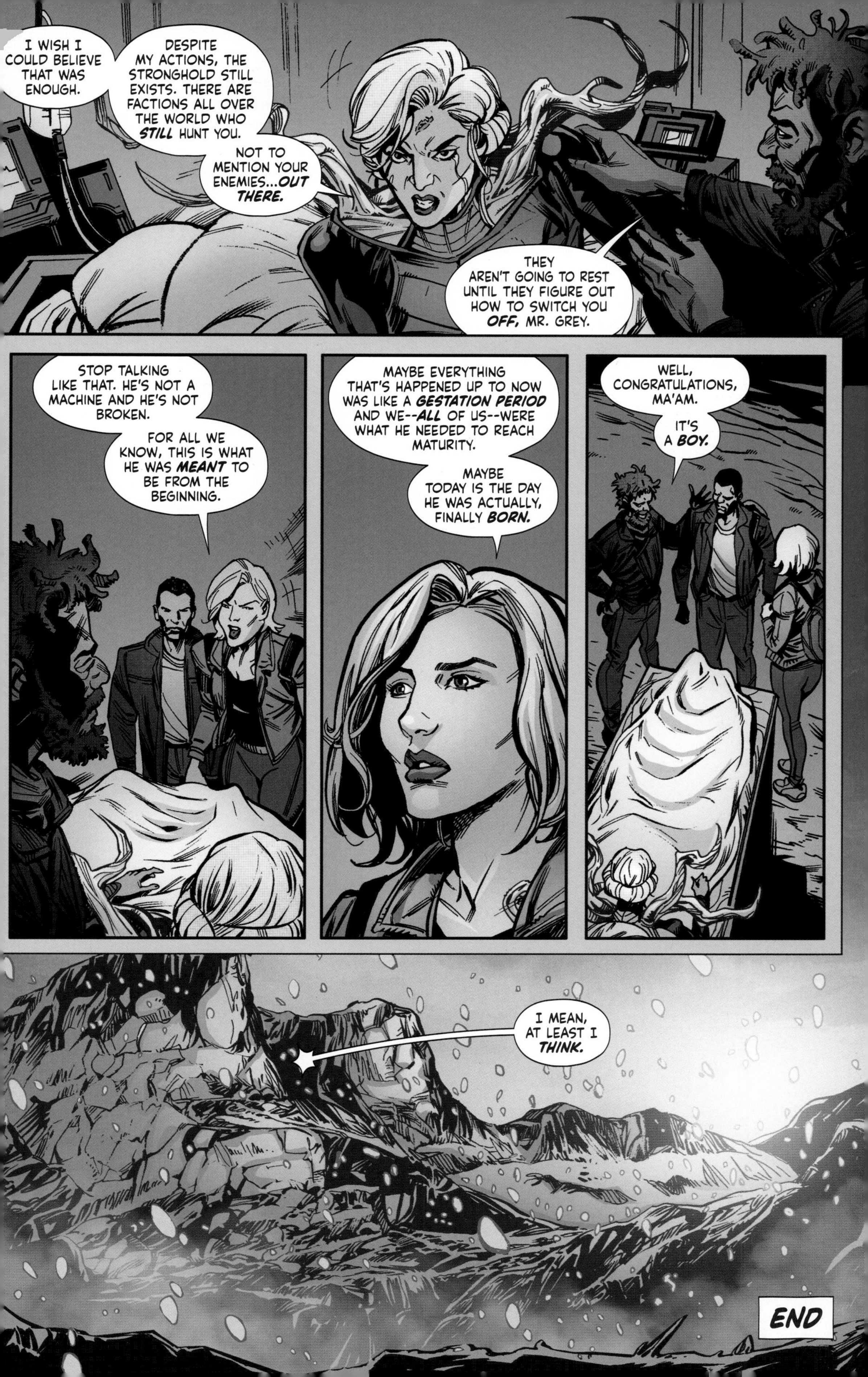
I WISH I COULD BELIEVE THAT WAS ENOUGH.
DESPITE MY ACTIONS, THE STRONGHOLD STILL EXISTS. THERE ARE FACTIONS ALL OVER THE WORLD WHO *STILL* HUNT YOU.
NOT TO MENTION YOUR ENEMIES...*OUT THERE.*
THEY AREN'T GOING TO REST UNTIL THEY FIGURE OUT HOW TO SWITCH YOU *OFF,* MR. GREY.
STOP TALKING LIKE THAT. HE'S NOT A MACHINE AND HE'S NOT BROKEN.
FOR ALL WE KNOW, THIS IS WHAT HE WAS *MEANT* TO BE FROM THE BEGINNING.
MAYBE EVERYTHING THAT'S HAPPENED UP TO NOW WAS LIKE A *GESTATION PERIOD* AND WE--*ALL* OF US--WERE WHAT HE NEEDED TO REACH MATURITY.
MAYBE TODAY IS THE DAY HE WAS ACTUALLY, FINALLY *BORN.*
WELL, CONGRATULATIONS, MA'AM.
IT'S A *BOY.*
I MEAN, AT LEAST I *THINK.*
END

Issue #1
TYLER WALPOLE
Cover B

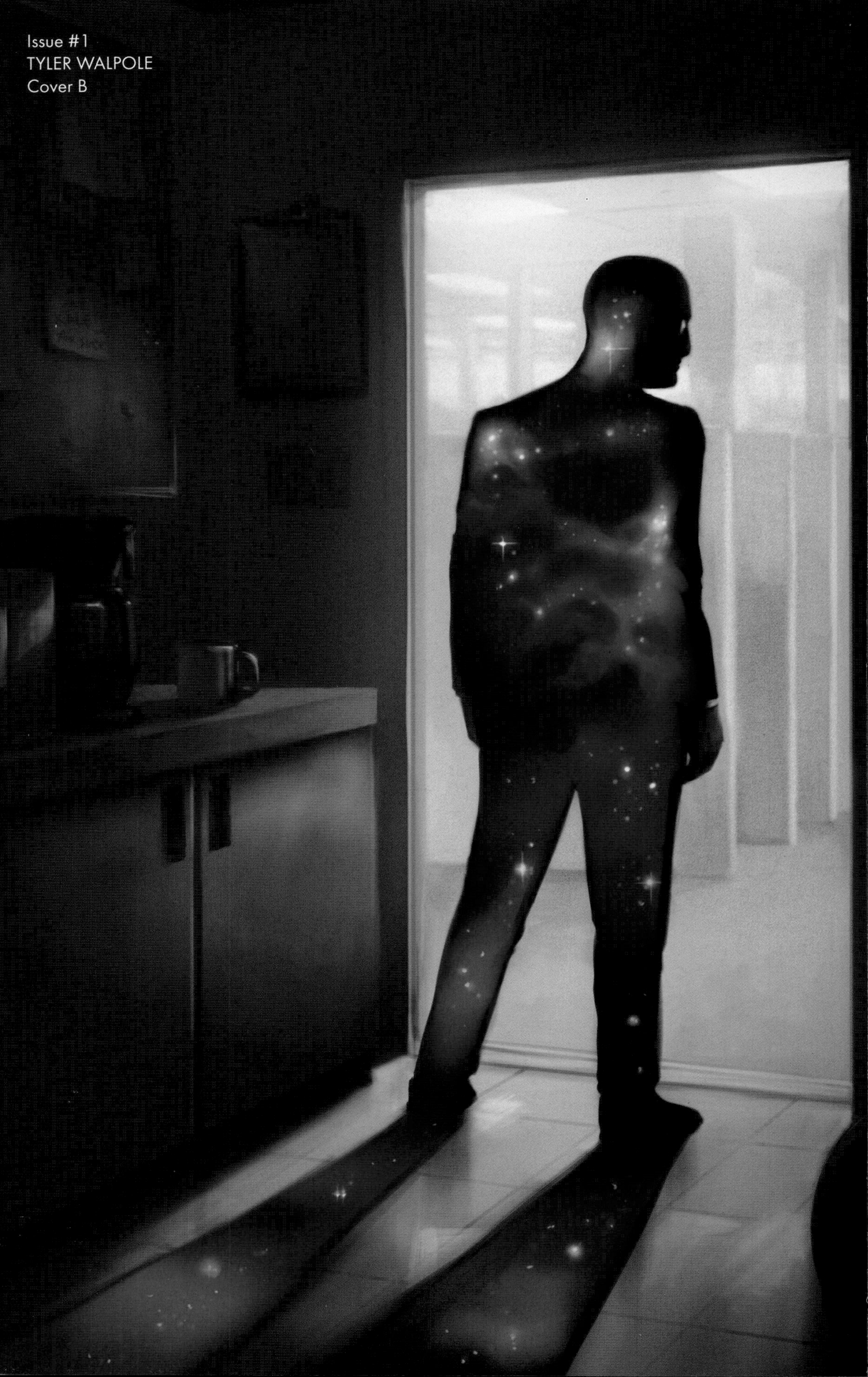

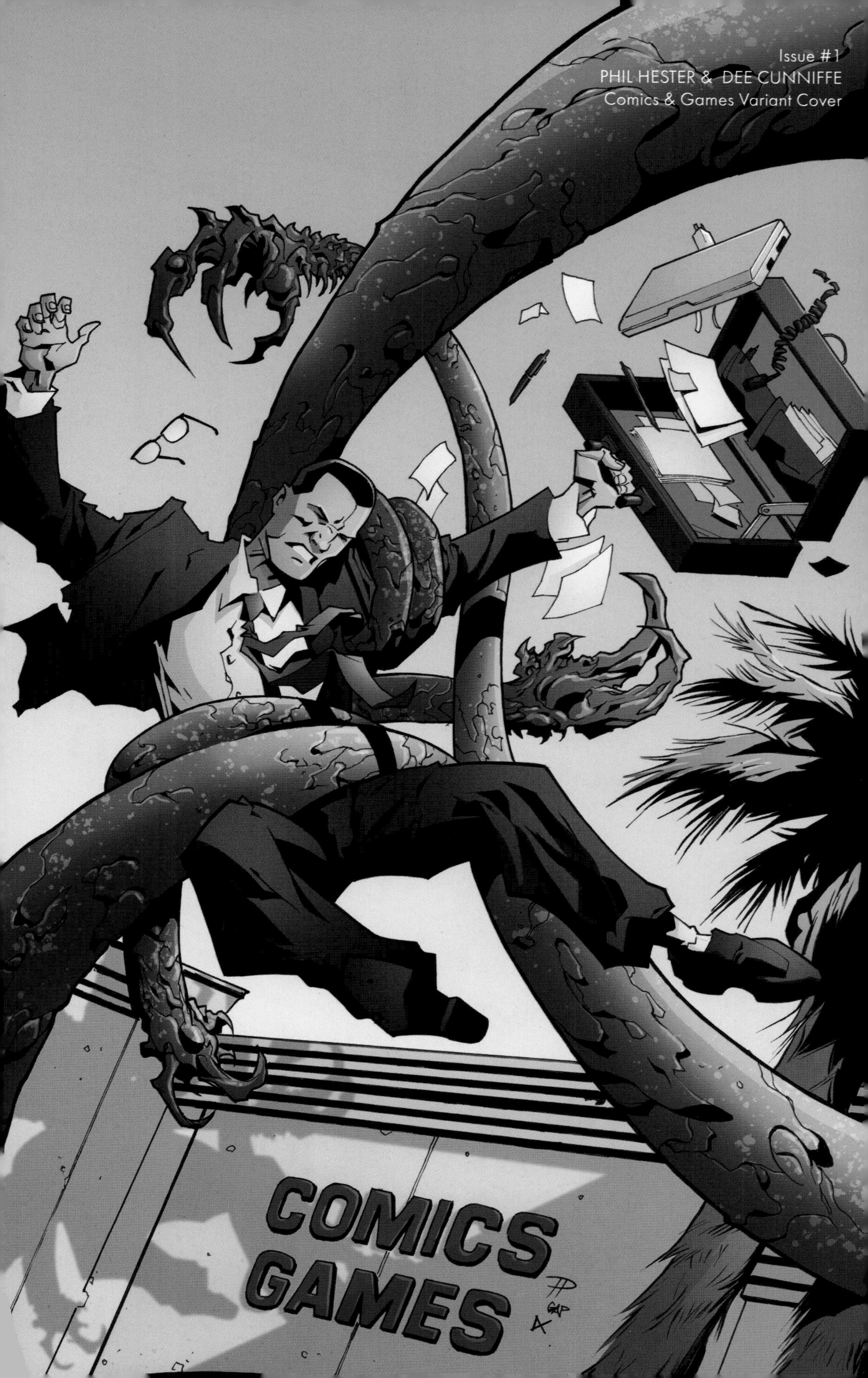
COMICS
GAMES

Issue #1
PHIL HESTER & DEE CUNNIFFE
Comics & Games Variant Cover

STRONGHOLD™

sketchbook

art by RYAN KELL

Michael Grey

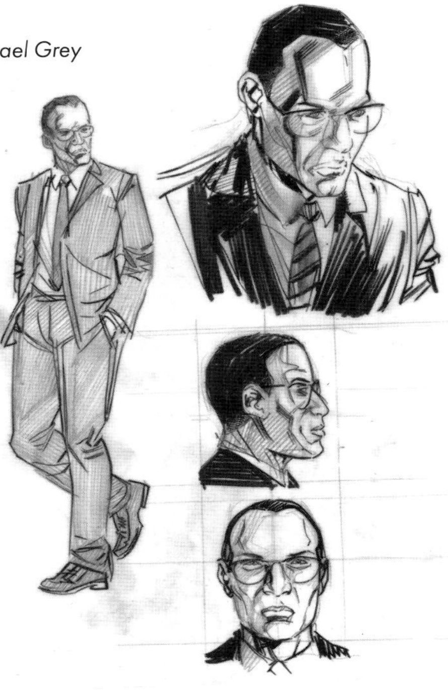

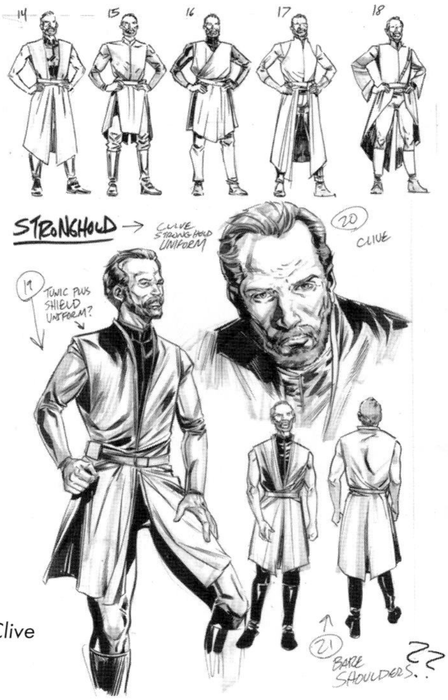
14
15
16
17
18
STRONGHOLD
CLIVE STRONGHOLD UNIFORM
20
CLIVE
19
TUNIC PLUS SHIELD UNIFORM?
21
BARE SHOULDERS..??

Clive

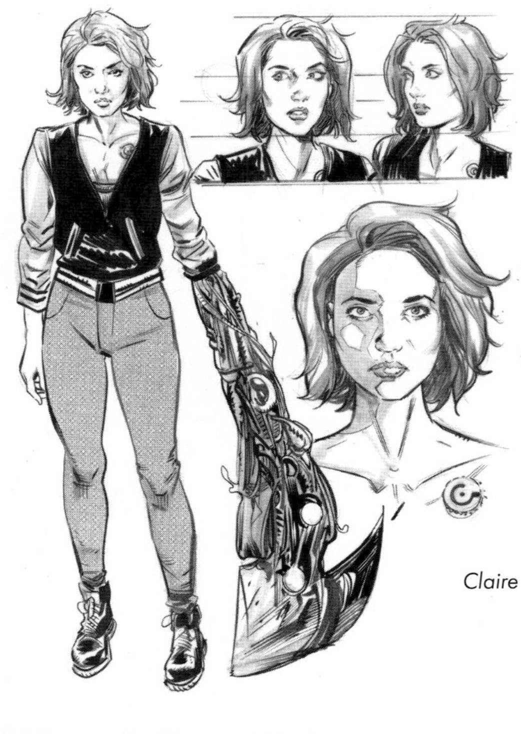

Claire

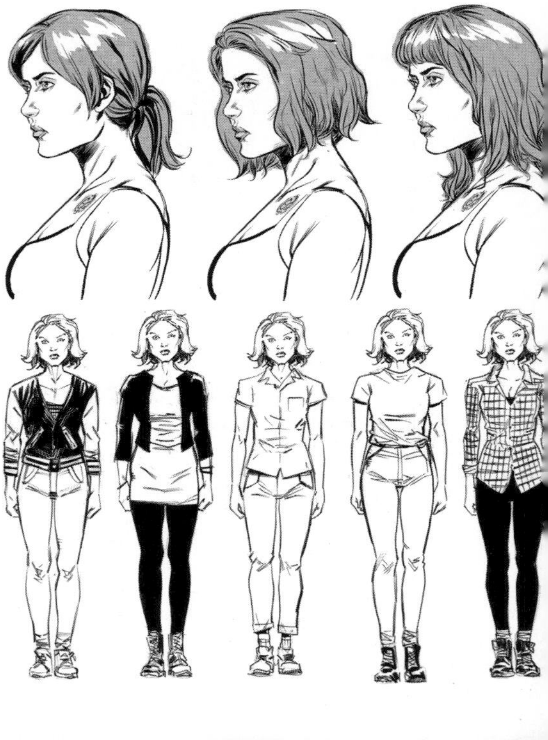

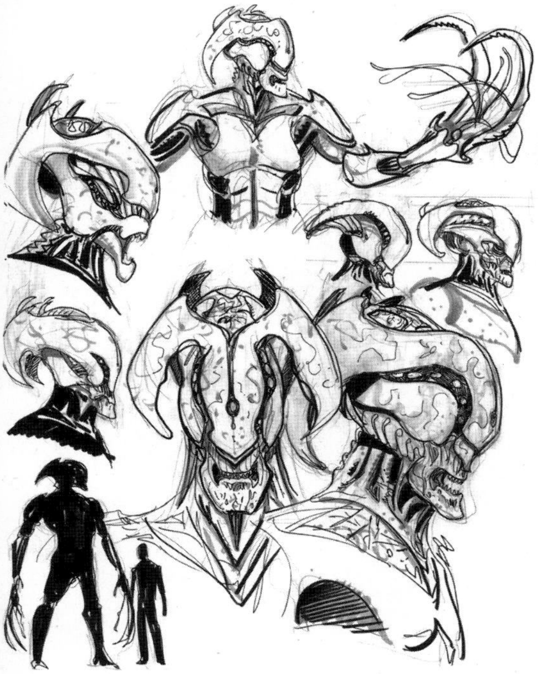

The Adversary

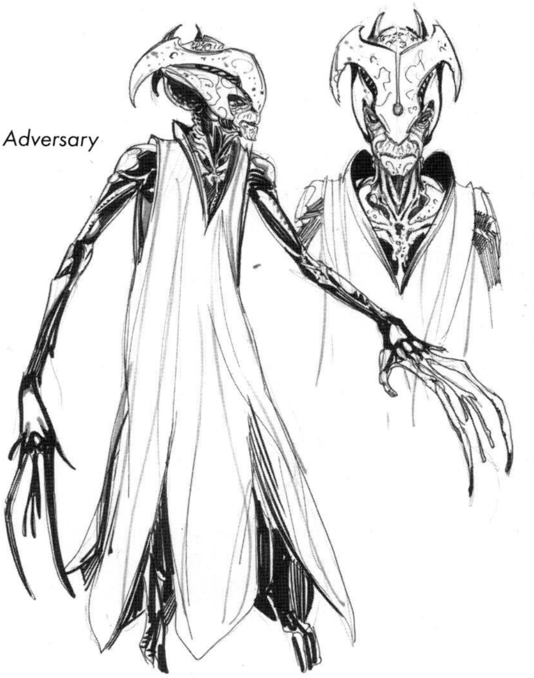

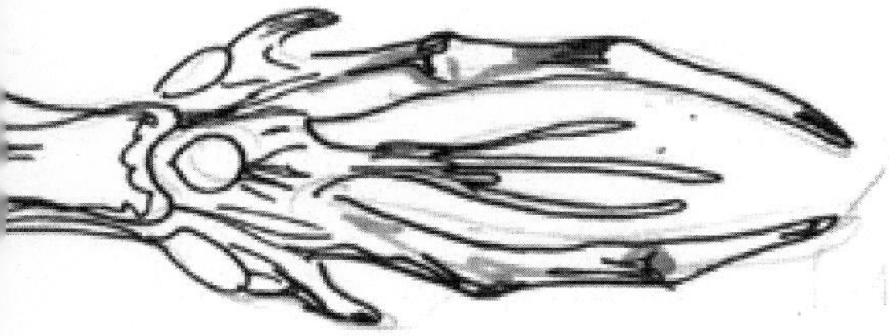

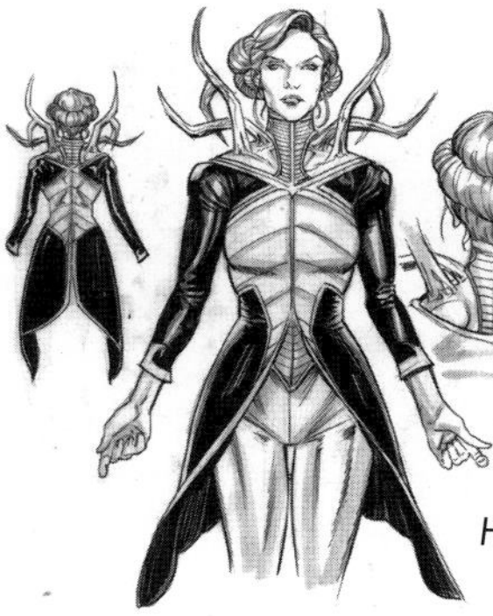

Holdmother

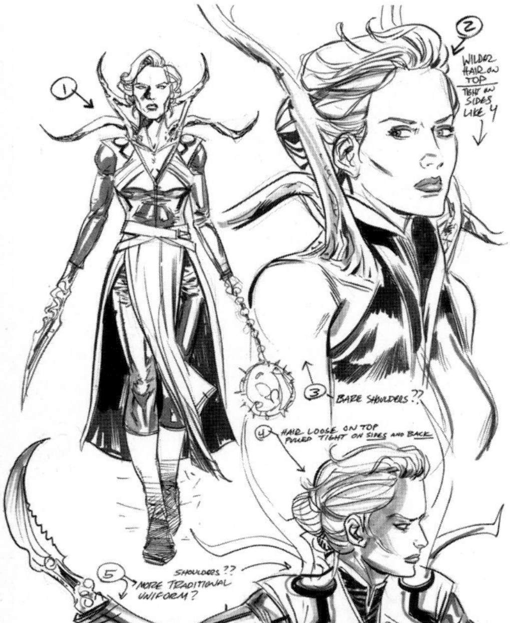
1
2
WILDER HAIR ON TOP TIGHT ON SIDES LIKE 4
3 BARE SHOULDERS??
4 HAIR LOOSE ON TOP PULLED TIGHT ON SIDES AND BACK
SHOULDERS??
5 MORE TRADITIONAL UNIFORM?

Holdmother

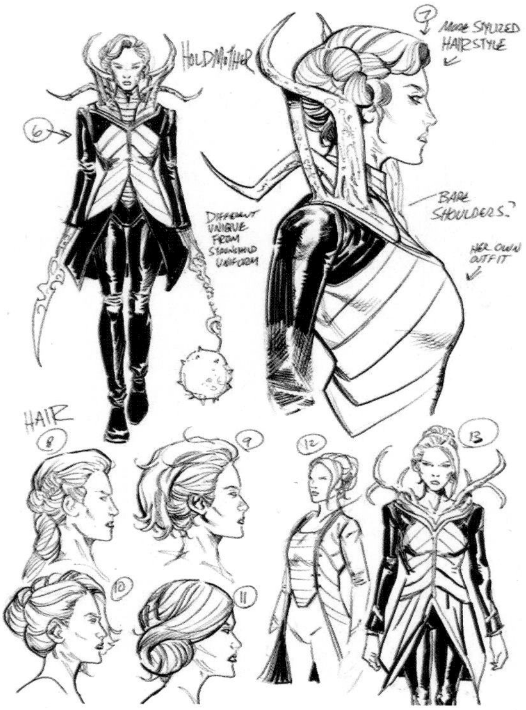
HOLDMOTHER
7 MORE STYLIZED HAIRSTYLE
6
DIFFERENT UNIQUE FROM STRONGHOLD UNIFORM
BARE SHOULDERS?
HER OWN OUTFIT
HAIR
8
9
10
11
12
13

ABOUT THE CREATORS OF

STRONGHOLD™

PHIL HESTER
writer

@PhilHester

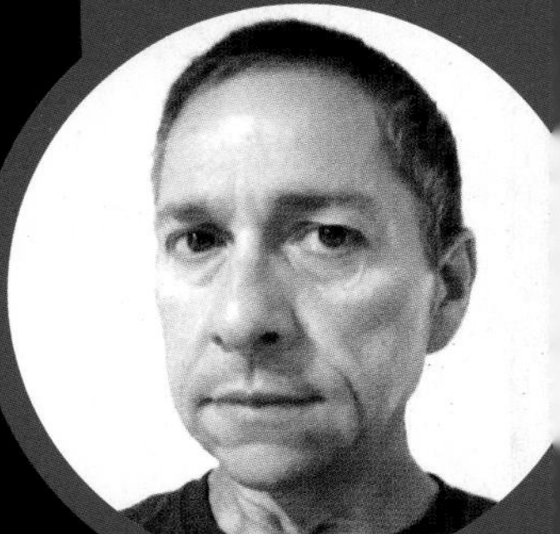

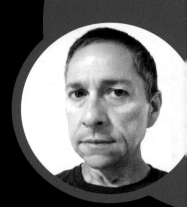

Phil has been writing and drawing comics for nearly three decades, beginning while still a student at the University of Iowa. He broke into the mainstream with a long run as artist of DC's *Swamp Thing* with writer Mark Millar. He also wrote and drew the Eisner Award nominated series *The Wretch*. Phil drew Kevin Smith's revival of DC's *Green Arrow*. He wrote the original graphic novels *The Coffin* and *Deep Sleeper* with artist Mike Huddleston. At Image Comics, he created *Firebreather* with artist Andy Kuhn.

His work, as both artist and writer, has been featured in hundreds of comics from nearly every American publisher, and includes runs on such titles as *The Darkness, Wonder Woman, Ant-Man, Ultimate Marvel Team-Up, Nightwing, Invincible Universe, Batman Beyond, The Flash: Season Zero, Deathstroke* and *Mythic*.

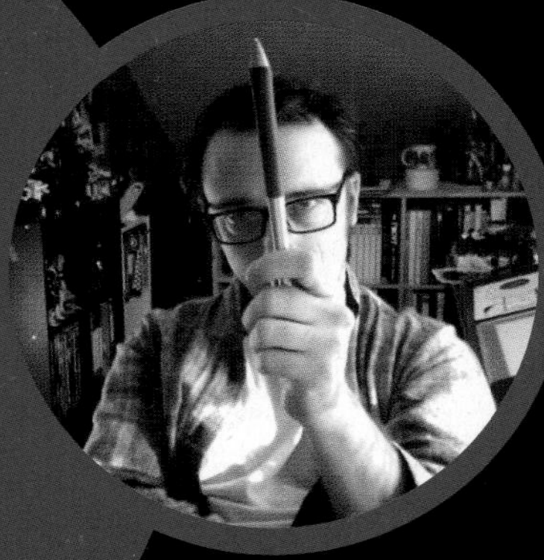

RYAN KELLY artist

@funrama

Ryan Kelly has been drawing comic books for over twenty years, and along the way has co-created numerous original books and series. He's done drama with *Local* and *The New York Four* (as well as Eisner Award-nominated *The New York Five*). Ryan has illustrated horror in *Survivors Club* and the supernatural in *Cry Havoc*. He helped create the historically-based *Three* and the political sci-fi thriller *Saucer Country* (along with the sequel, *Saucer State*). Ryan lives in Minnesota with his lovely family and he likes to draw, paint and read in his free time.

DEE CUNNIFFE colorist

@deezoid

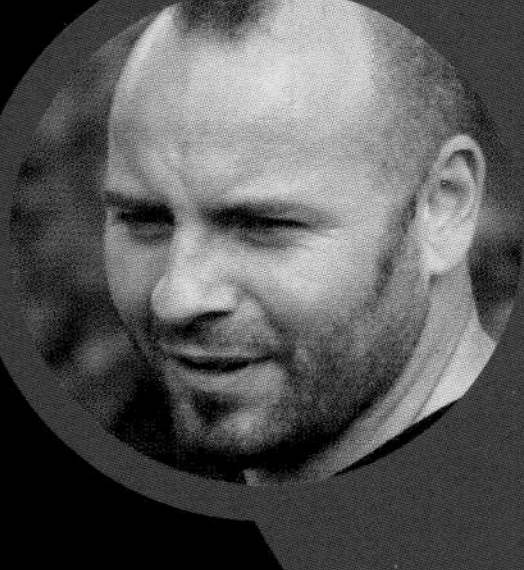

Dee is an award-winning Irish designer who worked for over a decade in publishing and advertising. He gave it all up to pursue his love of comics. Dee has worked for nearly every comic for every publisher as a flatter/color assistant to some of the world's top color artists. He has colored *The Dregs* and *Eternal* at Black Mask Studios, *The Paybacks* and *Interceptor* at Heavy Metal and *Redneck* at Skybound.

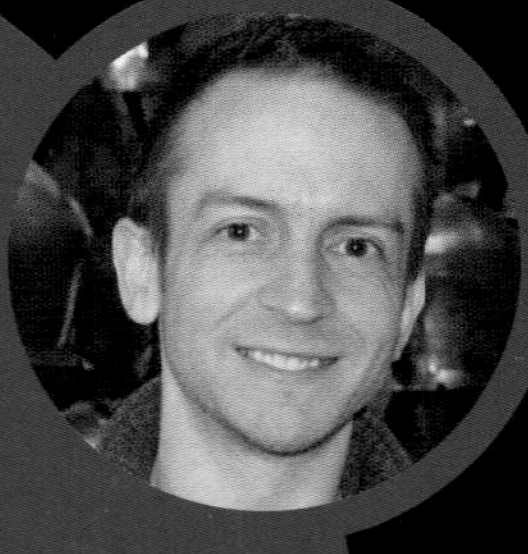

SIMON BOWLAND letterer

@SimonBowland

Simon has been lettering comics for over a decade and is currently working for DC, Image, Valiant, Dark Horse, Dynamite, 2000AD and IDW, amongst others. His debut AfterShock project is UNHOLY GRAIL. Born and bred in England, Simon still lives there today alongside his girlfriend and their tabby cat.